Janice Boucher Breuer
University of South Carolina
Dale Box
University College of the Fraser Valley
Ian McAskill
University College of the Fraser Valley

STUDY GUIDE

MICROECONOMICS
Principles and Tools

First Canadian Edition

Arthur O'Sullivan
Oregon State University
Steven M. Sheffrin
University of California, Davis
Rob Moir
University of New Brunswick, Saint John

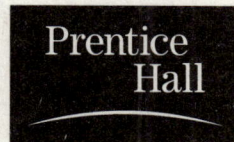

Prentice
Hall

Toronto

Executive Acquisitions Editor: Dave Ward
Developmental Editor: Laurie Goebel
Production Editor: Jennifer Therriault
Production Coordinator: Janette Lush

Original edition published by Prentice Hall, Inc., a division of Pearson Education, Upper Saddle River, New Jersey. Copyright ©1998 by Prentice Hall, Inc. This edition is authorized for sale only in Canada.

1 2 3 4 5 05 04 03 02 01

Printed and bound in Canada

Table of Contents

PREFACE

About the study guide...

This study guide has been designed especially for you as a student of economics. The study guide is designed to promote your comprehension of economic principles and your ability to apply them to different problems since these are the skills that you will be required to use when you take an economics exam and other economics courses.

The study guide is different from any other economics principles study guide for a few reasons. First, it contains a section on performance enhancing tips (PETS). The PETS are tips that may help you through some of the rougher material in each chapter as well as with some basic principles that are used over and over again throughout the course. Second, the study guide is different from other study guides because it contains detailed answers to the practice exam multiple-choice questions and to the essay questions. For the multiple-choice questions, the correct answer is explained in detail and explanations are given for why the other options are not correct. In this way, you learn a lot more because you learn not only why an answer is right but also why other answers are wrong. This should help you when it comes time to take an exam. The study guide also provides detailed answers to the essay questions. Finally, since your professor may use terms different than those used in text, equivalent terms that your professor may use have been put in parentheses. For example, some professors use the term "resources" to mean land, labour, and capital whereas other professors use the term "factors of production."

The study guide is not a tool to help you memorize economic principles, nor should it be used as a tool for memorization. It has been our experience as instructors that students who understand basic economic principles perform much better than students who attempt to learn by memorizing material.

Some words of wisdom...

When we took our first principles of economics course we had heard from our roommates and other classmates that economics was a very difficult course, made only more difficult because the professor who was to be teaching the course was supposedly very hard on the students. Naturally, we were scared since it seemed like there was a real possibility that this might be one course that we (and a lot of other students) might fail. Much to our surprise, we actually liked economics! The words of wisdom that we would like to impart to you we owe a great deal to our Professors. These are words of wisdom we share every semester with the students we teach.

#1   Attend class.

Don't think to yourself "I don't have to attend class to learn; I can learn this material by reading the textbook." First, professors cover material in class that they will put on the exam. This means two things: (1) professors may include material in their lectures that is not in the textbook and test you on it and (2) material not covered in class will probably not show up on the exam. By attending class, you will have a better idea about what to spend time studying and what not to and your study time will be more focussed and thus more productive.

#2   Take notes in class and recopy them within three days after each class.

For us, recopying our notes was the most useful practice for learning that we engaged in during our undergraduate and graduate school career. Recopying notes forces you to review the material and confront any points on which you are not clear. You learn by recopying your notes. Also, by recopying your notes, you will have a well-organized, clear set of notes from which to study. And, that makes studying much easier.

When you recopy your notes, elaborate on major points from the lecture and supplement them with relevant material from the text. Write down questions about the material directly in your notes so that you can ask the professor later. Use coloured pens, stars, stickers, or whatever else you want to make your notes unique.

#3   Read or, at least, skim the assigned chapter(s) to be covered in each class before the class meets. Within three days after class, reread the chapter(s).

#4   Jump the gun with studying.

Begin studying for the exam four to five days prior to the exam date. You'd be surprised how much easier it is to learn when you don't feel pressured for time. Plus, the extra time to study gives you an opportunity, to review the material more than once or twice and to work through the study guide. You'll also have time to meet with your professor and ask questions about material which gives you trouble.

#5   Do things in reverse.

When your professor works through an example in class for which an "increase" is considered, work through the reverse case of a "decrease." When you are working through the practice exam multiple choice questions and essay questions in the study guide, it may also be useful for you to consider the reverse of each question. For example, if the multiple choice question asks you to consider an "increase," instead consider a "decrease" and then figure out whether there is any correct answer or how an answer would have to be modified to be correct. You should do likewise for questions where you are asked to consider a "rightward" shift in a curve, or a "negative" relationship, or which statement is "true."

#6   Meet with your professor to discuss material that you have trouble with.

All of these words of wisdom may be summed up as:

Expect to work hard if you want to do well. Hard work, in this course, or any course, usually has its rewards.

In our experience as a student and then later as a professor who has interacted with students, we have observed firsthand how hard work has transformed a D student into a C or B student and a C student into a B or A student.

CHAPTER 1
INTRODUCTION: WHAT IS ECONOMICS?

I.   OVERVIEW

In this chapter, you will be introduced to the basic ideas associated with the study of economics. You will learn about the basic economic problem of scarcity. You will learn about the resources a society has that enable it to produce goods and services (output). You will learn what a market is. You will also learn about some of the techniques used by economists for thinking about problems faced by individuals when dealing with scarcity. You will also be introduced to basic graphing principles and techniques that can help you analyse problems.

II.   CHECKLIST

By the end of this chapter, you should be able to:

- Explain the concept of scarcity.
- Use the production possibilities curve to reflect scarcity.
- List the resources or factors of production a society has that enable it to produce goods and services.
- Describe what it means for a society to be producing at a point inside, along, and outside the production possibilities curve.
- Define a market and explain why it exists.
- Describe the usefulness of making assumptions.
- Explain what is meant by "ceteris paribus."
- Draw a picture of a graph with a positive slope and a negative slope.
- Compute the slope of a graph.
- Determine what will cause a graph to shift and in what direction and what will cause a movement along a graph.
- Compute a percentage change and use it to make other calculations.

III.   KEY TERMS

Economics: the study of the choices made by people who are faced with scarcity.
Scarcity: a situation in which resources are limited and can be used in different ways, so we must sacrifice one thing for another.

Factors of production: labour and capital used to produce output.

Natural resources: things created by acts of nature and used to produce goods and services.

Labour: the human effort used to produce goods and services, including both physical and mental effort.

Physical capital: objects made by humans and used to produce goods and services.

Human capital: the knowledge and skills acquired by a worker through education and experience and used to produce goods and services.

Entrepreneurship is the effort used to co-ordinate the production and sale of goods and services.

Production possibilities curve: a curve that shows the possible combinations of goods and services available to an economy, given that all productive resources are fully employed and efficiently utilised.

Market: an arrangement that allows buyers and sellers to exchange things: a buyer exchanges money for a product, while a seller exchanges a product for money.

Planned economy: an economy in which the basic economic questions are answered by a committee of planners.

Mixed economy: the mixture of both market-based and planned economic systems.

Microeconomics: the study of the choices made by consumers, firms, and government; how these decisions affect the market for a particular product or service.

Marginal analysis: method of analysis that assumes people pay attention to the additional or incremental benefits and costs of the action under consideration.

Macroeconomics: the study of the nation's economy as a whole.

Variable: a measure of something that can take on different values.

Ceteris paribus: Latin for "other variables are held fixed."

Positive statement: a statement that follows logically from a model.

Normative statement: a statement which states what we should (or ought) to do.

From the Appendix

Positive relationship: a relationship in which an increase in the value of one variable increases the value of the other variable.

Negative relationship: a relationship in which an increase in the value of one variable decreases the value of the other variable.

Slope: the change in the variable on the vertical axis resulting from a one-unit increase in the variable on the horizontal axis.

IV.   PERFORMANCE ENHANCING TIPS (PETS)

PET #1

A graph of the relationship between X and Y (use whatever variables you like) will SHIFT when other variables, like Z, G, and J (use whatever variables you like), which are relevant to the relationship between X and Y, change. Changes in the variables, X and Y, that are being graphed will NOT cause a shift of the curve but, instead, will cause a movement along the curve.

As your textbook discusses in the appendix to Chapter 1, a graph shows the relationship between two variables while holding fixed or constant (i.e., the *ceteris paribus* condition) other variables that are relevant to the relationship being graphed.

Generally speaking, a graph of the relationship between X and Y holds other variables that are relevant to the relationship between X and Y constant. That is, the relationship assumed to hold between X and Y is based on the current state of other variables believed to be relevant to X and Y. The relationship between X and Y is drawn for today, and what the values of Z, G, and J are today, not one year later. For example, a graph of the relationship between age and income-earning potential holds constant other variables, like level of education, skills, and perhaps even whether the federal government is liberal or conservative at the time the relationship is drawn.

Suppose that during your last year in high school you had not yet decided whether or not you wanted to pursue a post-secondary education. You went to your favourite teacher and asked for her advice. Your teacher proceeded to draw the following graph (Figure 1-1):

Figure 1-1

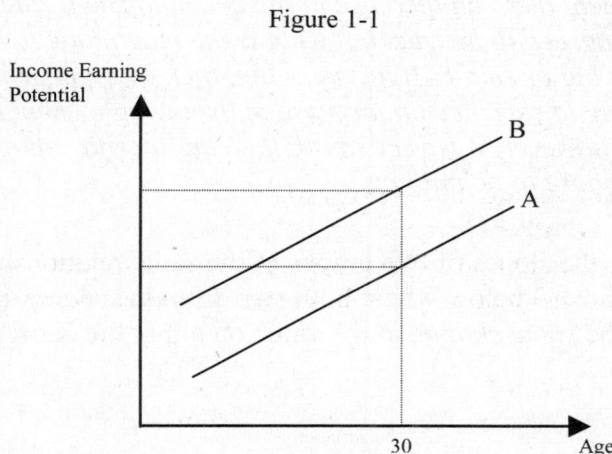

Figure 1-1 shows that, as you get older, your income earning potential increases (line A). This assumes all other factors remain the same including your current level of education.

Now, what would happen to the graph if you pursue post-secondary studies? You should expect that your income earning potential, *for any and every age,* will be higher since you are now more educated. How could you represent this with the graph? Since your income earning potential will be higher after you have completed your studies than if you had not pursued a post-secondary education, line A would be shifted up, to the left. The line labelled B represents this. Now, notice that, when you compare your income earning potential at *any and every age,* it is higher, which is consistent with the assumption that more education leads to higher income earning potential, regardless of age. That is, Figure 1-1 shows that, at age 30, the income earning potential of the college graduate exceeds that of the high school graduate. The same is true at age 40, 50, and so on. So, should you pursue a post-secondary education?

Suppose you are told that the earth's temperature had increased by 1 degree since Figure 1-1 had been drawn. What would this do to the line A? Nothing. The change in the earth's temperature is not a variable that is relevant to the relationship between age and income earning potential. Therefore, its change will not cause line A to shift.

Suppose you are asked what happens to line A when age increases? Since age is graphed on one of the axes, a change in age is simply represented by a movement along line A as age increases. An increase in age should not be represented by a shift in the curve. A shift in the curve can only occur when some other variable, besides age or income earning potential, that is relevant to the relationship, changes.

PET #2

The numeric value computed from a slope can be a very informative piece of information, especially when debating economic policy. For example, a statement like "an increase in the budget deficit will raise interest rates" may be agreed to be true, but what is the magnitude (or numeric value) of this relationship? Is it big or small? If it is very small, perhaps policymakers needn't worry about the effects of the budget deficit on interest rates. Similarly, a statement like "an increase in the unemployment rate will bring inflation down" may be agreed to be true, but what is the magnitude (or numeric value) of this relationship? Is it big or small? If it is very big, then a country that has a high rate of inflation may be willing to sacrifice an increase in its unemployment rate in order to bring down inflation. If, however, it is very small, then the sacrifice may be too large and the policy makers will choose to do nothing.

An easy way to compare the slopes of two graphs of the same relationship is to draw them as in Figures 1-2 and 1-3 below where both start from the same value on the X or Y-axis. Then, consider the *same change* in the value on either the X or Y.

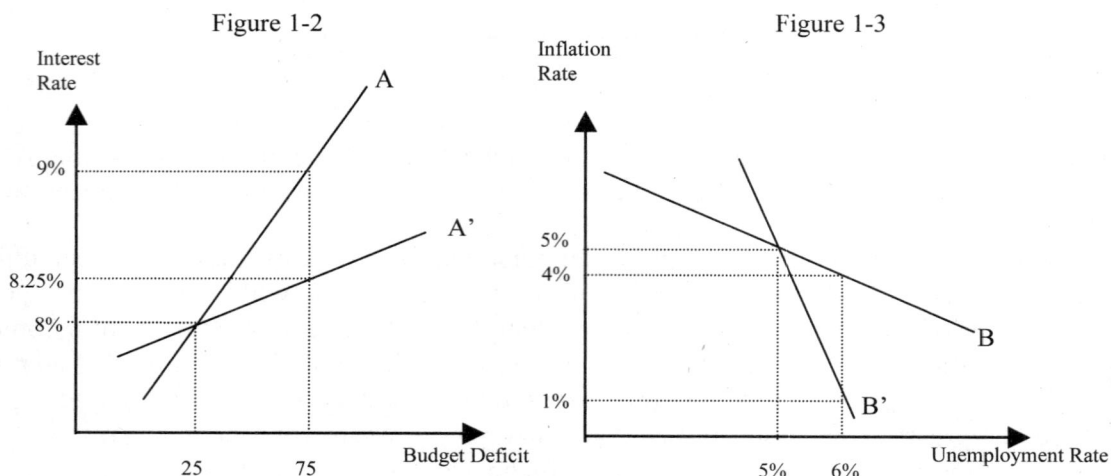

Figure 1-2

Figure 1-3

Is the slope of line A or A' larger in Figure 1-2? For the same $50 billion increase in the budget deficit, the interest rate rises by 1% along line A (slope = 1%/$50 billion) and by

0.25% along line A' (slope = 0.25%/$50 billion). That is, a $50 billion increase in the budget deficit will cause the interest rate to rise by 1% (and vice-versa for a decrease). Along line A', a $50 billion increase in the budget deficit will cause the interest rate to rise by 0.25% (and vice-versa for a decrease). Along line A, the interest rate is more responsive (or sensitive) to the change in the budget deficit than along line A'.

Is the slope of line B or B' bigger in Figure 1-3? In this case, the slope of each graph is negative and so "bigger" means in "absolute" terms (i.e., ignore the negative sign). For the same 1% increase in the unemployment rate, along line B', the reduction in inflation is bigger. Inflation falls by 4% compared to 1% along line B. That is, the slope of line B' is 4%/1% and along line B is 1%/1%.

V.   PRACTICE EXAM: MULTIPLE CHOICE

1. Which one of the following does NOT represent the concept of "scarcity"?

    a. A decision by your parents to put more of their savings to fund university expenses and less to life insurance.
    b. Public policy in British Columbia to reduce timber production so that more wildlife species will be preserved.
    c. A decision by a company to increase advertising expense for a new board game by decreasing its budget for telephone expense.
    d. A decision to commit more time to perfecting your volleyball serve and more time to perfecting your tennis serve.
    e. A decision by a student to spend more time studying and less time partying.

2. Which one of the following would **NOT** be considered a resource or factor of production?

    a. A conveyor belt.
    b. A financial analyst with a B.A. degree.
    c. Tin.
    d. A new house.
    e. A computer.

3. Which one of the following would cause the production possibilities curve (PPC) to shift to the *left?*

    a. A technological advancement.
    b. An increase in the skill level of workers.
    c. Deterioration in the highway system.
    d. A discovery of more oil.
    e. An increase in the amount of plant and equipment.

4. Which one of the following would **NOT** cause a rightward shift in the production possibilities curve (PPC)?

    a. An increase in the utilisation of workers.
    b. An increase in the pool of labour available to work.
    c. A technological breakthrough.
    d. A newer stock of physical capital.
    e. All of the above will cause a rightward shift in the PPC.

5. Consider a graph of grade point average versus hours studied. Which one of the following is most likely held constant in such a graph?

    a. The number of classes attended.
    b. The grade point average.
    c. The number of hours studied.
    d. The phases of the moon.
    e. All of the above are held constant.

6. Which one of the following statements is true?

    a. The production possibilities curve is positively sloped, which shows that, as society wants to produce more of one good, it must produce more of another.
    b. The production possibilities curve is negatively sloped because, with a limited set of resources, society can only produce more of one good by taking resources out of producing another good.
    c. At a point outside the production possibilities curve resources are fully employed.
    d. At a point inside the production possibilities curve, resources are efficiently used.
    e. A movement along the production possibilities curve shows that society can produce more of both goods.

7. Which one of the following statements is the most accurate?

    a. "If I increase the amount of time spent reading my economics textbook and working through the study guide, my course grade in economics should improve."
    b. "If the Canadian budget deficit is reduced, then interest rates will be lower."
    c. "If the tax on cigarettes is increased, fewer packages of cigarettes will be sold."
    d. "If my company lowers the price of its product, it should sell more, assuming our competition does not do likewise."
    e. "Lower interest rates will lead to consumers taking out more car loans."

8. Which one of the following illustrates a negative (inverse) relationship between two variables?

    a. As auto insurance rates decrease, the number of automobile purchases remains unchanged.
    b. As the number of police cars out on the road increase, highway speeding decreases.
    c. As highway speeding decreases, highway fatalities decrease.
    d. As drunken driving increases, auto insurance rates increase.
    e. (b) And (c).

Introduction: What is Economics?

9. Suppose you volunteer at a local food bank and find that, for every additional 100 brochures you send out seeking financial donations, the food bank sees an increase in the donations received of $1,500. If you convince the executive director of the food bank to send out 200 more brochures this year than last year, by how much can you expect donations to change?

   a. $3,000.
   b. $750.
   c. $30.
   d. $135.
   e. Cannot be determined from the information given.

Figure 1-4

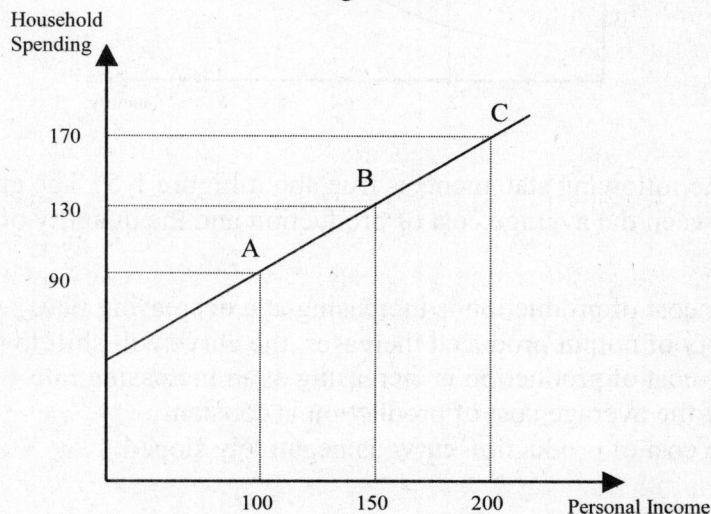

10. Which one of the following statements about Figure 1-4 is true? The graph shows the relationship between household spending and personal income.

   a. The slope is calculated at point A as 90/100 = 0.90.
   b. The slope is negative.
   c. An increase in personal income taxes would shift the curve up, to the left.
   d. An increase in interest rates would shift the curve up, to the left.
   e. The slope is 0.80.

11. Suppose you go out for coffee with your friends and your bill comes to $12. You thought the service that the table waiter provided was adequate, so you decide to leave a tip of 15%. What would be the amount of your tip?

   a. $1.25.
   b. $1.80.
   c. $7.40.
   d. $1.50.
   e. $0.18.

Figure 1-5

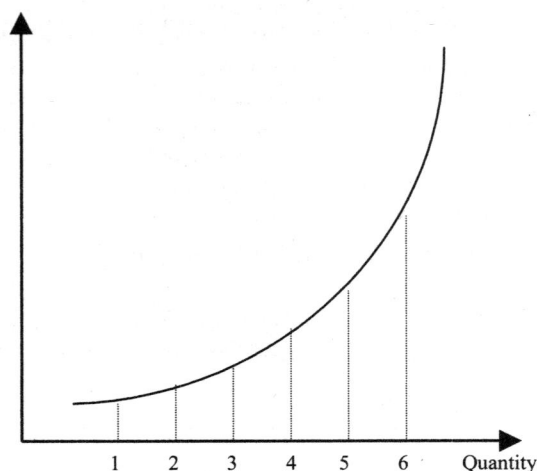

12. Which one of the following statements is true about Figure 1-5? The graph shows the relationship between the average cost of production and the quantity of output produced.

   a. The average cost of production is increasing at a decreasing rate.
   b. If the quantity of output produced increases, the curve will shift to the right.
   c. The average cost of production is increasing at an increasing rate.
   d. The slope of the average cost of production is constant.
   e. The average cost of production curve is negatively sloped.

VI.   PRACTICE EXAM: ESSAY QUESTIONS

13. Consider a society that is producing two types of goods: birdhouses and pianos. Explain what happens in the society if a decision is made to produce more birdhouses.

14. Suppose you hear a commentator on the radio state that, when interest rates fall, the stock market tends to rise. Draw a picture of such a relationship. Describe the slope. What factors would cause a movement along the graph? What factors might cause a shift in the graph?

VII.   ANSWER KEY: MULTIPLE CHOICE

1.   Correct Answer: d.

   Discussion: This statement does not represent the concept of scarcity because it does not reflect any sacrifice or trade-off. That is, you have decided to commit *more* of your limited amount of time to *both* activities. Thus, you are not giving up anything. Of course, you will obviously have to cut back time on other activities, (perhaps sleeping, studying, shopping, or whatever), but such trade-offs are not expressed in the answer.

Statements a, b, c and e all represent the concept of scarcity. Statement a represents the concept of scarcity because it reflects a sacrifice or trade-off made by your parents. Their decision to put more of their savings toward university expenses means that they will have less savings to devote to life insurance. That is, while your parents have to give up some funding of life insurance, in return, they are able to increase funding for university expenses. Statement b represents the concept of scarcity because it reflects a sacrifice or trade-off made by legislators representing the province's interests. The sacrifice is that some timber companies may be put out of business. In return, more wildlife species will be preserved. Statement c represents the concept of scarcity because it reflects a sacrifice or trade-off made by a business. The sacrifice is that its telephone budget will be reduced. In return, the company will be able to beef up its advertising expenses for the new board game. Statement e represents the concept of scarcity because it reflects a sacrifice or trade-off made by a student. The sacrifice is that the amount of partying will be reduced. In return, the student will be able to study more and, perhaps, earn higher grades.

Note: while there is a sacrifice, there is also something earned in return. Perhaps another way to think of sacrifice is "trade-off" whereby something must be given up in order to obtain more of something else.

2. Correct Answer: d.

    Discussion: A resource or factor of production is any good, service, or talent that enables a society to produce output -- other goods and services. A new house does not enable society, to produce more of other goods and services.

    Statements a, b, c, and e are all examples of factors of production. A conveyor belt is physical capital. A factory in its production process may use it. A financial analyst is both labour and human capital. The financial analyst provides physical and mental effort on the job and also brings with him or her skills acquired through formal education. Tin is a natural resource. It may be used in many different production processes -- bottling, sheeting, etc. A computer may be used in the production process of a service like banking or in manufacturing.

3. Correct Answer: c.

    Discussion: A leftward shift in the PPC means that society can now *produce fewer* goods and services of all types. This occurs because its resources or factors of production have, for whatever reason, been depleted. Deterioration in the highway system is a reduction in the physical capital resource that society uses to (indirectly) produce all types of goods and services.

    Statements a, b, d, and e are all examples that would be represented by shifting the production possibilities curve to the fight. A technological advancement makes it easier for society to produce more goods and services with its *existing* set of natural resources. An increase in the skill level of workers is an increase in the factor of production "human capital." More skilled workers tend to be more productive. That is, workers are able to produce more while on the job. A discovery of more oil is an increase in the factor of production "natural resources." With more natural resources available for production, more goods and services can be produced. An increase in the amount of plant and equipment is an increase in a society's capital stock that enables it to produce more of all types of goods and services. All of these would be represented with a rightward shift in the PPC. A rightward shift shows that society is able to produce more of all types of goods and services.

4. Correct Answer: a.

    Discussion: An increase in the utilisation of workers implies that workers must have been idle or under-utilised prior to the increase. Being at a point inside the PPC represents this. When the utilisation of workers (or, for that matter, production facilities) is increased, society moves from a point *inside* the PPC toward a point on the PPC. There is no shift in the PPC. Notice that society, in this case, does not face a trade-off. It can produce more of both types of goods.

    Statements b, c, and d will all cause a rightward shift in the production possibilities curve, not a movement to the PPC. An increase in the pool of labour available to work is an increase in the factor of production labour. With more labour available to work, more goods and services can be produced. This would be represented by a rightward shift in the PPC. A technological breakthrough enables a

Chapter 1

society with its given set of resources (factors of production) to produce more goods and services. This would be represented by a rightward shift in the PPC. A newer stock of physical capital enables society to produce more than before because its physical capital (equipment, factories, etc.) is not as old and, therefore, as subject to breakdown. This would be represented by a rightward shift in the PPC. Statement e cannot be correct since answer a is correct.

5. Correct Answer: a.

    Discussion: Number of classes attended is the only variable being held constant in this example. Since the graph will show a picture of grade point average versus hours studied, these variables will be on the axes of the graph. Suppose that grade point average is graphed on the vertical axis and hours studied on the horizontal axis; you should expect the graph to have a positive slope. Suppose it is drawn assuming that the full number of classes is attended. Now, if the number of classes attended drops, what would happen to the position of the graph? It would shift down, to the right, indicating that, for a given number of hours studied, the grade point average will, in all cases, be lower.

    Statements b and c are not correct because they are the variables being graphed and therefore are subject to change. Statement d is not correct because the phases of the moon are not relevant to the relationship between the two variables, so it doesn't matter whether it is assumed to be held constant or not. Statement e is not correct because the number of classes attended is held constant, as stated in a. It is reasonable to assume that this variable is relevant to the relationship between grade point average and number of hours spent studying.

6. Correct Answer: b.

    Discussion: Statement b is true. The production possibilities curve is negatively sloped, which shows that in order to produce more of one good, less of another good must be produced. The reason this trade-off arises is because, when society has a limited set of resources that are fully employed and efficiently used, the only way it can physically produce more of one good is to take resources out of the production of another good. Thus, production of the other good must necessarily decline.

    Statements a, c, d, and e are all false. Statement a is false because the production possibilities curve is not positively sloped; it is negatively sloped. Statement c is false because a point outside the production possibilities curve represents a combination of goods and services that is unattainable given society's current set of resources and its current state of technology. Society does not currently have enough resources to produce at a point outside the production possibilities curve. Thus, the issue of full employment is moot. Statement d is false because a point inside the production possibilities curve reflects a society that is either under utilizing its resources (there is some "idleness") or not using its resources efficiently. If society, were using its resources efficiently and the resources were fully employed, a point on the production possibilities curve, would be attained. Statement e is false because a movement along the production possibilities curve reflects a trade-off which means that more of one good can be produced but only at the expense of reducing production of another good.

7. Correct answer: d.

    Discussion: Statement d is the most accurate because it is the only statement that qualifies the relationship between the two variables, price and amount sold. For example, without the qualifier, a company may lower its price but find that its sales do not increase. This situation may arise because the company's competitors may also lower their price, making it harder for the company to sell more even though it has lowered its price. The qualifier, in effect, holds fixed other variables that may be relevant to the relationship between price and amount sold. The qualifier thus makes clearer what the expected relationship is between the two variables.

    Statements a, b, and c are not as accurate as statement d because none of these answers adheres to the *ceteris paribus* condition of holding other variables fixed that might also be important to a relationship between two variables. Statement a would be more accurate if it was qualified with a clause like "assuming that I continue to attend class regularly and take and recopy my notes." That is, even if you spend more time reading the textbook and using the study guide, if you decide, at the same time, to skip class and stop taking notes, you may not see any improvement in your grade at all. Statement b would be more accurate if it was qualified with a clause like "assuming that the central bank decides not to raise interest rates." That is, a lower budget deficit may not necessarily lead to lower interest rates if something else happens in the economy to change them. Statement c would be more accurate if it was qualified with a clause like "assuming tobacco companies do not increase their advertising and/or do not lower the price they charge for a pack of cigarettes." That is, an increased tax on cigarettes may not have the desired effect of reducing the packages of cigarettes sold if tobacco producers respond by, say, lowering the price they charge for a pack of cigarettes.

8. Correct Answer: b.

    Discussion: Statement b is the only response that shows a negative (or inverse) relationship. A negative relationship exists when one variable increases and the other decreases or when one variable decreases and the other increases. In statement b, as the number of police cars out on the road increases, highway speeding decreases.

    Statements a, c, and d do not illustrate a negative relationship. Statement a indicates that there is no relationship between auto insurance rate decreases and automobile purchases. Statement c illustrates a positive relationship. Even though both variables are decreasing, they move in the same direction. That is, you could also say that, as highway speeding increases, highway fatalities increase. In either case, there is a positive (or direct) relationship between both variables. Statement d, for the reason just mentioned, illustrates a positive relationship between drunken driving and auto insurance rates. Statement e cannot be correct because statement c is not correct.

9. Correct answer: a.

    Discussion: The information in the question reveals that the change in donations received is $1,500 for every 100 additional brochures mailed out. That is, every 1 additional brochure sent out returns $15 in donations. ($1,500 donations/100 brochures = $15 donations/1 brochure). So, if the food bank mails out 200 more brochures, it can expect to raise $15 per brochure * 200 brochures = $3,000.

    Statements b, c, and d are not correct based on the explanation above. Statement e is not correct because there is enough information to figure out the answer.

10. Correct answer: e.

    Discussion: We can calculate the slope of a line by taking two points on a curve and computing the change in the variable on the vertical axis (the rise) and dividing it by the change in the variable on the horizontal axis (the run). Taking any two points on the diagram (A to B, B to C, A to C) will produce a slope of 0.80.

    Statement a is not correct because a slope cannot be computed by using a single point on a graph. Remember this! Statement b is not correct because the graph shows a positive slope -- that is, as personal income increases, household spending increases (A to B) and, as personal income decreases, household spending decreases. (B to A.) Statement c is not correct because an increase in personal income taxes would be expected to lower the level of household spending for every level of personal income. Shifting the curve down, to the right would represent this. Statement d is not correct because an increase in interest rates would be expected to lower the level of household spending for every level of personal income. Shifting the curve down, to the right, too, would represent this.

11. Correct Answer: b.

    Discussion: You can use a few methods for calculating the tip. You could multiply $12 by 0.15 (15/100), which would yield $1.80. If you don't have a calculator or want to double-check your answer, you could compute 10% of $12, which is $1.20. Since 10% of $12 is $1.20, 5% of $12 must be $0.60 (half of $1.20). Then, add $1.20 + $0.60 to get $1.80.

    Statements a, c, d, and e are all incorrect. Statement a reflects a tip of just a nickel over a 10% tip. Statement c reflects a tip of 20% ($12 * 0.20 = $2.40). Statement d reflects a tip of [($1.50/$12)]*100 = 12.5%. Statement e reflects a tip of 1.5% ($12 * 0.015 = $0.18).

12. Correct Answer: c.

Discussion: The average cost of production is increasing at an increasing rate. You can figure this out by comparing several points on the graph. Compare the change in the average cost of production from an increase in output of one unit from 1 to 2 units to the change in the cost of production from an increase in output of 5 to 6 units. You will see, even without numbers, that the change in the average cost of production will be greater when output increases by one unit from 5 to 6 than when output increases one unit from 1 to 2. Alternatively, you could look at the change in the average cost of production as you move from producing 1 unit to 2 units to 3 units, and so on. Again, you will see that the average cost of production increases by more when going from producing 2 to 3 units than from 1 to 2 units. Thus, the average cost of production is increasing at an increasing rate.

Statement a is not correct because the average cost of production is increasing at an increasing rate, as explained above. Statement b is not correct. As the quantity of output increases (or decreases), this would be represented by a movement along the curve, not a shift in it. Remember that a shift in a curve only occurs when a variable that is relevant to the relationship to the two being graphed changes. When a variable on the axis itself changes, a movement along the curve represents this. Statement d is not correct because the average cost of production is increasing at an increasing rate. If the slope were constant, then the change in the average cost of production from producing 1 to 2 units, compared to 5 to 6 units would be exactly the same (as it would from 2 to 3 units, as well). Statement e is not correct because the graph is positively sloped. The graph shows that, as output increases, the average cost of production increases (and vice-versa).

VIII. ANSWER KEY: ESSAY QUESTIONS

13. If the society decides that it wants to produce more birdhouses, then it must give up (sacrifice) the production of some pianos. Since the resources a society has available to help produce output are scarce (limited, fixed amount) at a point in time, the only way the society can produce more birdhouses would be to cut back piano production. By cutting back piano production, the society frees up resources from producing pianos and can then allocate those resources (labour, capital, etc,) into birdhouse production. However, if the amount of resources available to the society were to increase, then these new resources could be devoted to producing more birdhouses without having to cut back on piano production.

14. The commentator is pointing out a relationship between two variables -- the interest rates and stock prices. The stated relationship is negative since the two variables move in opposite directions. That is, when interest rates fall, stock prices rise and vice-versa. Thus, a graph of the relationship should have a negative slope. Factors that would cause a movement along the graph are the two variables that would be labelled on each axis, which are the interest rate and stock prices. Of course, there are other factors that could affect interest rates and stock prices. Such factors are held constant (not permitted to change) when drawing the relationship between interest rates and stock prices. For example, one factor that might be held constant is whether the Liberal party of Canada or the Canadian Alliance party is currently in power. If the relationship is drawn based on the Liberals being in power, the graph may shift (be further to the right or left) when the party changes to the Canadian Alliance (assuming the political party is relevant to the relationship between interest rates and stock prices). Another factor that might be held constant is the unemployment rate. That is, the relationship is drawn assuming a certain unemployment rate. If the unemployment rate were to change (assuming it is relevant to the relationship between interest rates and stock prices), the graph may shift.

CHAPTER 2
KEY PRINCIPLES OF ECONOMICS

I.   OVERVIEW

In this chapter, you will learn fundamental economic principles that will be used throughout this course. You will learn that decisions made by individuals generally involve an opportunity cost; choosing one option means that other options must be given up or sacrificed or foregone. You will learn about the marginal principle. The marginal principle can be used to guide decisions. It requires that the marginal benefit be compared to the marginal cost of undertaking an activity. You will learn about the principle of diminishing returns. The principle of diminishing returns means that more and more effort devoted to an activity leads to smaller and smaller increases (or improvements) in the activity. Diminishing returns arise because some factors remain fixed. As more and more effort is exerted in one factor, other factors begin to have an increasingly greater limiting effect. You will learn about the spillover principle. The spillover principle means that the benefits and costs of an activity may "spill over" to other parties not directly involved in the activity. Lastly, you will learn about the reality principle. The reality principle requires that you think in "inflation-adjusted" terms. That is, you must always consider the effects of rising prices (inflation) on your income, pay raises, and interest and dividend earnings from financial investments, as well as on your debt. A true picture of the national economy also requires that you think of its performance in inflation-adjusted terms.

II.   CHECKLIST

By the end of this chapter, you should be able to do the following:

- ❑ Evaluate the opportunity cost that is encountered when choosing an activity (e.g., attending a party on Saturday night, furthering your education, opening up a new factory, building more schools, cutting tax rates).
- ❑ Use the production possibilities curve to compute the opportunity cost of producing one good or bundles of goods instead of another.
- ❑ Explain why opportunity costs increase in moving either up or down the production possibilities curve.
- ❑ Use marginal analysis to decide the level at which an activity should be undertaken.
- ❑ Explain why picking an activity level where "marginal benefit" = "marginal cost" is the best choice.

❑ Explain why fixed costs are not relevant for marginal analysis, i.e., why it is that fixed costs do not matter in selecting an activity level.

❑ Explain the circumstances under which diminishing returns occur and under what circumstances it does not occur.

❑ Explain the spillover principle and give examples of spillover benefits and spillover costs.

❑ Use the reality principle to assess how well off you are based on the income you earn, any pay raises you might get, or any interest earnings you might receive from financial investments. Use the reality principle to get a true picture of the state of the economy.

❑ Explain the difference between nominal and real variables.

III.   KEY TERMS

Principle: a simple truth that most people understand and accept.
Marginal benefit: the extra benefit resulting from a small increase in some activity.
Marginal cost: the additional cost resulting from a small increase in some activity.
Fixed costs: costs that do not change as the level of an activity changes.
Variable costs: costs that change as the level of an activity changes.
Explicit costs: costs in the form of actual cash payments.
Implicit costs: the opportunity cost of non-purchased inputs.
Economic cost: the sum of explicit and implicit costs.
Diminishing returns: as one input increases while the other inputs are held fixed, output increases but at a decreasing rate.
Short run: a period of time over which one or more factors of production is fixed; in most cases, a period of time over which a firm cannot modify an existing facility or build a new one.
Long run: a period of time long enough that a firm can change all the factors of production, meaning that a firm can modify its existing production facility or build a new one.
Spillover (or externality): a cost or benefit experienced by people who are external to the decision about how much of a good to produce or consume.
Nominal value: the face value of a sum of money.
Real value: the value of a sum of money in terms of the quantity of goods the money can buy.

IV.   PERFORMANCE ENHANCING TIPS (PETS)

<u>PET #1</u>

Throughout this course, it is wise to always consider the best-foregone alternative (option that is given up) when a household, firm, or government makes a decision. An understanding of what is being given up in order to have something else may alter your opinion about the proper course of action.

For example, suppose that a political candidate is proposing that tax rates be cut. What opportunity costs might arise if the proposal is adopted? On the surface, you might think that a tax cut is great because your take-home pay will be higher and allow you to buy more goods and services (assuming prices don't rise; remember the reality principle). However, as with most decisions, there is a cost – something that is given up. In this case, a tax cut means that the government has less money to spend. So, the government may have to cut funding for Medicare, education, or social services, or whatever. These are opportunity costs of the tax cut. Which one of these government programs is the "best" foregone alternative depends on your viewpoint. If you value good schools, then the cut in education would be considered the opportunity cost associated with the tax cut. As you can see, debate over the opportunity costs of the proposal to cut taxes can lead to quite a lively discussion and may mean that not everybody agrees that a tax cut is such a good thing.

PET #2

*When you see the term "marginal" you should always think of computing the **change** in a variable. Computing the change requires that you have some numeric value before the change and some numeric value after the change. The difference between the two is the change in the variable.*

For example, suppose you have computed the revenue that your company earns from selling 5,000 jewellery boxes is $100,000. Furthermore, you have forecasted that, if the company sells 6,000 jewellery boxes the revenue will be $108,000. What is the addition to revenue (marginal revenue)? It is $8,000 (for 1,000 more boxes). Suppose that the cost of producing 5,000 jewellery boxes is $90,000 and you forecast that the cost of producing 6,000 boxes will be $95,000. What is the additional cost (marginal cost) associated with producing 1,000 more jewellery boxes? It is $5,000.

Now, use the marginal principle to answer whether your company would be better off by increasing production by 1,000 boxes. Since the marginal revenue (benefit to the company) is $8,000 and the marginal cost (cost to the company) is $5,000, the marginal principle dictates that production be increased since the marginal benefit exceeds the marginal cost. That is, the company will add more to its revenue than it will incur in costs by raising production. This means that the company's profits will increase.

PET #3

*The marginal cost or marginal benefit associated with **fixed** costs or fixed benefits are zero. When costs and/or benefits are fixed, the change in the costs or benefits must, by definition, be zero. This is why fixed costs and benefits are not considered when using the marginal principle to decide the best activity level.*

For example, suppose that the fixed costs of operating a factory are the rent and interest on loans (debt) that it must pay every month. Suppose these fixed costs total $3,400 per month. Consider the other monthly costs of operating a factory, including paying employees and paying for raw materials. Suppose these costs are $6,600. If the factory decides to increase production, it must hire more employees and purchase more raw materials. Suppose these costs rise to $8,900. What about rent and interest? Do they change when the company decides to produce more? No, they are fixed costs. So, what is the *marginal* cost associated with increasing production? All you have to do is compute the change in costs – the cost of rent and interest on loans went from $3,400 to $3,400, which is a change of zero. There is no addition to fixed costs and, thus, no marginal cost associated with them. The cost of employees and raw materials has increased from $6,600 to $8,900, which is an increase of $2300. The change in costs or marginal cost associated with increasing production is $0 + $2,300 = $2,300.

PET #4

Diminishing marginal returns means that, as an activity level (such as production) increases, it increases but at a decreasing rate. Just because the term "diminishing" is used does not mean that an activity level (such as production) decreases or diminishes.

For example, which table below illustrates the principle of diminishing returns?

Table 2-1		Table 2-2	
# of workers	Output	# of workers	Output
1	100	1	100
2	98	2	110
3	95	3	117
4	91	4	122

The correct answer is Table 2-2. In Table 2-2, output is increasing as more workers are hired. However, the rate at which output is increasing is decreasing. Output increases by 10 units (110-100) from hiring one additional worker, then by 7 units (117-110), and then by 5 (122-117). In Table 2-1, output is decreasing as more workers are hired. This is not the definition of diminishing marginal returns. This shows negative marginal returns.

PET #5

Compare the inflation rate to the rate of change in any nominal variable to determine whether the variable has increased, decreased, or remained unchanged in real terms.

For example, suppose your boss gives you a raise of 15% for the coming year. You may be quite happy about this until one of your economist friends points out that inflation is expected to be 18% this year. In this case, while your nominal income will grow by 15%, your real income (inflation-adjusted) will be expected to decrease by 3% (15%-18%). Maybe you should go back to your boss and ask for a bigger raise!

For another example, suppose that you invested $1,000 in the stock market at the beginning of this year. At the end of the year, your investment is now worth $1,200. What is the percent return on your investment? In nominal terms, it is 20% –

[(1,200 - 1,000)/1,000] * 100. What is the percent increase in real terms? First, you'll need the inflation rate for that year. Suppose inflation was 4%. Then, in real terms, your investment has increased in value by 16% (20% - 4%).

V.   PRACTICE EXAM: MULTIPLE CHOICE QUESTIONS

1. The "bowed out" shape of the production possibilities curve (PPC) arises because:

    a. as we move farther inside the PPC, an economy loses increasing amounts of both goods.
    b. the opportunity cost associated with a move from a point on the PPC to a point outside the PPC increases in terms of what must be given up to get there.
    c. to continue to get the same increment in the production of a particular good requires that more and more of the other good be given up.
    d. since resources are scarce, producing more of one good means we must produce less of another.
    e. none of the above.

Figure 2-1

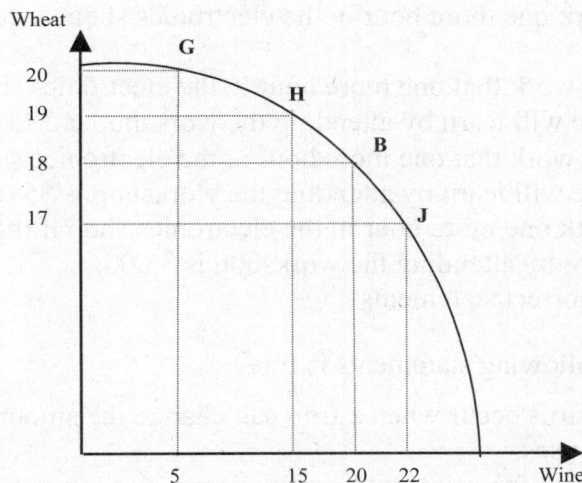

2. Based on Figure 2-1, which statement is correct?

    a. Moving from G to H incurs an opportunity cost of 1 bushel of wheat.
    b. As the economy moves along the PPC, more wheat can be obtained along with more wine.
    c. The opportunity cost of moving from G to H to B increases while the opportunity cost of moving from B to H to G decreases.
    d. Moving from H to B incurs an opportunity cost of 5 barrels of wine.
    e. Moving from G to J entails no opportunity cost.

3. Which one of the following is an example of a fixed cost?

   a. Electricity.
   b. Raw materials.
   c. Telephone.
   d. Supplies.
   e. Rent.

4. Suppose you are debating whether to open up your own pet shop. Which one of the following is an example of an implicit cost?

   a. Cost of fish tanks.
   b. Cost of a computerized bookkeeping system.
   c. Cost of your time spent setting up the shop and monitoring it.
   d. Cost of sales clerks.
   e. Cost of pet food.

5. Suppose Fred computes the marginal benefit of working one more hour as a sales clerk in an electronics store to be $7.75. However, by working one more hour, he must give up the opportunity to attend a free, one-hour workshop on how to start your own business. However, Fred believes he will learn a lot by attending the workshop. Based on this information, which one of the following statements is correct?

   a. Fred should work one more hour in the electronics shop since the workshop is free.
   b. Fred should not work that one more hour in the electronics shop if the implicit value of what he will learn by attending the workshop is $25.00.
   c. Fred should not work that one more hour in the electronics shop if the implicit value of what he will learn by attending the workshop is $5.00.
   d. Fred should work one more hour in the electronics shop if the implicit value of what he will earn by attending the workshop is $5.00.
   e. (b) and (d) are correct statements.

6. Which one of the following statements is true?

   a. Diminishing returns occur when a firm can change the amount of all of the factors of production it uses.
   b. If Helena finds that the marginal benefit of eating an ice cream cone is equal to the marginal cost of eating an ice cream cone, then Helena would be better off to eat one more ice cream cone.
   c. The short run is defined as a period during which some workers are idle.
   d. The production possibilities curve is positively sloped.
   e. None of the above is true.

7. Use Table 2-3 to answer the following question.

Table 2-3	
# of workers	Output
1	5
2	15
3	30
4	37
5	40
6	38

Diminishing returns occur:

a. Between the first and second worker.
b. Between the second and third worker.
c. Between the third and fourth worker.
d. Between the fourth and fifth worker.
e. Between the fifth and sixth worker.

8. Which one of the following activities is least likely to generate a spillover?

a. Wearing perfume.
b. Smoking a cigarette.
c. Reading a comic book.
d. Picking up trash from the roadside.
e. Repainting the exterior of your house.

9. Suppose that your boss informs you that you will receive a raise of 8% for this coming year. Suppose further that you have heard economic forecasts that the inflation rate for this coming year will be 9%. Based on this information, you might think to yourself:

a. "Wow, they must really like me – I'm effectively getting a 17% pay raise! I need to call home and tell Mom!"
b. "Gee, thanks for the raise, but the raise isn't actually a raise at all since my real income will decline by 1%."
c. "This isn't much of a raise, but at least my real income will increase by 1%."
d. "Well, this isn't really a raise – my real income is going to decline by 0.72%."
e. "This isn't really a raise – my real income is going to decline by 7.2%."

10. Suppose an old high school friend calls you up and desperately pleads to borrow $1,000 from you. You've been out working for a few years and have a little bundle in savings and decide that this is a good friend who really needs your help. So, you lend him $1,000 with the promise that he pays you the $1,000 back, without interest, at the end of the year. In one year after you are paid back:

   a. In real terms, the money you will be paid back will be worth less than $1,000 if inflation was greater than 0%.
   b. In real terms, the money you will be paid back will be worth more than $1,000 if inflation was greater than 0%.
   c. In real and nominal terms, you will be paid back $1,000.
   d. In nominal terms, the money you will be paid back will be worth less than $1,000 if inflation was greater than 0%.
   e. In nominal terms, the money you will be paid back will be worth more than $1,000 if inflation was greater than 0%.

VI.   PRACTICE EXAM: ESSAY QUESTIONS

11. Explain what happens when a country decides to move from one point on its production possibilities curve to another. Be sure to discuss opportunity cost and the allocation of scarce resources.

12. What advice would you give to a friend who has received two job offers? Both jobs offer the same starting salary of $30,000 and the same benefits package and the jobs are basically the same. However, one job is located in Toronto and the other in Edmonton.

VII.   ANSWER KEY: MULTIPLE CHOICE QUESTIONS

1.   Correct Answer: c.

Discussion: The bowed-out shape of the PPC reflects increasing opportunity costs (which arise because resources are not equally-well adapted to producing one good as another). Statement c is the only one that expresses that opportunity costs are increasing, i.e., that more and more of one good must be given up in order to get back the same increment (say, 1 unit) of the other good. For example, to produce 1 more motorboat may require that an economy give up producing 100 rolls of carpet: if the economy wants to produce 1 more boat, the economy now has to give up producing 125 rolls of carpet: and if the economy wants to produce yet 1 more motorboat, the economy now has to give up producing 175 rolls of carpet.

The question asks about the bowed-out shape of the PPC and so requires an answer that addresses a movement along the PPC, not to or from it. Statements a and b are incorrect because they address movements from a point not on the PPC to a point on it (or vice-versa), neither of which deals with a movement along the PPC. Statement d is incorrect because it only explains why the PPC has a negative slope, not why it has a bowed-out shape. Statement e is incorrect because answer c is correct.

2. Correct answer: a

    Discussion: Opportunity cost is measured by how much is given up or sacrificed. In this case, the graph shows that in moving from G to H, the economy foregoes producing (reduces production by) 1 bushel of wheat. In return, however, the economy is able to produce 10 more barrels of wine.

    Statement b is incorrect because it is not true that, as the economy moves along the PPC, more wheat can be obtained along with more wine. The concept of opportunity cost means that the economy can only have more wheat if it produces less wine (and vice-versa). Statement c is incorrect because increasing opportunity costs are encountered moving in both directions along the PPC. To see this, note that as the economy moves from G to H, it must give up producing 1 bushel of wheat but gets back 10 barrels of wine. As the economy moves from H to B, it must give up 1 bushel of wheat, but this time only gets back 5 barrels of wine. That is, it is more costly to produce wine because less is gotten back in return for the same 1 bushel of wheat. Thus, opportunity costs of producing more wine are increasing as the economy moves from G to H to B. If the economy moves from B to H to G, opportunity costs will also be increasing. To see this, note that, as the economy moves from B to H, it must give up producing 5 barrels of wine, while it gets back 1 bushel of wheat. In moving from H to G, the economy must now give up 10 barrels of wine while still only getting back 1 bushel of wheat. This just means that producing wheat has become more costly (i.e., the opportunity cost has increased). Statement d is not correct. Opportunity cost is measured by how much is given up; in moving from H to B, the economy has gotten back (not given up) 5 barrels of wine. Statement e is not correct because there is an opportunity cost; the opportunity cost is 3 bushels of wheat.

3. Correct answer: e

    Discussion: Rent is the only example of a cost that will not change with a firm's production level. That is, whether a firm produces 0, 1, or 1,000,000 skateboards, for example will not change the cost of the rent the firm pays for the production facility.

    Electricity, raw materials, telephone, and supplies are all examples of costs that will change with a firm's production level. The more a firm produces, the more electricity it will need to operate the factory, the more raw materials it will need to produce the product, the more telephone calls it will have to make to coordinate distribution and sales, and the more supplies (packaging, etc.) it will need in production.

4. Correct Answer: c

    Discussion: An implicit cost is a cost for which a cheque does not have to be written. The cost of your time spent setting up the shop and monitoring it is time that you, as owner, could have spent elsewhere, perhaps working for a company. While you will be compensated for your time as shop owner through any profits the pet shop makes, you are not explicitly paid for your time, i.e., there is not a set salary or wage per hour.

    Fish tanks, a computerized bookkeeping system, sales clerks, and pet food are all expenses that you must explicitly write a cheque for. They are explicit costs that arise from operating a pet shop.

5. Correct answer: e

    Discussion: Statement e is correct because statements b and d are both correct. Statement b is correct because the marginal cost of not working one more hour (or of attending the workshop) is $7.75 – i.e. Fred will give up $7.75 by attending the workshop. However, Fred will benefit. The marginal benefit of using that one-hour to attend the workshop has a value of $25.00. In this case, the marginal benefit of attending the workshop exceeds the marginal cost of attending the workshop so Fred would be better off by attending the workshop. Statement d is also correct but for the reverse reasons. In this case, if Fred assesses the marginal benefit of the one-hour of attending the workshop at $5.00, the marginal benefit exceeds the marginal cost of attending the workshop ($7.75 loss in wages from not working that one hour). Here, Fred would be better off working and not attending the workshop.

    Statement a is not correct. Even though the workshop is free, it does not mean that there is no benefit to attending it. Thus, it is not correct to compare the marginal cost of attending the workshop of $7.75 to a zero benefit. Statement c is not correct. If the marginal benefit of attending the one-hour workshop is $5.00 and the marginal cost of attending it is $7.75 (loss in wages from not working that one hour), then Fred would be better off working that one-hour. Here, the marginal benefit of attending the workshop is less than the marginal cost of attending the workshop. So, the workshop should not be attended. Statements b and d are both correct; however, option (e) allows you to pick both statements so that it is the correct answer.

6. Correct answer: e

Discussion: Statements a, b, c, and d are not true.

Statement a is incorrect because diminishing returns occur because a firm CANNOT change the amount of all of the factors of production it uses. Statement b is incorrect because, if Helena found the marginal benefit to eating an ice cream cone just equal to the marginal cost, then she is as happy as she can be. She should neither eat one more ice cream cone nor one fewer. She is eating just the right amount. Statement c is incorrect by definition. The short run is a time period during which a firm is not able to change the level of all of the factors of production that it uses to produce output. Statement d is incorrect because the production possibilities curve is negatively sloped.

7. Correct answer: c

Discussion: Diminishing returns occur when the addition of one more input (a worker in this example) adds less to output than the previous worker. Between the third and fourth worker, output increases by 7 units but had previously increased by 15 units (from 15 to 30). Thus, diminishing returns have set in.

Statement a is incorrect. Output has increased by 10 units from hiring one more worker but diminishing returns cannot yet be inferred until you are able to make one more comparison. Statement b is incorrect because, in this case, output has increased by 15 units from hiring one more worker (2 to 3 workers) and had previously increased by 10 units. This is an example of output increasing at an *increasing* rate, not a decreasing rate as is true of diminishing returns. (See PET #4.) Statement d is not correct because the point at which diminishing returns has set in is where the rate of increase in output slows down: this happens between the third and fourth worker, not the fourth and fifth worker. While statement d does show that the addition to output is decreasing (it had been 7 units from the previous worker and is now 3), it is not the point at which diminishing returns has set in. Statement e is not correct because output actually *decreases* by hiring one more worker. That is, output goes from 40 units to 38 units (-2) by hiring one more worker. This is not an example of diminishing returns (see PET #4).

8. Correct answer: c

Discussion: Statement c is correct because it is the only activity that does not generate any benefits or costs to those who are not reading the comic book. That is, reading a comic book does not impose a cost or those around you, nor does it create a benefit for those around you.

Wearing perfume can generate a spillover cost to others who are allergic to perfume or are bothered by the scent. The same is true for smoking a cigarette. Picking up trash from the roadside can generate a spillover benefit to others who use the road. They get to enjoy a more picturesque road trip. Repainting the exterior of your house can generate a spillover benefit for your neighbours. The benefit is that they don't have to look at a rundown-looking house. Also, by keeping up the appearance of your house, you may help to keep the property values in your neighbourhood from declining.

9. Correct answer: b

Discussion: Since your nominal income is going to grow by 8% but prices are expected to go up by 9%, then, in real terms, your income will decline by 1% (8% - 9%). (See PET #5.)

Statement a is not correct. This statement assumes that you have added the two numbers. It is not correct to add the growth rate of your nominal income and the inflation rate to determine the effect on your real income. Statement c is not correct. This statement assumes that you should take the inflation rate and subtract the growth rate of the nominal variable. This is not correct: it is the other way around. Statements d and e are not correct. These statements assume that you have multiplied the numbers. This is not the correct method for computing the real value of a variable.

10. Correct answer: a

Discussion: If you have agreed to be paid back $1,000 without interest and inflation is greater than 0%, then, in real terms, your $1,000 will be worth less than $1,000. In other words, your $1,000 will not be able to buy as much as it had the year before if inflation was greater than 0%. You should note that, in nominal terms, you are still getting back $1,000 but, in real terms, you are getting back less than $1.000.

Statement b is incorrect. If inflation is greater than 0%, then the $1,000 you are paid back will not be able to buy as much as the year before. Thus, in real terms, the money you will be paid back is less than $1,000. Statement c is not correct. In nominal terms, you will be receiving $1,000. However, in real terms, you may be getting back more or less than $1,000 depending on whether prices have fallen (deflation) or risen (inflation). Statement d is not correct because, in nominal terms, you will be getting back $1,000. Statement e is not correct because, again, you will be getting back $1,000 in nominal terms. Inflation affects how much you earn in real terms, not nominal terms.

VIII. ANSWER KEY: ESSAY QUESTIONS

11. When a country moves from one point on its production possibilities curve to another, it has made a decision to produce fewer units of one good (e.g., apparel) and more of another (e.g., electronics). The country faces an opportunity cost – the opportunity cost is that the country must cut back on production of apparel goods if it wants to produce more electronics. This is because resources are scarce. In order to produce more electronics, more resources – land, labour, capital – will have to be devoted to the electronics industry which means that there will be fewer resources available to produce apparel goods. That is, there will be a re-allocation of resources from the apparel industry, to the electronics industry. With fewer resources available to the apparel industry, apparel production will contract; the opposite will happen in the electronics industry. While the movement along the production possibilities curve assumes that resources remain fully employed (and efficiently used), there may be an adjustment phase (setting up new factory floors, training apparel workers to work in the electronics industry) during which some resources may become idle.

12. The advice I would give to my friend would be to consider the cost of living in Toronto compared to that in Edmonton. That is, I would have them consider the price of food, rent, clothing, etc., in one city compared to the other in determining which job offer provides the higher "real" salary. Since Toronto is known to be a very expensive city and Edmonton, where the cost of living is typically lower than in Toronto, I would suggest to my friend that, in real terms, the salary offer from the company in Edmonton is better than the other offer. I would suggest to my friend that, if she really wants to live in Toronto, the company must offer her a higher nominal salary to entice her to work for them.

CHAPTER 3
MARKETS AND GOVERNMENT IN THE GLOBAL ECONOMY

I.   OVERVIEW

In this chapter, you will learn what markets are. You will learn that markets exist because people find it easier and mutually beneficial to specialize in producing certain types of goods and to exchange what they have produced with what others have produced, than to produce for all of their own needs. You will learn that specialization and exchange can increase the set and amount of goods and services that each participating party may ultimately acquire. You will learn about comparative advantage, which is an application of the principle of opportunity cost. You will learn that comparative advantage can be used to determine which goods and services households, firms, and countries should specialize in, i.e., produce, and which they should exchange. You will learn that households, firms, the government, and foreign countries all participate in markets as both buyers and sellers. You will learn what role the government plays in a market-based economy. You will also learn of different methods the government uses to finance its activities. You will learn that international trade may also be based on comparative advantage and that it, too, can be mutually beneficial. You will also learn about different types of trade protection and that trade protection inhibits international trade based on comparative advantage. You will learn about the foreign exchange market, what an exchange rate is, and how to convert the dollar price of a good or service to a foreign currency price, and vice-versa.

II.   CHECKLIST

By the end of this chapter, you should be able to do the following:

- ❑ Explain why specialization and exchange can benefit all participating parties.
- ❑ Determine comparative advantage by comparing opportunity costs of production.
- ❑ List the different markets of exchange and explain in which market who is doing the buying and who is doing the selling.
- ❑ Explain the roles government plays in a market-based economy.
- ❑ List different methods of taxation and define what they are.
- ❑ List different types of trade protection and define what they are.
- ❑ Define an exchange rate and use it to convert the dollar price of a good or service to a foreign currency price, and vice-versa.

III.   KEY TERMS

Market system: a system under which individuals and firms use markets to facilitate the exchange of money and products.

Absolute advantage: the ability of one person or nation to produce a particular good at a lower absolute cost than another person or nation.

Comparative advantage: the ability of one person or nation to produce a good at an opportunity cost that is lower than the opportunity cost of another person or nation.

Multinational corporation: an organization that produces and sells goods and services throughout the world.

Benefit-tax approach: the idea a person's tax liability should depend on how much he or she benefits from government programs.

Horizontal equity: the notion that people in similar economic circumstances should pay similar taxes.

Vertical equity: the notion that people with higher income or wealth should pay higher taxes.

Progressive tax system: involves wealthier individuals paying an increasing percentage of extra income in taxes.

Marginal tax rate: the percentage of extra income paid as taxes.

Export: a good produced in the "home" country (for example, Canada) and sold in another country.

Import: a good produced in a foreign country and purchased by residents of the "home" country (for example, Canada).

Trade Barriers: rules that restrict the free flow of goods between nations, including **quotas** (limits on total imports), **voluntary export restraints** (agreements between governments to limit imports), **tariffs** (taxes on imports), and **non-tariff trade barriers** (subtle practices that hinder trade).

Worldwide sourcing: the practice of buying components for a product from nations throughout the world.

General Agreement on Tariffs and Trade (GATT): an international agreement that has lowered trade barriers between member nations.

Most favoured nation clause: a clause in the GATT that forced nations to give the same tariff rates to all member nations.

World Trade Organization (WTO): an organization that oversees GATT and other international trade agreements.

Free trade agreement (FTA): an agreement between Canada and the United States to remove tariffs and trade barriers (signed in 1993).

North American Free Trade Agreement (NAFTA): an international agreement that lowers barriers to trade between the Canada, Mexico, and the United States (came into effect in 1994).

European Union (EU): an organization of European nations that has reduced trade barriers within Europe.

Asian Pacific Economic Cooperation (APEC): an organization of 18 Asian nations that attempts to reduce trade barriers between their nations.

Foreign exchange market: a market in which people to exchange one currency for another.

Exchange rate: the price at which currencies trade for one another.

IV.   PERFORMANCE ENHANCING TIPS (PETS)

PET #1

Opportunity cost calculations used to determine comparative advantage should be based on a per unit comparison.

Suppose you are given the following information of production per hour for two countries:

Table 3-1

	Country A	Country B
Wood Products	10 units/hour	8units/hour
High-tech products	15 units/hour	4units/hour

The information in the Table 3-1 tells you that Country A can produce 10 units of wood products in one hour (with its resources) and 15 units of high-tech products in one hour. Country B can produce 8 units of wood products in one hour (with its resources) and 4 units of high-tech products in one hour. How can this information be used to determine which country has a comparative advantage in wood production and which country has a comparative advantage in high-tech production?

As a side point, you may wish to note that Country A has an absolute advantage in the production of both wood and high-tech products since it can produce more per hour of either good than can Country B. But, absolute advantage does NOT determine the basis for trade.

The easiest way to compute comparative advantage is to determine what the opportunity cost of production is for each good for each country, on a per unit basis. To do this, you must first answer how much Country A must give up if it were to specialize in the production of wood. For every additional hour of effort devoted to producing wood products, Country A would give up the production of 15 units of high-tech products. (Of course, it is then able to produce 10 more units of wood products.) On a per unit basis, Country A must give up 1.5 units of high-tech products for each 1 unit of wood products (15 high-tech products/hour)/(10 wood products/hour). You would read this as follows: "for Country A, the opportunity cost of 1 wood product is 1.5 high-tech products." For Country B, for every additional hour of effort devoted to producing wood products, it must give up 4 units of high-tech products. (Of course, it is then able to produce 8 more units of wood products.) On a per unit basis, Country B must give up 0.5 units of high-tech products for each 1 unit of wood products (4 high-tech products/hour)/(8 wood products/hour). You would read this as follows: "for Country B, the opportunity cost of 1 wood product is 0.5 high-tech products." Thus, Country B has the lower opportunity cost of producing wood products since it has to give up fewer high-tech products.

Since Country B has the lower opportunity cost of wood production, it should specialize in wood production. (Wood production is "less costly" in Country B than in Country A).

If this is true, then it must also be true that Country A has the lower opportunity cost of high-tech production and thus should specialize in producing high-tech goods.

Let's see if this is true using the numbers from the Table 3-1. For Country A, the opportunity cost of producing more high-tech products is that for every additional hour of producing high-tech products, it must give up producing 10 units of wood products. (Of course, it is then able to produce 15 more units of high-tech products.) On a per unit basis, Country A must give up 0.67 wood products for every 1 high-tech product (10 wood products/hour)/(15 high-tech products per hour). You would read this as follows: "for Country A, the opportunity cost of 1 high-tech product is 0.67 wood products." For Country B, the opportunity cost of producing more high-tech products is that for every additional hour of producing high-tech products, it must give up producing 8 units of wood products. (Of course, it is then able to produce 4 more units of high-tech products.) On a per unit basis, Country B must give up 2 wood products for every one unit of high-tech products (8 wood products/hour)/(4 high-tech products/hour). Thus, Country A has the lower opportunity cost of producing high-tech products since it has to give up fewer wood products. (High-tech production is "less costly" in Country A than in Country B.)

PET #2

Household savings helps to fund firms' purchases of machinery, buildings, equipment, and technology (physical capital).

This performance-enhancing tip may not be especially useful in this chapter, but when you get to the chapters on Macroeconomics, it will be important to remember.

PET #3

If a government spends more for its programs than it collects in taxes, it finances its overspending by borrowing money from households, firms, and foreign countries. The government borrows by selling securities (bonds or IOUs) to households, firms, and foreign countries that in turn lend their saving to the government. The government, of course, promises to pay back the lenders with interest.

PET #4

Trade protection increases the price a country pays for goods it imports from other countries.

Your textbook mentions different types of trade protection – tariffs, quotas, and non-tariff barriers, all of which act to raise the price of the goods and services that a country imports from other countries.

The exchange rate is the price of one currency in terms of another. It can be thought of just like the price of any good or service.

Think about the price of any good or service; say a painting priced at $200, i.e., $200/painting. The item in the denominator is what is being priced. This is also true for an exchange rate. Suppose the exchange rate is expressed as 1.50 Canadian dollars/1 US dollar. In this case, the currency that is being priced is the US dollar. Its price is $1.50. The inverse of this exchange rate would be 0.667 US dollars/1 Canadian dollar. Now, the currency that is being priced is the Canadian dollar. One Canadian dollar is priced at (or costs) 0.667 US dollars.

If the price of a painting rises, we would say the painting has appreciated in value. If the price of a painting falls, we would say the painting has depreciated in value. This is also true for an exchange rate. If the exchange rate decreased from 1.50 Canadian dollars/1 US dollar to 1.40 Canadian dollars/1 US dollar, we would say that the US dollar has depreciated since it now worth $1.40 instead of $1.50. If the US dollar has depreciated against the Canadian dollar, then it must be true that the Canadian dollar has appreciated. To see this, the inverse of 1.40 Canadian dollars/1 US dollar is 0.714 U.S. dollars/1 Canadian dollar. Thus, the Canadian dollar has appreciated in value since it is now worth 0.714 US dollars instead of 0.667 US dollars.

V.   PRACTICE EXAM: MULTIPLE CHOICE QUESTIONS

1. Which one of the following is true of a corporation?

    a. A single individual owns it.
    b. Two or more partners own it.
    c. Stockholders own it.
    d. It is held in trust.
    e. A bank owns it.

2. Which one of the following statements is NOT true?

    a. France has the largest tax burden whereas the United States has the lowest.
    b. The major source of tax revenue for the federal government is the goods and services tax (GST).
    c. About 72% of income earned by households comes from wages and salaries.
    d. One of the three biggest spending programs for provinces is education.
    e. The two biggest federal government-spending programs are health and social services and government services.

3. Which one of the following is NOT a role of the government?

   a. Redistributing income from richer households to poorer households.
   b. Providing national defence, parks, and public safety, among other things.
   c. Regulating businesses.
   d. Making international trade policy.
   e. All of the above are roles of the government.

4. Suppose a province has in place a 5% sales tax. Further, suppose for that year, businesses throughout the province have collectively made $100,000,000 (100 million) in sales. How much in sales tax revenue will the government collect?

   a. $50,000,000.
   b. $5,000,000.
   c. $500,000.
   d. $50,000.
   e. $500,000,000.

5. Under a vertically equitable tax system:

   a. Every household would pay the same dollar amount of taxes. For example, every, household would be required to pay $2,500.
   b. Every household would pay the same percentage of their income in taxes. For example, every household would be required to pay 20% of their income in taxes.
   c. Wealthier households would pay a higher percentage of their incomes in taxes. For example, wealthier households would be required to pay 35% of their income in taxes whereas poorer households would pay 10% of their income in taxes.
   d. Every household would pay taxes based on the amount of government services they used over a year.
   e. Every household would pay taxes based on a three-year average of their income.

6. Which of the following is NOT a criterion for evaluating the tax system?

   a. Easy to understand.
   b. Maximizes government revenue.
   c. Fair.
   d. Not disruptive to markets that otherwise operate effectively.
   e. All of the above are criteria for evaluating the tax system.

7. Which one of the following is **NOT** an example of a trade barrier?

   a. Tariffs.
   b. Quotas.
   c. Health and safety laws.
   d. The General Agreement on Tariffs and Trade.
   e. Slow and inefficient customs systems.

8. Use Table 3-2 to answer the following question.

Table 3-2

	Country A	Country B
Toys	50 units per day	20 units per day
Ships	2 units per day	1 unit per day

Which country has the comparative advantage in producing toys, and which country has the comparative advantage in producing ships?

   a. Country A has the comparative advantage in producing both toys and ships.
   b. Country B has the comparative advantage in producing both toys and ships.
   c. Country A has the comparative advantage in producing toys and Country B has the comparative advantage in producing ships.
   d. Country B has the comparative advantage in producing toys and Country A has the comparative advantage in producing ships.
   e. Need information on exchange rates to answer the question.

9. Which one of the following statements is correct?

   a. The top three Canadian exports are machinery and equipment, automotive products and energy products.
   b. NAFTA is a free-trade agreement between Canada, Mexico, and the United States.
   c. The countries of the European Union plan on joining the governments of all of the participating countries into one federal government.
   d. Canada responded to the Smoot-Hawley Tariff Act imposed by the United States in the 1930s by raising Canadian tariffs by 3%.
   e. All of the above are correct statements.

10. Suppose that you are going to buy a cuckoo clock from Germany and the German Euro price for the clock is 250 Euros. If the current exchange rate is 2 Euros/1 Canadian dollar, you will pay $_____. If the exchange rate changes to 1.8 Euros/1 Canadian dollar, the _____will have depreciated.

   a. $125; dollar.
   b. $125; Euro.
   c. $500; dollar.
   d. $500; Euro.
   e. $250; dollar.

VI. PRACTICE EXAM: ESSAY QUESTIONS

11. What is the purpose of taxation? What types of taxes are there? How do taxes affect people's behaviour?

12. What are the roles of government in a mixed economy?

VII. ANSWER KEY: MULTIPLE CHOICE QUESTIONS

1. Correct answer: c.

   Discussion: those individuals who have purchased stock in the corporation own a corporation. They are the stockholders, and they effectively own the company. Stockholders are paid dividends on the shares of stock they own. This is sort of like earning interest, except that dividend payments do not necessarily offer the same yield every quarter or every year as would be typical with an investment in an interest-bearing asset.

   Statement a would be true if the question was about a sole proprietorship. Statement b would be true if the question was about a partnership. Statement d is an irrelevant concept. Statement e is incorrect because stockholders, not a bank, own a corporation.

2. Correct answer: b.

   Discussion: Statement b is not true. The major sources of tax revenues for the federal government are income taxes. Statements, a, c, d, and e are all true.

3. Correct answer: e.

   Discussion: All of the above statements are listed in your textbook as roles of the government. The book includes one more role that is the role of taxing. Statements a, b, c, and d are all true statements.

4. Correct Answer: b.

   Discussion: To compute the amount collected in sales tax revenues, multiply 100,000,000 times (5/100) or (0.05). This equals $5,000,000.

   Statement a would be correct if the sales tax rate was 50%. Statement c would be correct if the sales tax rate was 0.5% (or a half percent). Statement d would be correct if the sales tax rate was 0.05%. Statement e would be correct if the sales tax rate was 500%.

5. Correct answer: c.

   Discussion: A vertically equitable tax system (sometimes called a "progressive" tax system) is one in which the wealthier citizens pay a higher percentage of income in taxes than do the poorer citizens. This type of tax system reduces to some extent the differences in income between the citizens of a country.

   Statement a is an example of a tax system in which every household is assessed a lump-sum fee that they must pay regardless of their income or family size. Statement b is an example of a horizontally equitable tax system (sometimes referred to as a flat tax). Statement d is an example that applies the benefit-tax approach to assessing taxes. Statement e computes taxes paid by an individual based on the last three years' worth of income.

6. Correct answer: b.

   Discussion: Statements a, c, and d are all true statements. All of the statements are listed in your textbook as criteria we should use when evaluating a tax system. Statement b is incorrect because the role of the government in a mixed economy is not to maximize its revenue through taxation but to redistribute income and help the market work more effectively.

7. Correct answer: d.

Discussion: The General Agreement on Tariffs and Trade (GATT) is an agreement between countries to work together to reduce tariff rates amongst themselves.

A tariff is a tax on an imported good which raises the price that a country must pay to buy it from another country. This acts as a trade barrier. A quota is a restriction on the quantity of imports of a particular good that a country may purchase from another country. It is also a trade barrier and acts to raise the price of the imported good. Health and safety laws are non-tariff trade barriers. These laws may effectively make it more difficult for a country to import a product from another country. For example, the health and safety laws of European countries restrict them from importing genetically altered food. This meant that they could not buy some Canadian agricultural products. Slow and inefficient customs laws also act as a trade barrier. For example, if a product must pass through several layers of administration and paperwork before being admitted into the importing country, this raises the cost of the good and thus its price. This effectively makes it harder and more expensive for the importing country to buy the good and more of a hassle for the exporting country to deliver its products to another country.

8. Correct answer: c.

Discussion: Country A must give up 50 toys to produce 2 ships. On a per unit basis, Country A must give up 25 toys to produce 1 ship. On the other hand, Country B must give up 20 toys to produce 1 ship. Since Country B has to give up fewer toys to produce 1 ship, Country B incurs a smaller opportunity cost of building one more ship. That is, it is less costly to produce a ship in Country B than in Country A. So, Country B should produce ships which means Country A should produce toys. The two countries will be able to acquire more of both goods by trading or exchanging toys for ships and vice-versa.

Statement a is not correct. It would be correct if the question had been "Which country has an absolute advantage in toy production and which in ship production?" The table shows that Country A can produce more toys and more ships per day than can Country B. However, this is not the concept of comparative advantage. Statement b is not correct for similar reasons just mentioned. Statement d is not correct because it is the other way around – Country A has a comparative advantage in toy production and Country B in shipbuilding. Statement e is not correct because comparative advantage can be computed using the table of numbers given.

9. Correct answer: b.

Discussion: NAFTA is the North American Free Trade Agreement. It is an agreement to eliminate all tariffs and trade barriers between the U.S., Canada, and Mexico.

Statement a is incorrect because the top three exports for Canada are machinery and equipment, automotive products and industrial goods and machines. Statement c is incorrect; the countries of the European Union are planning on having completely free trade and a single currency. Statement d is incorrect because Canada responded by increasing tariffs by 30%, not 3%. Statement e is not correct because not all of the statements are true.

10. Correct answer: a.

Discussion: To figure out the dollar price of the clock, the Euro price must be converted to dollars using the exchange rate. Since the exchange rate is expressed as Euros/dollar, you can determine the dollar price by multiplying 250 Euros * (1 dollar/2 Euros) = $125. (The Euros in the numerator and denominator cancel each other out.) Since the exchange rate is expressed as Euros/dollar, it is best to think of the exchange rate as the price of a dollar. Since the exchange rate has changed from 2 Euros/dollar to 1.8 Euros/dollar, the price of a dollar has decreased (See PET #5), i.e., the dollar has depreciated (which also means that the Euro must have appreciated).

Statement b is not correct because the Euro appreciated, not depreciated. Statement c is not correct because the conversion of the Euro price of the clock to a dollar price leads to a price of $125, not $500. Statement d is not correct for the reasons mentioned for b and c. Statement e is not correct because the dollar price of the clock is $125, not $250.

VIII. ANSWER KEY: ESSAY QUESTIONS

11. Taxes serve the purpose of paying for goods and services that a society may collectively want to have but which may be too expensive to pay for on an individual basis. By pooling money collected from households and corporations across the country, goods like national defence, highways and bridges, prisons, national parks, school buildings, etc., may be easier to pay for. Taxes also serve a purpose of funding the poorer segments of society or those who have fallen on hard times. For example, your tax dollars may be used to fund unemployment compensation, drug rehabilitation, health care, etc. So your tax dollars not only pay for goods and services from which you might directly benefit, but also pay for goods and services which you may or may not ever use. There are three basic types of taxes: taxes on households/workers, taxes on corporations, and excise taxes which are taxes on specific goods like gasoline, cigarettes, and imported goods. Households/workers pay personal income taxes, payroll taxes, sales taxes, and property taxes, to name a few. Corporations pay corporate income taxes, payroll taxes, sales taxes, and property taxes as well. Households and corporations, to the extent that they purchase goods that have an excise tax levied on them, also pay taxes to the government. Taxes can distort people's behaviour by altering the actual price that they pay for a good or service or for providing a good or service. A higher personal income tax rate may cause people to spend less and/or save more. A tax on gasoline may cause people to use gasoline more frugally. A tax on air travel may cause people to be less likely to fly to get somewhere. A city property tax may cause fewer people to want to live in the city. A tax on paper may cause a publishing company to be more likely to produce electronic versions of their product than paper versions.

12. A government plays several roles in a mixed economy. It provides goods and services like parks, public safety, consumer information, etc., to its citizens. A government also redistributes income from richer citizens to poorer citizens. This is done in the interest of creating a more equitable distribution of income. In order for the government to be able to provide goods and services and transfer income from richer citizens to poorer citizens, it must collect taxes. A government also regulates business practices for different reasons. A government may regulate an industry, to ensure that it doesn't impose undue hazards on its citizens (nuclear fuel); a government may regulate an industry to ensure that its citizens aren't charged an unfair price for the product (utilities or cable industry); or a government may regulate industries to ensure that its citizens are not being sold unsafe products (automobiles, food, medicine). Finally, a government enacts trade policy. A government may set the rules of the game that are used between countries that engage in trading goods and services with each other. It should also be mentioned that a government establishes a legal system to assign and enforce property rights.

CHAPTER 4
SUPPLY, DEMAND, AND MARKET EQUILIBRIUM

I. OVERVIEW

In this chapter, you will learn about two basic economic constructs: demand and supply. These two constructs can be used to answer questions like: what might happen to housing prices in a subdivision if a new mall is built near the subdivision? What might happen to the share price of a health services company when the government revamps the health care system? What might happen to the price of bread when former Soviet-bloc countries begin to trade with Canada? What might happen to the price of tea when the price of coffee rises? Not only can demand and supply be used to guide your thinking about what will happen to prices, it can also be used to guide your thinking about whether more or less will be bought and sold. In this chapter, you will learn how to use graphs of demand and supply to determine what happens to a market price and the quantity bought and sold. Thus, in this chapter it is imperative that you familiarize yourself with shifts of a curve versus movements along a curve (see Chapter 1 of the Study Guide).

II. CHECKLIST

By the end of this chapter, you should be able to do the following:

- ❏ Explain the Law of Demand and the Law of Supply (for both price increases and price decreases).
- ❏ Understand what will cause a movement along a demand or supply curve and what will cause the curves to shift.
- ❏ Explain what happens to equilibrium price and equilibrium quantity when:
    - ❏ Demand increases (shifts right)
    - ❏ Demand decreases (shifts left)
    - ❏ Supply increases (shifts right)
    - ❏ Supply decreases (shifts left)
- ❏ Explain whether you can determine for certain what happens to equilibrium price and equilibrium quantity when demand and/or supply both shift.
- ❏ List factors that will cause demand to shift (and in which direction).
- ❏ List factors that will cause supply to shift (and in which direction).
- ❏ Explain what causes a shortage and what causes a surplus and be able to depict them with a supply and demand graph.

III.   KEY TERMS

Perfectly competitive market: a market with a large number of firms, each of which produces the same standardized product and is so small that it does not affect the market price of the good it produces.

Demand curve: a curve showing the relationship between price and the quantity that consumers are willing to buy during a particular time period.

Law of demand: the lower the price, the larger the quantity demanded.

Substitution effect: The change in consumption resulting from a change in the price of one good relative to the price of other goods.

Income effect: The change in consumption resulting from an increase in the consumer's real income, *ceteris paribus*.

Change in quantity demanded: a change in quantity resulting from a change in just the price of the good; causes movement along a demand curve.

Change in demand: a change in quantity resulting from a change in something other than the price of the good; causes the entire demand curve to shift.

Normal good: a good for which an increase in income, *ceteris paribus*, increases demand.

Inferior good: a good for which an increase in income, *ceteris paribus*, decreases demand.

Substitutes: two goods for which an increase in the price of one good, *ceteris paribus*, increases the demand for the other good.

Complements: two goods for which an increase in the price of one good, *ceteris paribus*, decreases the demand for the other good.

Supply curve: a curve showing the relationship between price and the quantity that producers are willing to sell during a particular time period.

Law of supply: the higher the price, the larger the quantity supplied, *ceteris paribus*.

Change in quantity supplied: a change in quantity resulting from a change in the price of the good; causes movement along a supply curve.

Change in supply: a change in quantity resulting from a change in something other than the price of the good; causes the entire supply curve to shift.

Complement in production: a good that is produced as a by-product of the production of some other good.

Substitute in production: a good that can be produced instead of some other product.

Market equilibrium: a situation in which the quantity of a product demanded equals the quantity supplied, so there is no pressure to change the price.

Shortage: a situation in which consumers are willing to buy more than producers are willing to sell; there is excess demand.

Surplus: a situation in which producers are willing to sell more than consumers are willing to buy; there is excess supply.

IV.   PERFORMANCE ENHANCING TIPS (PETS)

PET #1

Since price is a variable on the axis of a graph of the demand and supply of a particular good, a change in the price will NOT cause the demand or supply curve for that good to shift but will instead be represented by a movement along the demand and supply curves.

Remember from Chapter 1 of the Study Guide that in a graph of Y and X, where Y and X are drawn on either axis, changes in Y or X will not cause the curve(s) to shift but instead cause movements along the curve. It may be wise to review practice question 10 and PET #1 from Chapter 1 to reinforce your memory of this principle.

PET #2

*When the price of good X rises (falls), the quantity demanded falls (rises). Do **NOT** say that the **demand falls** (rises) since this means the whole curve shifts left (right).*

For example, suppose you read on the exam a statement that says, "What happens in the market for peanut butter when the price of peanut butter falls?" One of the test options might be "the demand for peanut butter increases." This is not the correct answer. Shifting the whole demand curve out to the right would represent a statement like "the demand for peanut butter increases". However, since the price of peanut butter has fallen and is a variable on the axis for which the demand and supply of peanut butter are drawn, moving along the demand curve will represent the decline in the price of peanut butter. As the price of peanut butter falls, the *quantity of peanut butter demanded* increases. This would be the correct answer.

PET #3

*When the price of good X rises (falls), the quantity supplied rises (falls). Do **NOT** say that the **supply rises** (falls) since this means the whole supply curve shifts right (left).*

For example, suppose you read on the exam a statement that says, "What happens in the market for jelly when the price of jelly falls?" One of the test options might be "the supply of jelly decreases." This is not the correct answer. Shifting the whole supply curve to the left would represent a statement like "the supply of jelly decreases". However, since the price of jelly has fallen and is a variable on the axis for which the demand and supply of jelly are drawn, moving along the supply curve will represent the decline in the price of jelly. As the price of jelly falls, the *quantity of jelly supplied* decreases. This would be the correct answer.

PET #4

A rightward shift in the demand curve can be expressed in the following ways:

(a)   At every price, the quantity demanded that buyers' want is now higher.
(b)   At every quantity demanded, the price buyers would be willing to pay is now higher.

To see this, look at Figures 4-1 and 4-2. Demand curve (a) corresponds to statement (a) because, at every price, the quantity demand is now higher. Demand curve (b) corresponds to statement (b) because, at every quantity demanded, the price buyers would be willing to pay is now higher. In both cases, the demand curve is further to the right after the shift than before.

Figure 4-1

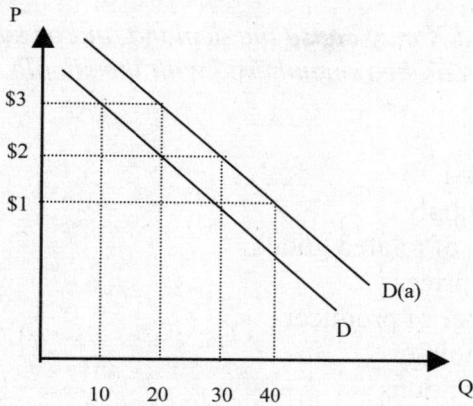

Figure 4-2

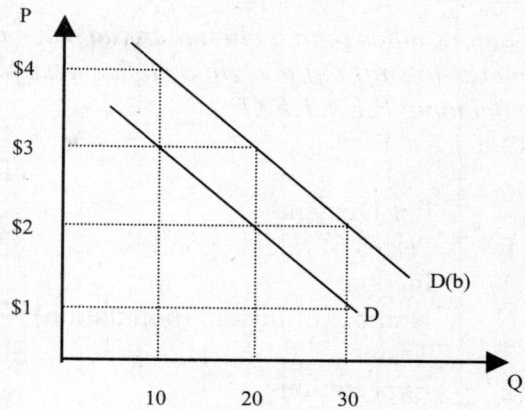

You should be able to rewrite statements (a) and (b) for a leftward shift in demand.

PET #5

A rightward shift in the supply curve can be expressed in the following ways:

(a)   At every price, the quantity that producers are willing to supply is now higher.

(b)   At every quantity supplied, the price at which producers would be willing to sell is now lower.

To see this, look at Figures 4-3 and 4-4. Supply curve (a) corresponds to statement (a) and supply curve (b) corresponds to statement (b). In both cases, the supply curve is further to the right after the shift than before.

Figure 4-3

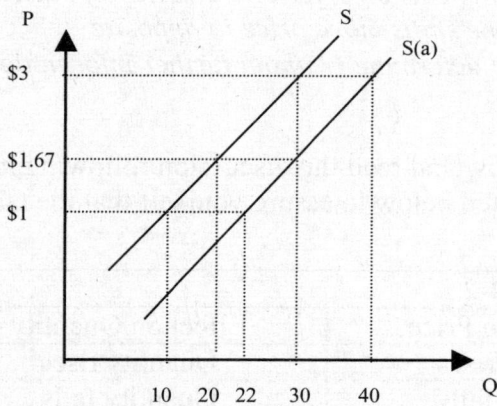

Figure 4-4

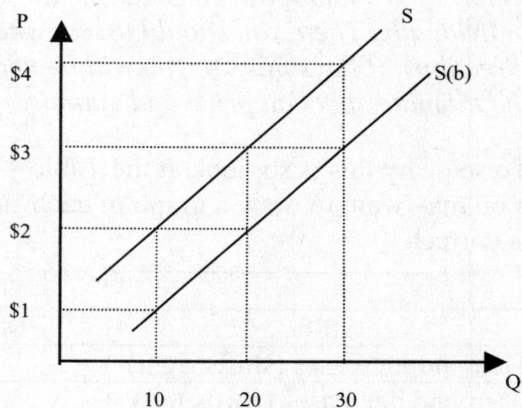

You should be able to rewrite statements (a) and (b) for a leftward shift in supply.

PET #6

Factors other than a change in the price of good X may cause the demand and/or supply curves to shift to the right or left. These factors can be remembered with the simple mnemonic P.I.N.T.E.O.

Table 4-1

	For Demand	For Supply
P -	Prices of related goods	Prices of related goods
I -	Income	Input prices
N -	Number of buyers (population)	Number of producers
T -	Tastes	Technology
E -	Expectations	Expectations
O -	Other (advertising, fads. etc.)	Other (weather, strikes, taxes on producers, etc.)

While this mnemonic should help you if basic logic fails you during an exam (perhaps due to exam-induced stress), you should not simply memorize these lists. They should make sense to you. So, for example, if there is a technological improvement in producing computer chips, it should make sense that the technological improvement makes production of chips more efficient and less costly, which you would represent by shifting the supply curve for computer chips to the right. That is, supply increases. Likewise, it should make sense to you that, when the price of peanut butter goes up, the demand for jelly (a complement) will decrease, which you would represent by shifting the demand curve for jelly to the left. You should work through different examples of each to ensure that your logic is correct.

PET #7

When you are asked to consider the effects of a shift in demand together with a shift in supply, you should first consider the directional effects on price and quantity of each shift individually. Then, you should assess whether the shifts move price in opposite directions. If the shifts do, you will be unable to determine (without further information) the ultimate effect on price and quantity.

To see why this is so, look at the Table 4-2 below and read the discussion following it. You may want to draw a graph of each shift listed below to assure yourself that the table is correct.

Table 4-2		
Shift	Effect on Price	Effect on Quantity
Demand increases (shifts right)	Price rises	Quantity rises
Demand decreases (shifts left)	Price falls	Quantity falls
Supply increases (shifts right)	Price falls	Quantity rises
Supply decreases (shifts left)	Price rises	Quantity falls

Suppose you are given a test question that asks what happens in the market for bicycles when rollerblades becomes the rage and when the price of aluminium used in making bicycles increases.

First, you must categorize the rollerblade rage as one of the four shift factors above and the increased price of aluminium as one of the four shift factors above. The rollerblade rage would be categorized as a leftward shift in the demand for *bicycles,* and the increased price of aluminium as a leftward shift in the supply of bicycles. Since rollerblades and bicycling are substitutes, the increased rollerblade rage might decrease the demand for bicycles (leftward shift), which is to say that, at every price, the quantity demanded would now be lower. Since aluminium is an input into bicycles, the increased price of aluminium makes bicycle production more costly which is to say that at every quantity supplied, the price that producers would be willing to accept would be higher (to cover their costs). That is, the supply of bicycles decreases (shifts left).

Now, the decrease in demand for bicycles will lower the equilibrium price and quantity of bicycles. The decrease in the supply of bicycles will raise the equilibrium price and lower the equilibrium quantity of bicycles. In this case, the two shifts move price in the opposite direction but have the same directional effect on the equilibrium quantity. Therefore, you can only answer for sure what happens to the equilibrium quantity. (It falls.) If you knew the magnitudes of the shifts in demand and supply, you would be able to answer what happens to the equilibrium price.

V   PRACTICE EXAM: MULTIPLE CHOICE QUESTIONS

1. Which one of the following statements is correct about the Law of Demand?

    a. As the price of oranges decreases, the demand for oranges increases.
    b. As the price of oranges increases, the demand for oranges increases.
    c. As the price of oranges decreases, the quantity of oranges demanded increases.
    d. As the price of oranges increases, the quantity of oranges demanded increases.
    e. As the price of oranges decreases, the demand for oranges shifts left.

2. Consider the market for flavoured mineral water. If the price of soda (a substitute for flavoured mineral water) increases, which one of the following might be an outcome?

    a. The demand for soda will decrease.
    b. The demand for mineral water will increase (shift right).
    c. The price of mineral water will fall.
    d. The equilibrium quantity of mineral water will fall.
    e. (b) and (c).

3. Which one of the following statements is correct about the Law of Supply?

    a. As the price of dog bones decreases, the supply of dog bones increases.
    b. As the price of dog bones increases, the supply of dog bones increases.
    c. As the price of dog bones decreases, the quantity of dog bones supplied decreases.
    d. As the price of dog bones increases, the quantity of dog bones supplied decreases.
    e. As the price of dog bones increases, the supply of dog bones shifts right.

4. Consider the market for mattresses. If the price of foam used in making mattresses declines, which one of the following might be an outcome?

    a. The supply of mattresses will increase (shift right).
    b. The demand for mattresses will increase.
    c. The price of mattresses will rise.
    d. There will be a shortage of mattresses.
    e. (a) and (b).

5. Which one of the following would **NOT** cause the supply of bananas to decrease?

    a. A technological advance in banana production.
    b. A decrease in the number of producers of bananas.
    c. An increase in the price of a fertilizer used in growing bananas.
    d. A severe rain shortage.
    e. A tax placed on banana producers.

6. Which one of the following would **NOT** cause the demand for walking shoes to increase?

    a. An advertising campaign that says walking is good for your health.
    b. An increase in income.
    c. A decrease in the price of rubber used in producing walking shoes.
    d. An increased preference for walking rather than running.
    e. All of the above will cause the demand for walking shoes to increase.

7. Consider the market for chocolate candy. What is the effect on the equilibrium price and equilibrium quantity of a decrease in demand for and an increase in the supply of chocolate candy?

    a. Equilibrium price rises; equilibrium quantity falls.
    b. Equilibrium price falls; equilibrium quantity rises.
    c. Equilibrium price is uncertain; equilibrium quantity falls.
    d. Equilibrium price rises; equilibrium quantity rises.
    e. Equilibrium price falls; equilibrium quantity is uncertain.

8. Pretend that you are an economic detective and are given the following clues about the market for wine: the price of wine rose and the equilibrium quantity of wine declined. In writing your investigative report, which one of the following would you conclude might be responsible for the outcome?

    a. A decrease in the demand for wine.
    b. A decrease in the supply of wine.
    c. All increase in the demand for wine.
    d. An increase in the supply of wine.
    e. A decrease in the demand for wine and an increase in the supply of wine.

9. Use Figure 4-5 to answer the following question.

Figure 4-5

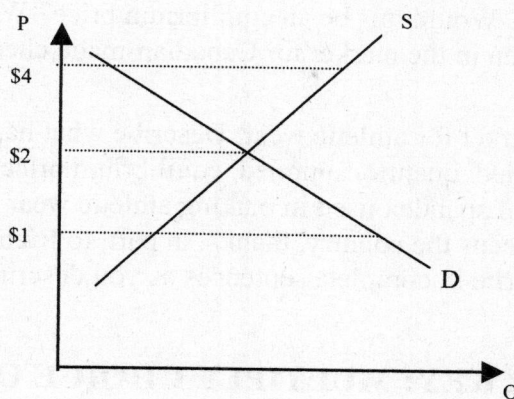

Which one of the following statements is true about Figure 4-5?

   a. There is a shortage at a price of $4.
   b. There is a surplus at a price of $4.
   c. At a current price of $1, there is pressure for the equilibrium price to fall.
   d. If the price fell from $4 to $2, quantity supplied would increase.
   e. If the price fell from $4 to $2, demand would shift right.

10. Canada imports a lot of cars from Japan. Suppose that the price of steel that Japan uses in making cars declines. What effect might this have in the Canadian market for cars?

   a. The supply of Japanese-made cars to Canada will decrease.
   b. The price of Japanese-made cars sold in Canada will decrease.
   c. The price of Japanese-made cars sold in Canada will increase.
   d. The demand for Japanese-made cars will increase.
   e. The quantity of Japanese-made cars sold in Canada will decrease.

11. Which one of the following statements would be true of an increase in demand for cameras?

   a. Equilibrium price rises and the supply of cameras increases.
   b. Equilibrium price rises and the supply of cameras decreases.
   c. Equilibrium price falls and the quantity of cameras supplied decreases.
   d. Equilibrium price rises and the quantity of cameras supplied increases.
   e. Equilibrium price falls and the supply of cameras falls.

VI. PRACTICE EXAM: ESSAY QUESTIONS

12. Consider the market for Canadian-made cheese. Suppose that the current equilibrium price is $10 per kg. Suppose that the French develop a preference for Canadian-made cheese. Describe what would be true in the market if, after this development, the price remained at $10. Would this be an equilibrium price? Why or why not? What would eventually happen in the market for Canadian-made cheese?

13. Consider the market for athletic wear. Describe what happens to demand, supply, quantity demanded, quantity supplied, equilibrium price, and equilibrium quantity when the price of spandex used in making athletic wear rises and at the same time a fitness craze sweeps the country, thanks, in part, to Richard Simmons. Do not simply draw graphs. Write in complete sentences as you describe what happens.

VII. ANSWER KEY: MULTIPLE CHOICE QUESTIONS

1. Correct Answer: c.

   Discussion: The law of demand expresses an inverse or negative relationship between the price of a good and the quantity demanded (holding other factors constant). Thus, when the price of X rises, the quantity of X demanded falls and when the price of X falls, the quantity of X demanded rises.

   Statement a is incorrect because demand does not increase (which would be represented by the demand curve shifting right). The law of demand is about a movement along a demand curve, not a shift in the curve. Statements b and e are incorrect for similar reasons. Statement d is incorrect because it infers a positive relationship between price and quantity demanded.

2. Correct answer: b.

   Discussion: Since mineral water and soda are substitutes, when the price of soda rises, consumers may switch to buying mineral water instead. Thus, the demand for mineral water increases, represented by a rightward shift in demand.

   Statement a is incorrect because the price of soda is not a shift factor in the market for soda: a fall in the price of soda causes a movement along the demand curve for soda and thus causes the quantity of soda demanded (not the Demand) to decrease. Statement c is not correct because when the demand for mineral water increases, the price of mineral water will rise. Statement d is not correct because when the demand for mineral water increases, the equilibrium quantity will rise. Statement e is not correct because statement a is not correct.

3. Correct answer: c.

   Discussion: The Law of Supply states that there is a positive relationship between the price of X and the quantity of X supplied, holding other factors constant. This means that, when the price of X increases, the quantity of X supplied increases, and when the price of X decreases, the quantity of X supplied decreases. Statement c describes a positive relationship between the price of dog bones and the quantity of dog bones supplied.

   Statements a, b, and e are incorrect because a change in the price of dog bones will not cause the supply curve to shift in either direction but rather cause a movement along the supply curve (quantity supplied changes). Statement d is not correct because there is a positive relationship between the price and quantity supplied, not a negative relationship as implied in statement d.

4. Correct answer: a.

   Discussion: Foam is an input into mattresses. When the price of foam decreases, it makes mattress production less costly. Shifting the supply of mattresses to the right (increasing supply) would represent this.

   Statement b is not correct because the price of foam will not shift the demand for mattresses. What will happen, however, is that, as the supply of mattresses increases, which will cause the price of mattresses to fall, the quantity of mattresses demanded will rise in response. Thus, b would have been correct if it had said, "quantity demanded." Statement c is not correct because an increase in the supply of mattresses caused by the decrease in the price of foam will decrease the price of mattresses. Statement d is not correct because there is no reason given to think a shortage would occur. Statement e is not correct because statement b is not correct.

5. Correct answer: a.

   Discussion: A technological advance in banana production would increase the supply of bananas, not decrease it.

   Statements b, c, d, and e are all factors that would cause the supply of bananas to decrease. A decrease in the number of producers would obviously reduce the supply of bananas. An increase in the price of fertilizer raises the cost of producing bananas and would be represented by a leftward shift in supply, i.e. supply decreases. A severe rain shortage would obviously reduce the banana crop and thus decrease the supply of bananas. A tax on banana growers has the effect of raising the cost of doing business. This acts just like an increase in the price of fertilizer, i.e., the supply of bananas would shift left (decrease).

6. Correct answer: c.

   Discussion: A decrease in the price of rubber used in producing walking shoes will lower the cost of producing walking shoes and cause the supply of walking shoes to increase, not the demand. However, quantity demanded would rise since the lower cost of production would translate to a lower price of walking shoes, which would raise the quantity of walking shoes demanded (movement along the demand curve).

   Statements a, b, and d would lead to an increase in the demand for walking shoes. However, it may be worth noting that, if walking shoes were considered an inferior good, then an increase in income would actually reduce the demand for walking shoes. Statement e is not correct because statement c should have been selected.

7. Correct answer: e.

   Discussion: A decrease in demand for chocolate candy will lower the equilibrium price and lower the equilibrium quantity. An increase in the supply of chocolate candy will lower the equilibrium price and raise the equilibrium quantity. You can see these two cases by drawing graphs of them, separately. Since the demand and supply shifts only push the price in the same direction, price will decline for sure. However, the demand and supply shifts push the equilibrium quantity in opposite directions, so the effect is not known for certain.

8. Correct answer: b.

   Shifting the supply curve to the left represents a decrease in the supply of wine. A leftward shift in supply raises the equilibrium price and reduces the equilibrium quantity. You can see this by drawing a graph where supply shifts to the left and sketching out what happens to the equilibrium price and quantity.

   Statement b is not correct because a decrease in demand would reduce the equilibrium price and reduce the equilibrium quantity. Statement c is not correct because an increase in demand would raise the equilibrium price and raise the equilibrium quantity. Statement d is not correct because an increase in supply would lower the equilibrium price and raise the equilibrium quantity. Statement e is not correct because the effects of these two shifts will have an uncertain effect on price but lower the equilibrium quantity for certain.

Chapter 4

9. Correct answer: b.

At a price of $4, the quantity supplied exceeds the quantity demanded which is the case of a surplus. Just take the price of $4 and draw a line over to the demand and supply curves and then drop those points down to the quantity axis. You will see that the quantity supplied exceeds the quantity demanded.

Discussion: Statement a is not correct because there is not a shortage but rather a surplus. Statement c is not correct because there would be pressure for the price to rise to the equilibrium price of $2. In fact, at a price of $1, there is a shortage. Statement d is not correct because, if the price fell from $4 to $2, the quantity supplied would decrease. Statement e is not correct because, if the price fell from $4 to $2, the quantity demanded (not demand) would increase.

10. Correct answer: b.

Discussion: A decrease in the price of steel reduces the cost of manufacturing cars and thus increases the supply of Japanese-made cars. The increase in supply of Japanese-made cars will lower the price that Canadian buyers pay for the cars. You can see this by drawing a graph where supply shifts to the right along the demand curve.

Statement a is not correct because the supply will increase, not decrease. Statement c is not correct because the price will decrease, not increase. Statement d is not correct because the event will not cause demand to shift; quantity demanded will however rise. Statement e is not correct because the quantity of cars sold in the U.S. will increase, not decrease.

11. Correct answer: d.

Discussion: shifting the demand curve to the right would represent an increase in the demand for cameras. The increase in demand raises the equilibrium price and quantity. As the equilibrium price rises, there is a movement along the supply curve which shows that the quantity, supplied increases. You may wish to draw a graph to see this.

Statement a is not correct because the supply curve for cameras does not shift to the right; the quantity, of cameras supplied increases. Statement b is not correct because the supply curve does not shift. Statement c is not correct because the equilibrium price rises, not falls, and the quantity of cameras increases, not decreases. Statement e is not correct because the price of cameras rises and because the supply curve does not shift.

VIII. ANSWER KEY: ESSAY QUESTIONS

12. An increased preference by the French for Canadian-made cheese would mean that there would be an increase in the demand for Canadian-made cheese. Shifting the demand curve for Canadian-made cheese to the right as Figure 4-6 shows. At every price, the quantity demanded is now higher (or at every quantity, the price that buyers would be willing to pay is now higher). If the price remained at $10 (rather than rising as it should), there would be a shortage of Canadian-made cheese. That is, if the price remained at $10, the new quantity demanded would now exceed the quantity supplied at a price of $10. This would not be an equilibrium price any more. The shortage should not persist for too long because the shortage creates upward pressure on the price of cheese. Eventually, the price of cheese will rise to a new equilibrium price that is above $1. As the price rises, two things happen to eliminate the shortage. (1) As the price rises, the quantity supplied increases as the arrows along the supply curve indicate (Law of Supply; movement along supply curve): this helps eliminate the shortage. (2) As the price rises, the quantity demanded decreases as the arrows along the demand curve indicate (Law of Demand; movement along demand curve). This also helps eliminate the shortage. Eventually, a new equilibrium price will be reached where the new quantity supplied is equal to the new quantity demanded.

Figure 4-6

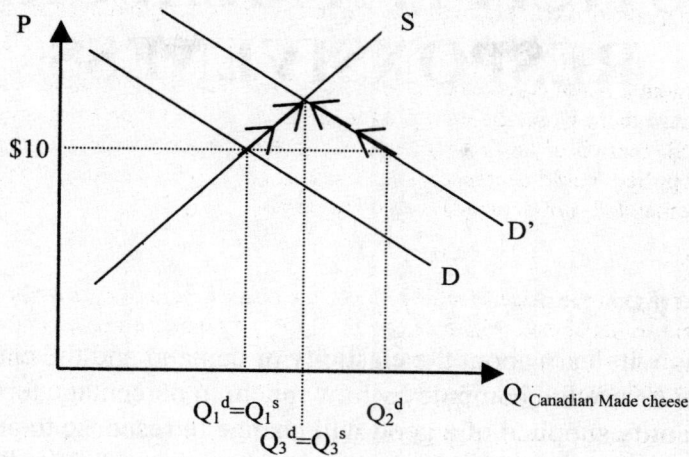

13. I will analyze the two events of an increase in the price of spandex and the fitness craze separately for their effect on the equilibrium price and quantity of athletic wear. Then, I will consider the combined effect of the two events on price and quantity. First, the increase in the price of spandex used in making athletic wear is an increase in an input price. As such, the increased input price raises the costs of producing athletic wear at every quantity supplied. Shifting the supply curve of athletic wear to the left. The shift reflects that, at every quantity supplied, the price that producers would be willing to accept in order to produce various amounts of athletic wear is now higher. By itself, this raises the equilibrium price of athletic wear and lowers the equilibrium quantity. (Notice that the price increase caused by supply shifting left will cause a *movement along the demand curve* which means that the *quantity* of athletic wear demanded will decrease). The fitness craze spawned in part by Richard Simmons will increase the demand for athletic wear. That is, at every price, the quantity demanded will now be higher than before. Shifting the demand curve for athletic wear to the right represents an increase in demand. By itself, the rightward shift raises the price of athletic wear and increases the equilibrium quantity. (Notice that the price increase caused by demand shifting right will cause a *movement along the supply curve* which means that the *quantity* of athletic wear supplied will increase.)

When the effects of the shifts in demand and supply are combined, we know for certain that the equilibrium price will increase since both events cause price to increase. However, we do not know for sure what the effect is on the equilibrium quantity since, in the first case, the equilibrium quantity declines but, in the second case, the equilibrium quantity increases.

CHAPTER 5
ELASTICITY: A MEASURE OF RESPONSIVENESS

I.   OVERVIEW

In this chapter, you will learn about the elasticity of demand and the elasticity of supply. Price elasticity can be used to compute by how much, in percentage terms, quantity demanded and quantity supplied of a good will change in response to an X% change in the price of that good. You will also learn that the elasticity of demand can be used to figure out what will happen to the total revenue of a firm when it lowers or raises the price of one of its products or services by X%, *ceteris paribus*. You will learn that the elasticity of demand and supply can be used to determine by what percentage the equilibrium price of a good will change when either demand or supply shifts. You will learn why the elasticity of demand for some products is very high and for others very low and you will learn what factors affect the elasticity of demand. You will learn that the concept of elasticity has important applications for business decision-making or policymaking. Since you will be using formulas that require that you compute percentage changes, you may wish to review Chapter 1 appendix of the text and the Basic Algebra chapter of the study guide.

II.   CHECKLIST

By the end of this chapter, you should be able to:
- ❑ Explain, in words, elasticity of demand and supply.
- ❑ Use formulas to compute the elasticity of demand and supply.
- ❑ Use the elasticity of demand and supply to determine the percentage price change for a given percentage quantity change.
- ❑ Use the elasticity of demand and supply to figure out the percentage quantity change for a given percentage price change.
- ❑ Use the elasticity of demand to determine what happens to a firm's total revenue when it raises or lowers the price of one of its products.
- ❑ Use the elasticity of demand to determine whether a particular policy enacted by the government will have the desired effects.
- ❑ Use the elasticity of demand and supply to determine what happens to the equilibrium price when demand or supply shifts.

III. KEY TERMS

Price elasticity of demand: a measure of the responsiveness of the quantity demanded to changes in price; computed by dividing the percentage change in quantity demanded by the percentage change in price and taking the absolute value.

Absolute value: a mathematical operation that makes any numerical value positive.

Unitary elastic: a good with a price elasticity of 1.

Price elasticity of supply: a measure of the responsiveness of the quantity supplied to changes in price; computed by dividing the percentage change in quantity supplied by the percentage change in price.

Price-change formula: a formula that calculates the change in equilibrium price due to a change in demand or supply; calculated by dividing the percentage change in demand or supply by the sum of the price elasticity of demand and supply.

From the Appendix:

Income elasticity of demand: a measure of the responsiveness of the quantity demanded to changes in consumer income; computed by dividing the percentage change in the quantity demanded by the percentage change in income.

Cross elasticity of demand: a measure of the responsiveness of the quantity demanded to changes in the price of a related good; computed by dividing the percentage change in the quantity demanded of one good (X) by the percentage change in the price of another good (Y).

IV. PERFORMANCE ENHANCING TIPS (PETS)

<u>PET #1</u>

Elasticity is quoted on a per "unit basis."

Maybe this statement doesn't make sense quite yet, but it will after you look at the following example. Suppose you are told that the elasticity of demand is 2. What does that mean? You know that the elasticity of demand (E_d) for good X is given by the formula $\%\Delta Q^d_x / \%\Delta P_x$. You may think that, when you are given the number 2, all you have is the number in the numerator. Since, 2 is equal to 2/1, you do have a number for the numerator and denominator of the elasticity of demand formula. The number in the denominator is 1. Thus, an elasticity of demand of 2 means that a 1% increase in the price of good X leads to a 2% decline in the quantity of good X demanded. Once you know the elasticity, of demand on a per unit basis, you can also scale up or down the percentage changes in price and quantity but keeping the proportion equal to 2. For example, you could say that with an elasticity of demand of 2, a 10% increase in the price of good X leads to a 20% decline in the quantity of good X demanded.

PET #2

For any formula, if you are given two of three missing components, you can always figure out the third component. Likewise for three of four, four of five, and so on.

This performance-enhancing tip will prove useful in this chapter as you apply it to elasticity and will also prove useful in other chapters of this textbook.

Let's see how this works by applying it to the elasticity of demand. Suppose you are told that the elasticity of demand is 0.5 and that a firm is considering reducing the price of one of its products by 10%. Can you determine by how much quantity demanded would change? All of you have to do is plug the numbers that you are given into the formula:

$$E_d = \%\Delta Q^d_x / \%\Delta P_x$$
$$0.5 = \%\Delta Q^d_x / 10$$
$$0.5 * 10 = \%\Delta Q^d_x$$
$$5 = \%\Delta Q^d_x$$

Thus, a 10% reduction in the price of the product will lead to a 5% increase in the quantity of the good demanded.

Let's try another example. Suppose you are told that the elasticity of demand is 4 and that a firm wants to increase the quantity it sells by 20%. By how much must it lower price in order to generate a 20% increase in the quantity it sells? The elasticity formula could be rewritten to solve for $\%\Delta P_x$ as:

$$\%\Delta P_x = \%\Delta Q^d_x / E_d$$
$$\%\Delta P_x = 20/4$$
$$\%\Delta P_x = 5$$

Thus, the firm would have to lower the price of the product by 5% in order to generate a 20% increase in quantity demanded.

PET #3

Lowering the price of a good does not always lower the total revenue that a firm will earn nor does raising the price of a good always increase the total revenue that a firm will earn.

Let's see why the statement above is true. First, total revenue is computed as (price * quantity demanded). In order to understand the effect on total revenue of a given percentage price change, you must also know by how much quantity demanded will change in percentage terms. Obviously, a lower price will reduce total revenue but only if the quantity demanded does not increase but instead remains the same (no change). Likewise, a higher price will raise total revenue but only if the quantity demanded does not decrease but remains the same (no change). However, it is usually the case that, when the price of a good is lowered, the quantity demanded increases and, when the price of a good is raised, the quantity demanded declines. In the case of a lower price, the lower price by itself reduces total revenue but, since quantity demanded will increase, this will tend to raise total revenue. In the case of a price increase, the higher price will by itself raise total revenue but, since quantity demanded will fall, this will tend to decrease total revenue. Thus, the combined effects on price and quantity must be determined.

Suppose you are told that the elasticity of demand is 2 and that a firm is going to raise the price of its product by 5%. What will be the effect on total revenue? With an elasticity of demand of 2, the percentage change in quantity demanded can be figured out. It will decrease by 10% (See PET #2). The net effect on revenue is based on a comparison of the percentage change in price to the percentage change in quantity demanded. A 5% increase in the price by itself would raise total revenue by 5%. A 10% decrease in the quantity demanded would by itself reduce total revenue by 10%. The combined effect depends on which one is larger. Since the 10% reduction is bigger in magnitude than the 5% increase, total revenue will decline.

V   PRACTICE EXAM: MULTIPLE CHOICE QUESTIONS

1. Which one of the following is the correct formula for the elasticity of demand?

    a. $\Delta P_x / \Delta Q^d_x$
    b. $\%\Delta Q^d_x / \%\Delta P_x$
    c. $\Delta Q^d_x / \Delta P_x$
    d. $\%\Delta P_x / \%\Delta Q^d_x + \%\Delta Q^s_x$
    e. $\%\Delta P_x / \%\Delta Q^d_x$

2. Suppose the elasticity of demand for bowling is 1.5 and the manager of the bowling alley decides to raise the price of a game by 5%. By what percentage will quantity demanded change?

    a. Decline by 7.5%.
    b. Rise by 7.5%.
    c. Decline by 3%.
    d. Rise by 3%.
    e. Not enough information to answer the question.

3. Suppose the government wants to reduce teenage smoking by 50%. Suppose further that the government knows that the teenage elasticity of demand for a pack of cigarettes is 2. By what percentage would the government have to increase the price of a pack of cigarettes (through a tax) in order to cut teenage smoking by 50%?

    a. 100%.
    b. 25%.
    c. 50%.
    d. 250%.
    e. 20%.

4. Which one of the following defines an inelastic demand?

   a. $E_d > 1$
   b. $E_d = 1$
   c. $0 < E_d < 1$
   d. $E_d > 0$
   e. $E_d < 0$

5. Which one of the following factors would tend to reduce the elasticity of demand for a particular product?

   a. More time to shop around.
   b. No close substitutes.
   c. Big part of budget.
   d. Luxury item.
   e. All of the above reduce the elasticity of demand.

6. Which one of the following goods would you characterize as being the most elastic?

   a. Insulin.
   b. Coffee.
   c. Cigarettes.
   d. Gasoline.
   e. Cookies.

7. Suppose the elasticity of demand for flowers at a local florist is estimated to be 4, as computed by a savvy economics student. If the florist raises the price of flowers by 5%, then:

   a. the revenue earned by the florist will decline.
   b. the quantity of flowers sold by the florist will decline by 1.25%.
   c. the quantity of flowers sold by the florist will decline by 0.2%.
   d. the quantity of flowers sold by the florist will decline by 20%.
   e. (a) and (d).

8. Total revenue _____ when the price of a good increases and its demand is inelastic, and total revenue _____ when the price of a good decreases and its demand is elastic.

   a. increases/increases
   b. increases/decreases
   c. increases/does not change
   d. decreases/decreases
   e. decreases/increases

9. What is the elasticity of supply of cows if the price of a cow increases from $500 to $550 and the quantity supplied rises from 100,000 to 130,000? (Do not use the midpoint formula).

    a. 3.33.
    b. 3.0.
    c. 5.0.
    d. 6.0.
    e. Cannot be determined without information on percentages.

10. Suppose that the supply of tweed jackets increases by 20%. Further, suppose that the elasticity of demand for tweed jackets is 1 and the elasticity of supply is 4. What will happen to the equilibrium price of tweed jackets?

    a. Rise by 8%.
    b. Fall by 8%.
    c. Rise by 4%.
    d. Fall by 4%.
    e. Fall by 5%.

VI. PRACTICE EXAM: ESSAY QUESTIONS

11. Discuss the short- and long-run effects of a government policy of imposing a tax that would raise the price of oil and gasoline by 20% assuming that the elasticity of demand for oil is currently estimated to be 0.5 and the elasticity of demand for gasoline to be 1.2. Be sure to address what factors might alter the elasticity numbers over time.

12. Suppose that you are an economic consultant for a large company that produces and sells lollipops that are shaped as the faces of Hollywood celebrities. The company has shops in the major cities around the country and also sells by mail-order catalogue. As an economic consultant, you have estimated the elasticity of demand for store-bought lollipops to be 0.75 and the elasticity of demand for mail-order lollipops to be 3. What advice would you give to the President of the company if she wanted to increase revenue from the shops and through mail orders? Now, suppose that the price of sugar increases causing a 20% reduction in the supply of celebrity lollipops. What information would you need to compute the effect of the reduction in supply on the equilibrium price?

VII. ANSWER KEY: MULTIPLE CHOICE QUESTIONS

1. Correct answer: b.

    Discussion: The elasticity of demand is the percentage change in the quantity of good X demanded by the percentage change in its price.

    Statement a is not correct because it is not expressed in percentage changes (but rather absolute changes) and has the numerator and denominator reversed. Statement c is not correct because it is expressed in absolute changes. Statement d is not correct because the elasticity of supply does not enter the formula. Statement e is not correct because the numerator and denominator should be reversed.

2. Correct answer: a.

Discussion: A rise in the price will always reduce the quantity demanded, so first you must look for an answer that has quantity demanded declining. The percentage change in quantity demanded is computed by multiplying E_d times $\%\Delta P = 1.5 * 5 = 7.5$.

Statement b is not correct because the quantity demanded will decline, not increase, when the price rises. Statement c and d are wrong based on the formula. Statement e is not correct because there is enough information to answer the question.

3. Correct answer: b.

Discussion: Since you are given the elasticity of demand and a desired percentage change in the quantity demanded, you can figure out the percentage change in price as $\%\Delta P_x = \%\Delta Q^d_x / E_d$. Thus, $\%\Delta P_x = 50\%/2 = 25\%$.

Statement a is not correct because the two numbers should not be multiplied. Statement c would only be correct if the elasticity of demand were 1. Statement d is not correct; it is off by a factor of 10. Statement e is also not correct.

4. Correct answer: c.

Discussion: An inelastic demand is defined as one for which E_d is less than 1 (in absolute value), which means that a 1% increase in price reduces the quantity demanded by less than 1% (and vice-versa for a price decrease).

Statement a defines an elastic demand. Statement b defines a unitary elastic demand. Statements d and e are not correct because elasticity is defined with respect to 1, not zero.

5. Correct answer: b.

Discussion: When there are no close substitutes for a product, the demand for a good tends to be more inelastic. That is, the price of the good can be raised by a big percentage but quantity demanded will not respond by very much because there are not close substitutes and consumers cannot easily switch their purchases to the substitute products. This describes a good that has an inelastic demand.

If consumers have more time to shop around, they are more likely to compare prices. This means that consumers will be more sensitive to price changes, i.e., demand will be more elastic. If a good is a big part of a consumer's budget, a small change in the price will have a bigger impact on his or her budget. Thus, consumers will be more likely to greatly reduce their purchases of the good even if its price goes up a little bit. This defines demand to be more elastic. (You may want to think about the effects on budget and spending if the price of a pen goes up by 10% to the price of housing going up by 10%). Luxury items, because they are not necessities, tend to have a more elastic demand. Since a, c, and d are likely to raise the elasticity of demand (make it more elastic), statement e cannot be correct.

6. Correct answer: e.

Discussion: Cookies are the only good that are not a "necessity." Goods that are not a necessity tend to have a more elastic demand. Furthermore, there tends to be a large number of good substitutes for cookies.

Insulin is a necessary good to a diabetic and there tends to few, if any, good substitutes. In this case, the elasticity of demand for insulin is likely to be very close to zero. The same, to a lesser degree, is true of gasoline. People must have transportation to their jobs, the grocery store, etc. Thus, gasoline is more of a necessity than cookies. A similar story can be told for coffee. Most people cannot seem to get through the day without at least one cup of coffee. This makes coffee more of a necessity than cookies. Cigarettes have an addictive property. This means that price increases will have less of an effect of reducing consumption than for a non-addictive good. Thus, cookies are likely to have a higher elasticity of demand than cigarettes.

7. Correct answer: e.

    Discussion: When the elasticity of demand is greater than 1, an X% price change will cause a greater than X% change in quantity demanded. In this case, the florist has chosen to raise, not lower, the price of flowers. With an elasticity of demand of 4, the 5% increase in the price will lead to a 20% decline in the quantity of flowers sold. Thus, statement d is correct. At the same time, since the percentage change in the price increase is swamped by the percentage reduction in the quantity of flowers sold, the revenue earned by the florist will drop. Thus, statement a is correct as well.

    Statement b is not correct. The effect on quantity is not determined by dividing 5 by 4. Statement c is not correct because it is off by a factor of 10.

8. Correct answer: a.

    Discussion: With an inelastic demand, the percentage rise (in this case) in the price of the good is greater than the percentage reduction in the quantity demanded, which means that, on net, total revenue (p * q) will increase. With an elastic demand, the percentage drop (in this case) will be less than the percentage increase in the quantity of the good demanded. (Remember price and quantity demanded move in opposite directions.) Thus, on net, total revenue will rise.

    Statement b is not correct: it would have been correct if the second part of the question asked what happened to total revenue when the price of a good with an elastic demand was increased. Statement c is not correct; only a unitary elasticity of demand leads to no change in total revenue when price is raised or lowered. Statement d is not correct; it would have been correct if the question had asked what happens to total revenue when price is decreased and demand is inelastic and what happens to total revenue when price is increased and demand is elastic. Statement e is not correct; it would have been correct if the first part of the question had asked what happens to total revenue when price is decreased and demand is inelastic.

9. Correct answer: b.

    Discussion: The percentage change in the price of a cow is 10% [($550-500)/500] * 100 and the percentage change in the quantity of cows supplied is 30% [(130,000-100,000)/100,000] * 100. The elasticity of supply is computed as the percentage change in the quantity supplied divided by the percentage change in the price which is 30%/10% = 3.

    For the reasoning just mentioned, statements a, c, and d are not correct. Statement e is not correct because you are given information that allows you to compute percentage changes.

10. Correct answer: d.

    Discussion: Since the supply of tweed jackets has increased, you should be looking for an answer that has the price of tweed jackets declining. The formula used to compute the percentage change in the equilibrium price is to take the percentage shift in supply (or demand, if that had been the question) and divide it by the sum of the elasticity of supply and demand. Thus, the percentage change in the equilibrium price will be 20%/(1 + 4) = 20%/5 = 4%.

    Statements a and c cannot be correct because a supply increase causes a drop in the equilibrium price (see Chapter 4 for review if you don't remember this). Statements b and e are not correct because the formula gives an answer of 4%.

VIII. ANSWER KEY: ESSAY QUESTIONS

11. Since the currently estimated elasticity of demand for oil is 0.5, a 20% increase in the price of oil will reduce the quantity demanded by 10% (0.5 * 20%), at least in the short run. The tax revenue collected by the government on oil will, however, increase. The tax revenue will increase because the percentage increase in the price of oil dominates the percentage decrease in the quantity demanded. For gasoline, a 20% increase in its price will reduce the quantity demanded by 24% (1.2 * 20%), at least in the short run. In the short run, the 20% increase in the price of gasoline is much more effective at reducing consumer use of gasoline than is the 20% increase in the price of oil at reducing consumer use of oil

(compare 10% to 24%). However, the tax revenue collected on gasoline sales will actually decline because the percentage decrease in the quantity demanded outweighs the percentage increase in the price. Thus, on balance, tax revenue collected by the government on gasoline will decline. While in the short run it may be difficult to find substitutes for oil or gasoline, in the long run, consumers may be able to modify their spending behaviour. They may find substitutes for oil or gasoline (perhaps because innovative companies will invent products like methanol or battery-run automobiles). Thus, in the long run, the estimated elasticity may increase. In fact, if the elasticity for oil increased above 1, then the tax increase of 20% would end up lowering the tax revenue collected by the government on oil consumption.

12. The advice I would give to the President of the Celebrity Lollipop Company is this: raise the price of lollipops purchased in shops throughout the country and lower the price of lollipops purchased through mail-order catalogue. However, be aware that, eventually, when consumers become aware of the price difference, you may see your revenue from the stores decline (rather than rise after you have raised the price), but your revenue from mail orders may eventually increase by more than originally estimated. This may happen because customers from the store-bought shops may begin to purchase by mail order. That is, they will have found an almost identical substitute for the store-bought lollipops.

If the price of sugar rises, the supply of celebrity lollipops will decrease (shift left). The decreased supply will raise the price of store-bought and mail-order lollipops. In order to know by how much the equilibrium prices would rise, you would need information on the elasticity of supply of store-bought and mail-order lollipops (in addition to the elasticity of demand) as well as on the percentage reduction in the supply of each type of lollipop. For example, if the supply of mail-order lollipops dropped by 40% and the elasticity of supply is 1 and you are given that the elasticity of demand is 3, then the equilibrium price will change by 40%/(1+3) = 40%/4 = 10%.

CHAPTER 6
GOVERNMENT INTERVENTION IN MARKETS

I.   OVERVIEW

In this chapter, you will learn about whether the interaction of consumers and producers leads to an efficient or inefficient outcome. You will learn that, when inefficient outcomes arise, the government may step in, in an effort to promote a better outcome. You will also learn why a government may intervene in a market that is already efficient and what effects it may create. You will learn that spillover benefits and costs generally create an inefficient outcome, either for producers or consumers, You will examine the effects of government price-setting policies such as rent control and dairy price supports on equilibrium price, quantities, and efficiency. You will also examine the effects of government restrictions on quantity such as quotas, voluntary export restraints, and licensing agreements. You will learn that there are always winners and losers of price-setting and quantity-restricting policies. You will see that there is an interface between economics and politics. You will learn about the difference between public and private goods and that there may be a role for the government in delivering public goods to the market.

II.   CHECKLIST

By the end of this chapter, you should be able to:
- ❑ Use a graph of demand and supply to show why, in the absence of spillover benefits and costs at the equilibrium price and quantity, neither a consumer nor a producer could benefit from there being one more transaction.
- ❑ Explain what an efficient market outcome is and what an inefficient market outcome is.
- ❑ Explain what a maximum price (price ceiling) policy is and the effects it creates on price, quantity demanded, and quantity supplied. You should also be able to discuss any other consequences that might arise from the policy.
- ❑ List some real world examples of price ceilings.
- ❑ Explain what a minimum price (price floor or price support) policy is and the effects it creates on price, quantity demanded and quantity supplied. You should also be able to discuss any other consequences that might arise from the policy.
- ❑ List some real world examples of price supports.
- ❑ Identify whom the winners and the losers are under different government policies.

- ❏ Define a public good and contrast it to a private good.
- ❏ Explain the free rider and chump problems.
- ❏ List some real world examples of public goods.

III. KEY TERMS

Efficient market: a market where *no* additional transactions exist that would mutually benefit a buyer and a seller.

Inefficient market: a market where transactions still exist that would mutually benefit a buyer and a seller.

Willingness to pay: the most a buyer will pay for a good or service.

Willingness to sell: the least a seller will accept as payment for a good or service.

Invisible hand: the phenomenon that leads individual consumers and producers to the market equilibrium, which is efficient in some circumstances.

Imperfectly competitive market: a market in which firms are large enough that they affect market prices.

Price ceiling: a maximum price set below the market equilibrium price; transactions above the maximum price are outlawed.

Rent control: a policy under which the government specifies a maximum rent that is below the equilibrium rent.

Price floor: a minimum price set above the market equilibrium price; transactions below the minimum price are outlawed.

Price support programs: a policy under which the government specifies a minimum price above the equilibrium price.

Taxi plate: a license to operate a taxi; sometimes called a medallion.

Import restriction: a law that prohibits the importation of a particular good.

Spillover benefit: the benefit from a good experienced by people who do not decide how much of the good to produce or consume.

Public good: a good that is available for everyone to consume, regardless of who pays and who doesn't.

Private good: a good that is consumed by a single person or household.

Free-rider problem: each person will try to get the benefit of a public good without paying for it, trying to get a free ride at the expense of others.

Spillover costs: the cost from a good experienced by people who did not decide how much of the good to produce or consume.

IV. PERFORMANCE ENHANCING TIPS (PETS)

<u>PET #1</u>

The prices corresponding to the quantities demanded and supplied along the demand and supply curves can be used to measure the marginal benefit to society of consuming and the marginal cost to society of producing at various quantities.

Suppose we are interested in determining the marginal benefit consumers derive from purchasing apples. The demand curve can be used to infer what the marginal benefit is to a consumer from buying one more apple. The marginal benefit is simply measured by the price a consumer would be willing to pay to buy one more apple. What is the marginal benefit of consuming apples for the demand curve shown in Figure 6-1?

The marginal benefit of the first apple (benefit to the consumer from buying the first apple) is $7; the marginal benefit of the second apple (benefit to the consumer from buying the second apple) is $6; and so on.

Figure 6-1

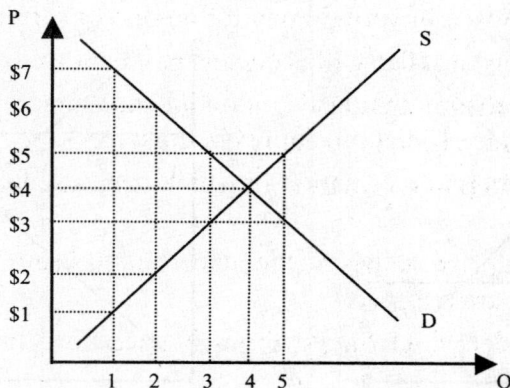

The supply curve can be used to infer what the marginal cost is from producing one more apple. The marginal cost of the first apple (cost to the producer of producing the first apple) is $1. The marginal cost of the second apple (cost to the producer of producing the second apple) is $2, and so on.

Notice that the marginal benefit of the third apple is $5. This exceeds the marginal cost of producing the third apple, $3. Thus, at a quantity of 3 apples, producers could profit by producing the third apple since consumers would be willing to pay $6. So producers should produce more apples.

Now, compare the marginal benefit of the fifth apple to the marginal cost. The marginal benefit is $3 while the marginal cost is $5. Thus, at a quantity of five apples, the marginal cost exceeds the marginal benefit, so it would not make sense for producers to produce an apple for which nobody is willing to pay them enough to cover the marginal cost of production.

At equilibrium, the marginal benefit of the fourth apple is $4 and equal to the marginal cost of producing the fourth apple. This is the efficient outcome; neither more nor fewer apples should be produced.

PET #2

Maximum prices (price ceilings) that are set below the equilibrium price create a shortage where quantity demanded exceeds quantity supplied. A price ceiling set above the equilibrium price is ineffective.

To see this, compare Figures 6-2 and 6-3 below. Figure 6-2 illustrates a price ceiling set below the equilibrium price and Figure 6-3, a price ceiling set above the equilibrium price. Remember that a price ceiling is a government-controlled price above which the equilibrium price may not rise.

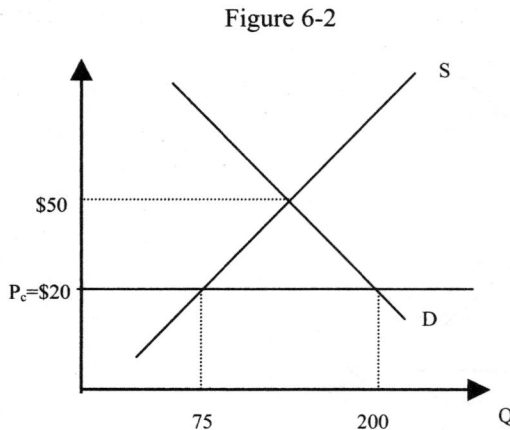

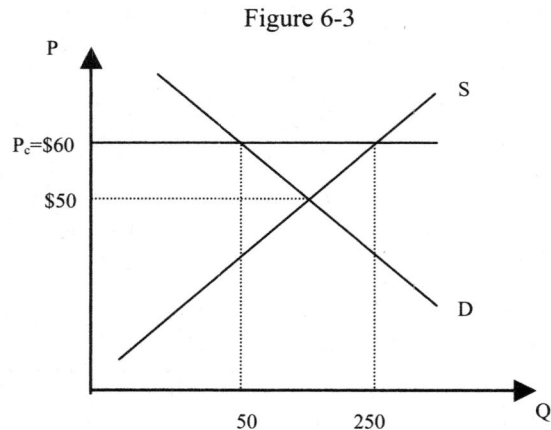

Figure 6-2

Figure 6-3

In Figure 6-2, at a price of $20, the quantity demanded is 200 units and the quantity supplied is 75 units.

Thus, there is a shortage of 125 units. If the government removed the price ceiling, the price would rise to $50 and the shortage would be eliminated as quantity demanded would decline and quantity supplied would increase (movements along the curves).

In Figure 6-3, at a price ceiling of $60, the quantity demanded is 50 units and the quantity supplied is 250 units. However, the equilibrium (or market-determined) price is $50. Thus, there is no tendency for the price to rise above the government-imposed price of $60, so the price ceiling, in this case, is not effective.

PET #3

Minimum prices (price floors or price supports) that are set above the equilibrium price create a surplus where quantity supplied exceeds quantity demanded. A price floor set below the equilibrium price is ineffective.

To see this, compare Figures 6-4 and 6-5 below. Figure 6-4 illustrates a price floor set above the equilibrium price and Figure 6-5, a price floor set below the equilibrium price. Remember that a price floor is a government-controlled price below which the equilibrium price may not fall.

In Figure 6-4, at a price floor of $15, the quantity demanded is 200 units and the quantity supplied is 500 units. Thus, there is a surplus of 300 units. If the government removed the price floor, the price would fall to $10 and the surplus would be eliminated as quantity demanded would rise and quantity supplied would decrease (movements along the curves).

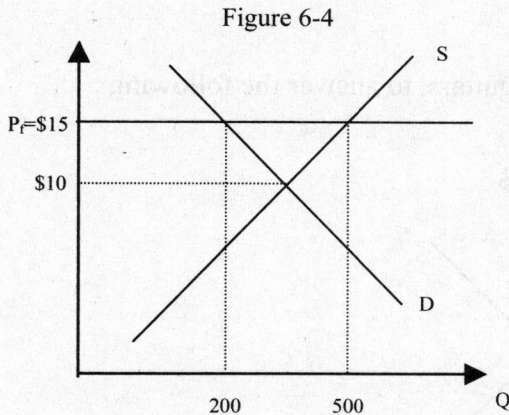

Figure 6-4

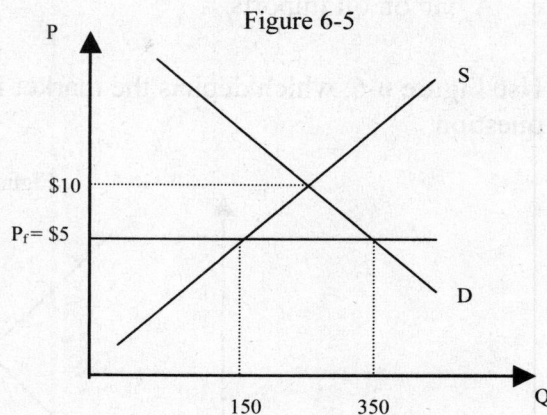

Figure 6-5

In Figure 6-5, at a price floor of $5, the quantity demanded is 350 units and the quantity supplied is 150 units. However, the equilibrium (or market-determined) price is $10. Thus, there is no tendency for the price to fall below $10 and so the price floor of $5 is not effective.

V.   PRACTICE EXAM: MULTIPLE CHOICE QUESTIONS

1. An efficient market outcome is one in which:

    a. the marginal benefit to consumers exceeds the marginal costs to producers.
    b. there are spillover benefits but no spillover costs.
    c. there are no free-rider problems.
    d. a third party can benefit from a transaction.
    e. no buyer or seller can benefit from any further transactions.

2. Who is responsible for the metaphor of the "invisible hand"?

    a. Adam Smith.
    b. Art O'Sullivan.
    c. John Maynard Keynes.
    d. Milton Friedman.
    e. Steven Sheffrin.

3. Which one of the following is NOT an example of a quantity restriction (control)?

   a. A quota on aircraft imports.
   b. A voluntary export restraint on automobiles.
   c. Subsidized housing.
   d. Licensing liquor stores.
   e. A ban on oil imports.

Use Figure 6-6, which depicts the market for guitars, to answer the following question.

Figure 6-6

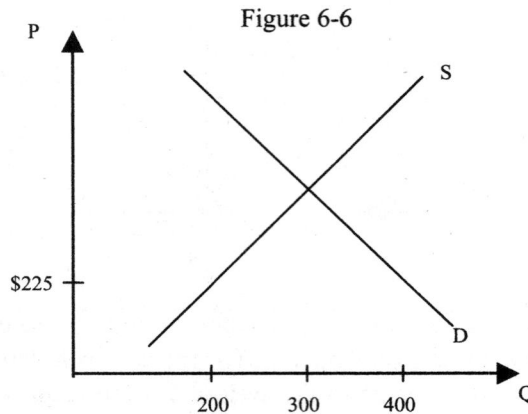

4. Which one of the following statements is true?

   a. At a quantity of 400, the marginal benefit of a guitar exceeds the marginal cost.
   b. At a quantity of 200, the marginal benefit of a guitar exceeds the marginal cost.
   c. If the price were $225 per guitar, there would be a surplus of guitars.
   d. One more consumer could be better off if 299 guitars were produced instead of 300.
   e. (b) and (c).

5. Suppose the government sets a maximum price (price ceiling) for pacemakers (a medical device that monitors the beats per minute of the heart). The maximum price is set at $1,299 and the equilibrium price is $1,750. Which one of the following would NOT be a likely result?

   a. Consumers may bribe their doctors for pacemakers or be willing to pay special hook-up fees.
   b. A surplus would develop.
   c. The quality of pacemakers may decline.
   d. The quantity of pacemakers supplied may decline in the long run.
   e. All of the above would be likely to develop.

6. Which one of the following is an effect of a minimum price (price floor) that is set above the equilibrium price?

    a. Quantity supplied increases.
    b. Quantity demanded decreases.
    c. An inefficient outcome is produced.
    d. Suppliers win and consumers lose.
    e. All of the above are effects of a minimum price.

Use Figure 6-7, which depicts the market for cheese, to answer the following question.

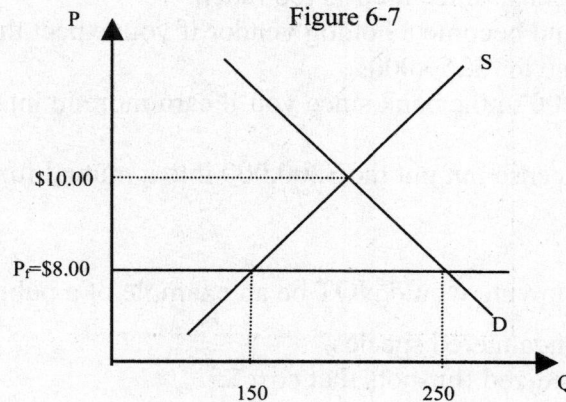

Figure 6-7

7. Suppose the government sets a minimum price (price floor) for cheese of $8.00 per kilogram. Based on Figure 6-7, which one of the following statements is correct?

    a. There will be a surplus of 100 pounds of cheese.
    b. There will be a shortage of 100 pounds of cheese.
    c. At $1.25, the marginal cost of production exceeds the marginal benefit of consumption.
    d. The price floor is ineffective.
    e. Supply will decrease.

8. Which one of the following would be an effect of the Canadian government imposing a quota on imports of automobiles?

    a. The price of imported automobiles will increase.
    b. The quantity of automobiles supplied by the foreign source will increase.
    c. The quantity of automobiles demanded will increase.
    d. Employment in the Canadian automobile industry will decrease.
    e. A surplus of foreign-made automobiles will be created in Canada.

9. Suppose you were debating whether to become a hotdog vendor in your town. You estimate that you can sell 40,000 hotdogs a year at a price of $2. You estimate the opportunity cost of your time to be $10,000 per year. You figure that you will operate the business for the next two years at which point you will go back to school. If you become a hotdog vendor, you must pay for a vending license. The license costs $200,000. Assume that you have $200,000 from an inheritance to pay for the license. The $200,000 is in a chequing account earning 3% interest per year. Which one of the following would be your best strategy?

   a. Buy the license and become a hotdog vendor since you'll make $80,000 a year.
   b. Do not buy the license since it costs too much.
   c. Buy the license and become a hotdog vendor if you expect that in two years you can sell the license for $250,000.
   d. Leave the $200,000 in the bank since you'll earn more in interest than working as a hotdog vendor.
   e. Do not buy the license but put the $200,000 into a mutual fund that earns 10% interest per year.

10. Which one of the following would NOT be an example of a public good?

    a. Preservation of endangered species.
    b. Provincially subsidized flu shots that cost $5.
    c. National defence.
    d. A city park.
    e. A bridge.

11. Which one of the following statements is true of public goods?

    a. They are generally paid for through taxes.
    b. It is impractical to exclude people who don't pay for them from using them.
    c. They are available for everyone to consume.
    d. They are associated with the free-rider problem.
    e. All of the above are true of public goods.

12. Which one of the following methods is the best way to overcome the free-rider problem?

    a. Ask people to make voluntary contributions.
    b. Tax people.
    c. Impose a price support.
    d. Subsidize the users of the good/program.
    e. Institute government-sponsored advertising campaigns for the good.

VI. PRACTICE EXAM: ESSAY QUESTIONS

13. Suppose that you are a lobbyist for the textile industry. Assume the industry is perfectly competitive and has no spillover benefits or costs associated with it. What government favours might you seek for your industry? Who will benefit if you are awarded a government favour? Who will be hurt? Will an efficient outcome occur if your lobbying is effective? Explain.

14. First, explain why a bridge is a public good. Also, why is it that some cities collect tolls for using a bridge? Second, explain why a rent-controlled apartment may not turn out to be as inexpensive as you may have thought based on the monthly payment?

VII. ANSWER KEY: MULTIPLE CHOICE QUESTIONS

1. Correct answer: e.

   Discussion: Statement e is correct because it is the only statement that points out that it is impossible to make someone better off by entering into another transaction. This defines an efficient outcome.

   Statement a is not correct. If the marginal benefit to consumers from consuming good Z exceeds the marginal costs to producers of producing good Z, then producers could make consumers better off by producing more and consumers could make producers better off by paying them. Since the marginal benefit of consumers exceeds the marginal costs of production, that means they would be willing to pay more than what it costs the producers to produce. This is just an application of the marginal principle from Chapter 2. Statement b is not correct because spillover benefits lead to inefficient outcomes, just as do spillover costs. Statement c is not correct because the absence of a free-rider problem does not define whether an outcome will be efficient or not. Statement d is not correct because, if a third party can benefit from a transaction, the outcome must not currently be the efficient one.

2. Correct answer: a.

   Discussion: Adam Smith, who wrote the Wealth of Nations is responsible for the metaphor of the "invisible hand" which is just that people acting in their own self-interest can frequently lead to outcomes in which all participating parties benefit.

   None of the other statements are correct. In fact, O'Sullivan and Sheffrin are two of the authors of your textbook.

3. Correct answer: c.

   Discussion: Subsidized housing is housing that is provided to people at a price below the market price.

   Quotas, voluntary export restraints, licenses, and bans all restrict or limit the quantity of a good to various degrees.

4. Correct answer: b.

   Discussion: At a quantity of 200, the marginal benefit is determined by drawing a line from the quantity level up to the demand curve and then over to the price line. The corresponding price is a measure of the marginal benefit of the 200th guitar. The marginal cost is determined by drawing a line from the quantity level up to the supply curve and then over to the price line. The corresponding price is a measure of the marginal cost of the 200th guitar. As you can see, the marginal benefit is greater than the marginal cost.

Statement a is not correct because the marginal cost exceeds the marginal benefit of the 400th guitar. Statement c is not correct because a price of $225 leads to a shortage, not a surplus. Statement d is not correct because the equilibrium quantity of 300 guitars is the efficient outcome, so nobody could be made better off by producing fewer (or even more) guitars. Statement e is not correct because statement c is not correct.

5. Correct answer: b.

Discussion: A maximum price that is set below the equilibrium price creates a shortage, not a surplus.

Since a maximum price set below the equilibrium price creates a shortage, several consequences emerge. One is that people may bribe their doctors with monetary or non-monetary gifts so that they can be one of the recipients of the limited supply of pacemakers. Second, the quality of pacemakers may decline because the shortage or excess demand for pacemakers doesn't give an incentive to the producers to produce a better product. They know that they can sell what they produce because, if one buyer makes demands on them, another buyer will be ready to pay the $1,299 for the pacemaker. Third, the quantity of pacemakers supplied may decline in the long run as pacemaker manufacturers decide that it is not as profitable to produce pacemakers (because of the government-imposed price) and so they may decide to produce other medical devices or get out of the business altogether.

6. Correct answer: e.

Discussion: A minimum price set above the equilibrium price creates a surplus. It does so by raising the price above the equilibrium. As the price is increased, quantity supplied increases (movement along the supply curve, Law of Supply) and quantity demanded decreases (movement along the demand curve, Law of Demand). An inefficient outcome is produced because we are no longer at the equilibrium level of output, which is where marginal benefit equals marginal cost. Suppliers win because they get a higher price for their product but consumers lose because they have to pay a higher price for it.

7. Correct answer: d.

Discussion: Since the price floor is set below the equilibrium price, it is ineffective. Remember that a price floor is a government-imposed price below which the price may not drop. By market forces, the price will naturally rest at $10.00.

Statements a and b are not correct because the price floor is ineffective, so neither a surplus, nor shortage will emerge. An equilibrium where the quantity demanded equals the quantity supplied at a price of $10.00 will emerge. Statement c is not correct because the quantity supplied and the quantity demanded at $8.00 is different, which means you can't compare the marginal benefit to the marginal cost. You have to look at the same quantity level for both demand and supply. Statement e is not correct because an ineffective price floor does not have the effect of decreasing supply (supply shifting left).

8. Correct answer: a.

Discussion: A quota restricts the supply of imports and, thus, reduces the overall supply of automobiles in the Canadian market. This raises the price of automobiles.

Statement b is not correct because the quota reduces the quantity of automobiles supplied by the foreign source, not increases it. Statement c is not correct because, as the price increases, the quantity of automobiles demanded will decrease not increase. Statement d is not correct because employment in the Canadian automobile industry may increase as they increase production to make up for the reduction from the foreign source. Statement e is not correct because a shortage of foreign-made automobiles will be created in Canada.

9. Correct answer: c.

Discussion: Your income over two years, after accounting for the opportunity cost of your time, will be $140,000, which is equal to [($2 * 40,0000) - $10,000] * 2 years. Plus, you will make $250,000 when you sell the license in two years. So, in total, you will have made $390,000 in two years. However, you had an expense of $200,000 to pay for the license. Thus, your profit across the two years is $190,000.

(You will learn in Chapter 18 that this profit figure is not quite correct. For now, however, it is close enough to the correct figure to allow us to answer this question.)

Statement a is not correct because you should not just consider how much you will make each year. You have to factor in the costs of your time and the license as well as earnings from selling the license.

Statement b is not correct for similar reasons. Statement d is not correct because, if you leave the $200,000 in the bank: for 2 years, you will earn $12,000 in interest, or $6,000 each year (200,000 * 3%). This is less than the $190,000 you could earn if you opened the hotdog stand. Statement e is not correct because, if you put the $200,000 in a mutual fund for two years, you will earn $40,000, or $20,000 each year ($200,000 * 10%).

10. Correct answer: b.

   Discussion: Flu shots are rival in consumption. The flu shot that I get means that somebody else can't have the exact same flu shot that I got. Each individual "consumes" his or her own flu shot. It is also excludable; if you don't pay for a flu shot, you can't get a flu shot.

   By contrast, preservation of an endangered species, a bridge, or a city park, or national defence is something that I can consume (use, get enjoyment out of) while at the same time, so can somebody else. Also, if I want a bridge or preservation of an endangered species or city park or national defense and pay for it myself, other people can consume (use and enjoy) it even if they don't pay for it.

11. Correct answer: e.

   Discussion: All of the above are characteristics of public good.

12. Correct answer: b.

   Discussion: The free-rider problem means that people recognize that they will be able to use a good without having to pay for it because they figure others will pay for it. Thus, a tax will force all people to indirectly pay for the good.

   Voluntary contributions will not overcome the free-rider problem. Nobody will make a voluntary contribution; they'll be waiting for other people to make contributions so that the good will is provided and then they can use it without having paid anything for it. A price support won't work and isn't related to the free-rider problem. Subsidizing users of the good/program makes no sense since that means the government would be paying the free riders to use it. This is the reverse of a tax. An advertising campaign won't work either.

VIII. ANSWER KEY: ESSAY QUESTIONS

13. If I were a lobbyist for the textile industry, I would probably seek out government favours that would lead to a higher, government-supported price for textiles. There are numerous government policies that could create a higher price for textiles. First, a minimum price policy (price support) which establishes a price below which the price of textiles may not fall and is above the equilibrium price would certainly generate a higher price for textiles and make the industry executives happy as they would see their profits rise (assuming nothing else happened to hurt profits). Second, any form of quantity, restriction, be it a quota or ban on imports of textiles from foreign countries, a quota on domestic industry output, or collecting a fee (paid for by textile producers) for a license to produce textiles, would ultimately reduce the textile industry output (supply of textiles would shift left) and the price of textiles would rise. A quota or ban on imports might also benefit employment in the textile industry since the loss of textiles due to a ban or quota on imports might mean that domestic industries might increase their production (and employment) to make up for the loss. While a fee for a license might lead to a higher price for textiles, the textile producers who are already in the industry may not be happy about having to pay the fee. The lobbyist might be smarter to ask that any new textile producers would have to buy a license in order to produce.

   Of course, any of these schemes will likely hurt consumers who ultimately end up having to pay a higher price for clothing made from textiles. (Obviously, clothing makers who buy textiles will also have to pay a higher price for textiles which they will pass on to consumers). Consumers may also find that the supply of clothing is smaller than before the lobbying. Producers of textiles would be the winners because they would see the profits of their companies increase, as the price they earned on the sales of textiles would be higher. However, the producers would have to factor into their profit calculation the expense of retaining a lobbyist.

If the lobbyist is very expensive, the producers may not make a profit after all.

An efficient outcome will not occur if the lobbying is successful. The price will be higher than the equilibrium price that would have occurred under a market-determined outcome, and the quantity available to consumers will be lower than that under a market-determined outcome.

14. A bridge is a public good because it satisfies the two criteria that determine a public good: non-rivalry and non-excludability. A bridge is a good that is non-rival in consumption because my use of the bridge does not restrict or eliminate somebody else's use of the bridge. The bridge is available for anybody to use. A bridge is also non-excludable, meaning that it is impractical to exclude people who don't pay for the bridge from using it. For example, if I want a bridge built across a river so it is quicker for me to get to work and I pay $1,000,000 to have the bridge built, it is going to be very difficult to exclude other commuters from using the bridge. Some cities collect tolls on their bridges as a way of getting those who use the bridge to pay proportionately more for it. Most citizens of a city pay for a bridge through their taxes; if they must also pay a toll to use the bridge, then those who use it the most will be paying more for the bridge than those who hardly use it.

A rent-controlled apartment may not turn out to be as inexpensive as the stated monthly payment suggests because of hidden fees. The apartment owners might add on some extra (rather costly) fees since they know there are lots of other people who would be willing to pay more than the rent-controlled price for the apartment. Thus, the apartment owners are just trying to rent to that person who is willing to pay what the true (market-determined or equilibrium) rental price would be. Alternatively, while the rent for the apartment may be controlled and, therefore, seem low relative to other rental rates around the city, the quality of the apartment may be pretty bad. The apartment may be very run down, poorly heated, with poor plumbing and peeling paint. Thus, while you may end up paying at the rent-controlled rate, you're paying for what you get. In this sense, even though your monthly payment may be low, you're not really reaping the benefits that you might have imagined (low monthly fee for a quality apartment).

CHAPTER 7
CONSUMER CHOICE

I.   OVERVIEW

In this chapter, you will learn about factors that affect an individual's decision about how much of a particular product or products to consume (or buy). Thus, you will consider an individual demand curve (instead of a market demand curve as in Chapters 4 and 5). You will learn about income and substitution effects. You will re-encounter the principle of opportunity cost, the reality principle that requires that you think in inflation-adjusted terms, and the marginal principle. You will learn about utility and marginal utility (economists way of measuring the satisfaction that consumers receive from the consumption of goods). You will learn about the law of diminishing marginal utility and the utility-maximizing rule. You will learn about consumer surplus and how to measure it using a demand curve.

II.   CHECKLIST

By the end of the chapter, you should be able to:

- Apply the principle of opportunity cost to consumption decisions.
- Explain the income and substitution effects that result from a change in the price of a good.
- Explain why each point on an individual demand curve represents a point at which the marginal benefit of consuming (using) a good equals the marginal cost to the consumer.
- Explain the law of diminishing marginal utility and represent it with a graph.
- Explain why consumers are willing to pay a higher price for consuming the first unit of a good than for any subsequent units.
- Explain the utility-maximizing rule and use it to decide whether a consumer should increase or decrease the consumption of one good and decrease or increase the consumption of another.
- Define consumer surplus and measure it using a graph.
- Explain why increases in price reduce consumer surplus and vice-versa.

III. KEY TERMS

Individual demand curve: a curve that shows the relationship between the price of a good and the quantity that a single consumer is willing to buy (the quantity demanded), *ceteris paribus*.

Substitution effect: the change in consumption resulting from a change in the price of one good relative to the price of other goods.

Real income: consumer's income measured in terms of the goods it can buy.

Normal good: a good for which an increase in income, *ceteris paribus*, increases demand.

Inferior good: a good for which an increase in income, *ceteris paribus*, decreases demand.

Income effect: the change in consumption resulting from an increase in the consumer's real income.

Utility: the satisfaction, or pleasure, measured in utils, that a consumer experiences when he or she consumes a good.

Marginal utility: the change in utility from the consumption of one additional unit of the good; also referred to as marginal benefit.

Law of diminishing marginal utility: as the consumption of a particular good increases, marginal utility decreases.

Utility-maximizing rule: pick the affordable combination of consumer goods that makes the marginal utility per dollar spent on one good equal to the marginal utility per dollar spent on a second good.

Consumer surplus: the difference between the maximum amount a consumer is willing to pay for a product and the price the consumer pays for the product.

IV. PERFORMANCE ENHANCING TIPS (PETS)

PET #1

When you see the term "marginal", you should always think of computing the change in a variable. Computing the change requires that you have some numeric value before the change and some numeric value after the change. The difference between the two is the change in the variable.

You have seen this PET in Chapter 2 of the Study Guide, but it is repeated again here because you will use it in this chapter to compute marginal utility.

Marginal utility is the change in utility or utils from increasing consumption (or cutting back on consumption) by one more unit of a good. The change in utility or utils is a way of measuring the change in satisfaction or benefits or "happiness" that consumers receive from consuming one more unit of the good.

Use the Table 7-1 to fill in the marginal utility reaped from buying potato chips.

Table 7-1		
Bags of Potato Chips	**Total Utility**	**Marginal Utility**
0	0 utils	
1	50 utils	
2	90 utils	
3	120 utils	
4	140 utils	
5	150 utils	
6	120 utils	

The marginal utility (change in utility) associated with consuming the first bag of potato chips is 50 utils since 0 bags of potato chips yields 0 utility. The total utility associated with consuming two bags of potato chips is 90 utils. This means that the change in utility (marginal utility) from consuming the second bag of potato chips is 40 utils (90-50). The marginal utility for the third bag is computed similarly as 30 utils, 20 utils for the fourth bag, and 10 utils for the fifth bag. However, the sixth bag actually *reduces* total utility from 150 to 120, so the marginal utility is negative 30. A rational consumer obviously would not consume any more than 5 bags of potato chips since that would reduce his overall level of satisfaction.

PET #2

Diminishing marginal utility means that the utility (or satisfaction) from consuming more and more of a good increases but at a decreasing rate. Just because the term "diminishing" is used does NOT mean that the total level of utility, (satisfaction) decreases or diminishes.

In Chapter 2, you encountered the principle of diminishing marginal returns or diminishing marginal output. In this chapter, the principle is applied to utility. In fact, if you look at Table 7-1 above, assuming you've now filled in the correct numbers, you will see that the numbers in the last column of the table reflect diminishing marginal utility. The marginal utility declines from 50 to 40 to 30 to 20 to 10 utils. The numbers are just a way of expressing that an individual gets less and less additional satisfaction from eating more and more bags of potato chips.

PET #3

The rule of utility-maximization is a marginal benefit-marginal cost comparison. If there is an inequality in the expression, then a consumer can rearrange his consumption choices and be better off (get more utility).

The rule of utility-maximization can be expressed two ways:

$$\frac{\text{Marginal Utility of Good X}}{\text{Price of Good X}} = \frac{\text{Marginal Utility of Good Y}}{\text{Price of Good Y}} \qquad \text{Equation 7 - 1}$$

This relationship can be rewritten as (see Basic Algebra appendix of the Study Guide if you need review):

$$\frac{\text{Marginal Utility of Good X}}{\text{Marginal Utility of Good Y}} = \frac{\text{Price of Good X}}{\text{Price of Good Y}} \qquad \text{Equation 7 - 2}$$

Equation 7-1 compares the marginal utility per unit price paid of good X to good Y. It says that the marginal utility (or marginal benefit) per unit of cost to the consumer of good X is equal to the marginal utility (or marginal benefit) per unit of cost to the consumer of good Y. If the equality sign was replaced with a > sign, then the marginal utility per unit price paid for good X would be greater than the marginal utility per unit price paid for good Y. Thus, a consumer could be better off (receive more utility) by rearranging his budget to consume more of good X and less of good Y (or vice-versa if the equality sign were replaced with a < sign).

Equation 7-2 compares the relative marginal utility of good X to good Y to the relative price paid for good X to good Y. Remember that, to the consumer, the price paid for one unit of a good represents the marginal cost to the consumer. Equation 7-2 says that the relative marginal utility (or marginal benefit} of good X to good Y is equal to the relative marginal cost to the consumer of good X to good Y. If the equality sign was replaced with a > sign, then the marginal utility of good X relative to good Y would be greater than the relative marginal cost of good X to good Y. Since the relative marginal benefit of good X is greater than the relative marginal cost of good X, a consumer could be better of by rearranging his budget to consume more of good X and less of good Y (or vice-versa if the equality sign were replaced with a < sign).

PET #4

The utility-maximizing rule is based on a consumer having a given budget (income) and facing fixed prices of the goods. A bigger budget (income) or changes in the price of the goods the consumer typically purchases could alter the quantities that a consumer would select based on the utility-maximizing rule.

Suppose based on the utility-maximizing rule, you decide to buy one chicken-salad sandwich and three soft drinks a day. Suppose that the price of a chicken salad sandwich is $2.00 and the price of a soft drink is $0.50. Furthermore, the marginal utility you receive from the one and only chicken salad sandwich is 8 utils and the marginal utility you receive from the third soft drink is 2 utils. Are you maximizing your total utility? Let's see:

Using Equation 7-1	Using Equation 7-2:
8 utils/$2.00 = 2 utils/$0.50	8 utils/2 utils = $2.00/$0.50
4=4.	4=4.

Thus, you are maximizing your total utility (for the given prices and your given income) by consuming one sandwich and three soft drinks since the two ratios are equal.

Now, suppose the price of a soft drink goes up to $1 but you continue to consume one chicken salad sandwich and three soft drinks. What would happen to the conditions above? Let's see:

Using Equation 7-1	Using Equation 7-2
8 utils/$2.00 = 4 utils/$1.00	8 utils/2 utils = $2.00/$1.00
4>2.	4>2.

By using Equation 7-1 we see that the marginal benefit per unit cost of one more chicken salad sandwich is greater than the marginal benefit per unit cost of one more soft drink. Thus, the consumer could be better off by increasing his consumption of chicken salad sandwiches and reducing his consumption of soft drinks.

By using Equation 7-2 we see that the marginal utility of chicken salad sandwiches relative to soft drinks is greater than the marginal cost of chicken salad sandwiches relative to soft drinks. Thus, the consumer could be better off by increasing his consumption of chicken salad sandwiches and reducing his consumption of soft drinks since he receives relatively more benefits than costs from chicken salad sandwiches.

Both of these examples illustrate what you probably already know: an increase in the price of a good (relative to others) will lead to a reduction in the amount consumed for a given income, tastes, etc.

Now, suppose that rather than the price of the goods changing, the income of the consumer changes. Let's suppose that the consumer gets an increase in his income. What will happen?

Without any price changes, the *ratio* of prices is still 4. However, since the consumer now has more income, he can consume more of both goods. When he does this, what will happen to the marginal utility of the goods? They will decline. Diminishing marginal utility tells you that, as you consume more of a good, the addition to utility (marginal utility) of consuming one more unit of that good declines. Thus, for example, a consumer may now consume 3 chicken salad sandwiches and 6 soft drinks a day. The third chicken salad sandwich may now yield a marginal utility of 4 utils and the sixth soft drink may now yield a marginal utility of 1 util. However, it is no accident that the ratio of marginal utilities remains at 4. The utility-maximizing rule dictates that the consumer continues to consume chicken salad sandwiches and soft drinks until the *ratio* of marginal utilities is equal to the ratio of the prices. Since the ratio of prices hasn't changed, the *ratio* of the marginal utilities must still be 4 even though the quantities consumed (and the respective marginal utilities) have changed.

PET #5

Consumer surplus is measured as the area underneath the demand curve but above the price line. It is measured using the formula for the area of a triangle, which is given by (0.5 * base * height) of triangle.

Suppose you were asked to compute the consumer surplus based on Figure 7-1 below assuming the price is $5.

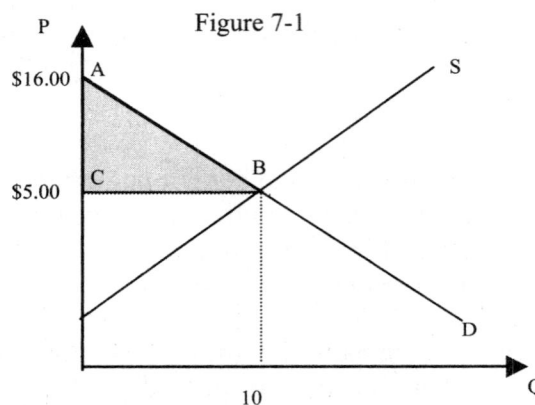

Figure 7-1

The letters ABC marks off the triangle. The triangle's base is 10 units long. The height of the triangle is ($16-$5) = $9. Thus, the area of consumer surplus is
1/2 * 10 units * $9/unit = $45.

V.   PRACTICE EXAM: MULTIPLE CHOICE QUESTIONS

1. Suppose you are given a monthly income of $200 to spend on food while at university. Further, suppose the price of a single serving of pizza is $4 and the price of a deli-sandwich is $2. Which one of the following consumption combinations is possible given these prices and income?

    a. 40 pizzas, 50 sandwiches.
    b. 15 pizzas, 80 sandwiches.
    c. 20 pizzas, 60 sandwiches.
    d. 10pizzas, 100 sandwiches.
    e. 50 pizzas, 20 sandwiches.

2. When the price of a normal good declines, the quantity demanded increases because:

    a. the opportunity cost of consuming the good declines.
    b. a consumer's real income increases and this enables him to buy more.
    c. the consumer's marginal utility of the good increases.
    d. the good is worth more.
    e. (a) and (b).

3. When the price of an inferior good declines,

    a. the substitution effect works to increase the quantity demanded and the income effect works to reduce the quantity demanded.
    b. the substitution and income effects both work to increase the quantity demanded.
    c. the substitution effect works to decrease the quantity demanded and the income effect works to increase the quantity demanded.
    d. the substitution and income effects both work to decrease the quantity demanded.
    e. the income effect dominates the substitution effect.

4. Which one of the following would be the best example of an inferior good?

    a. Steak.
    b. Lobster.
    c. A cruise.
    d. Macaroni and cheese.
    e. Jewellery.

5. Which one of the following could explain the observation that people in Ontario buy more automobiles per year than people in British Columbia?

    a. Differences in preferences/tastes for driving versus taking mass transit.
    b. A lower price of gasoline in Ontario relative to British Columbia.
    c. A bigger population in the Ontario.
    d. Mass transit is safer in British Columbia than in the Ontario
    e. All of the above.

6. Use the utility-maximizing rule and the information below to answer the following question.

    Marginal utility of 1 shrimp = 10   Marginal utility of 1 strawberry = 5
    Price of 1 shrimp = $0.25   Price of 1 strawberry = $0.10

    Based on this information, a consumer:

    a. is maximizing his or her utility.
    b. should eat more strawberries and fewer shrimp.
    c. should eat more shrimp and fewer strawberries.
    d. is minimizing his or her utility.
    e. (b) and (d).

Use Table 7-2 to answer the following question.

Table 7-2	
Number of Sweaters Purchased	**Total Utility**
1	25 utils
2	40 utils
3	50 utils
4	55 utils
5	58 utils

7. Which one of the statements based on Table 7-2 is true?

   a. The marginal utility of the fifth sweater is 33 utils (58-25).
   b. Total utility is diminishing.
   c. Total utility is increasing but at a decreasing rate.
   d. Marginal utility is negative.
   e. Marginal utility cannot be computed without more information.

8. Which one of the following terms is used in economics to describe the satisfaction that individuals receive from their consumption of goods and services?

   a. Utility.
   b. Opportunity cost.
   c. Totality.
   d. Plaisir.
   e. Hedonity.

9. Use the information below to answer the following question.

   Price of an ice cream cone = $1.50   Price of french fries = $0.75

   Which one of the following statements is true given the information above?

   a. If a consumer is maximizing utility, then the (marginal utility of an ice cream cone)/(marginal utility of french fries) = 0.50.
   b. If a consumer is maximizing utility, then the (marginal utility of an ice cream cone)/(marginal utility of french fries) = 2.00.
   c. A consumer will maximize utility by eating 2 bags of french fries for every ice cream cone.
   d. With an income of $600 a month, a consumer could eat 300 ice cream cones and 400 bags of french fries.
   e. (b) and (d).

10. Which one of the following statements is NOT true of a demand curve? Assume a normal good.

    a. The demand curve is negatively sloped.
    b. The demand curve will shift right as more consumers desire to buy the good.
    c. The demand curve is the sum of the quantities demanded by all consumers at various prices of the good.
    d. Increased preferences for the good will shift the demand curve to the left.
    e. Every point on the demand curve satisfies the marginal principle.

    Use Figure 7-2 to answer the following question.

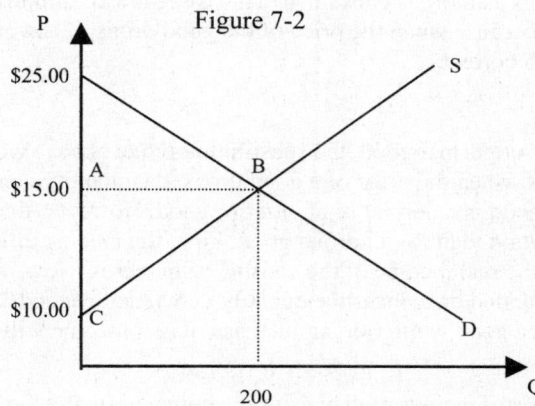

Figure 7-2

11. Which one of the following statements is true?

    a. Consumer surplus is measured by the triangle ABC.
    b. Consumer surplus equals $1,000.
    c. Consumer surplus will decrease if the price decreases.
    d. Consumer surplus will increase if the demand curve shifts to the right and the price increases.
    e. Consumer surplus will increase if the demand curve shifts to the left and the price increases.

VI. PRACTICE EXAM: ESSAY QUESTIONS

12. Explain the income and substitution effects for a normal good and for an inferior good.

13. Suppose that you are a member of a book club for which you have paid an annual subscription fee of $30. As a member, you may purchase books for $1 a book and no more than 12 books per year. Using economic principles, explain how you might decide how many books to buy.

VII. ANSWER KEY: MULTIPLE CHOICE

1. Correct answer: c.

    Discussion: The cost of 20 pizzas is $80 and the cost of 60 sandwiches is $120. The sum of these equals the monthly income of $200.

    Statements a, b, d, and e are all combinations of pizzas and sandwiches that require more than $200.

2. Correct answer: e.

    Discussion: Statement e is correct because (a) is just a way of restating the substitution effect and (b) is just a way of restating the income effect.

    Statement c is not correct because the marginal utility of increasing consumption (quantity demanded) would actually decline. More and more of a good adds progressively less to total utility which is to say that marginal utility declines as more is consumed. This is the law of diminishing marginal utility. Statement d is not correct because when the price of the good drops, it is worth less, not more. Statements a and b are both correct.

3. Correct answer: a.

    Discussion: For an inferior or normal good, the substitution effect always works to increase the quantity demanded. That is, when the price of a good drops, the quantity demanded will always rise regardless of whether the good is a normal or an inferior good. However, the income effect works differently for an inferior good than for a normal good. First, the income effect arises because, when the price of a good drops, the real income of the consumer increases. Now, whether the income effect increases the quantity demanded or reduces the quantity demanded depends on whether the good is normal or inferior. Since the good is inferior, an increase in real income will reduce the quantity demanded.

    Statement b would be correct if the question had asked about a normal good. Statement c is not correct because, when the price of a good falls, the substitution effect does not work to decrease quantity demanded but, rather, increase it. Also, with an inferior good, the income effect works to reduce quantity demanded, not increase it. Statement d is not correct because the substitution effect works to increase the quantity demanded. Statement e is not correct because it is not known whether the income effect dominates the substitution effect.

4. Correct answer: d.

    Discussion: When income increases, the consumption of macaroni and cheese is the most likely of the options listed to decrease.

    Steak, lobster, jewellery, and a cruise are all goods for which the amount consumed would be most likely to increase when income increases.

5. Correct answer: e.

    Discussion: Statement a means that consumers in Ontario simply prefer driving automobiles over mass transit as compared to people living in British Columbia. This would translate in the observation that the Ontario buys more automobiles than B.C. A lower price of gasoline in the Ontario means that it is less costly to drive an automobile in the Ontario than in B.C. Since gasoline is a complementary good to automobiles, the lower price of gasoline translates to a stronger demand for automobiles in the Ontario. A bigger population in the Ontario than in B.C means that there is a bigger market or more buyers for automobiles than in B.C. This too, could explain why Ontario buys more automobiles than B.C. If mass transit were safer in B.C. than in Ontario, people in B.C. would be more inclined to use mass transit than would people in Ontario. In other words, people in Ontario would be less inclined to use mass transit and, thus, more inclined to drive automobiles. This too, could explain why Ontario buys more automobiles than B.C.

6. Correct answer: b.

   Discussion: The ratio of the marginal utility of one shrimp to the price of one shrimp is 40. The ratio of the marginal utility of one strawberry to the price of one strawberry is 50. Since the marginal utility per unit cost to the consumer of a strawberry is greater than for shrimp, the consumer could be made better off by consuming more strawberries and fewer shrimp.

   Statement a is not correct. For the consumer to be maximizing utility, the ratios mentioned above would have to be equal to each other. (See PET #3.) Statement c is not correct since it should be the other way around. Statement d is not correct; while we know the consumer is not maximizing his utility, we can't say (without other information) whether the consumer is minimizing his utility. Statement e is not correct because statement d is not correct.

7. Correct answer: c.

   Discussion: This question requires that you compute the marginal utility associated with each sweater purchased. Thus, the marginal utility from the first sweater is 25 utils. The marginal utility or addition to utility from the second sweater is 15 utils (40-25); from the third sweater is 10 utils (50-40); from the fourth sweater is 5 utils (55-50); and from the fifth sweater is 3 utils (58-55). Thus, while total utility is increasing (from 25 to 58), it is increasing at a decreasing rate. Marginal utility is diminishing.

   Statement a is not correct because the marginal utility from the fifth sweater is measured by asking what the addition to utility is from buying the fifth sweater. Thus, the correct answer would be 3 utils. Statement b is not correct because total utility is increasing; marginal utility is diminishing. Statement d is not correct because in no case is marginal utility computed to be negative. Statement e is not correct because you can compute marginal utility from the table.

8. Correct answer: a.

   Discussion: Utility is the term used to describe the satisfaction or enjoyment individuals receive from the consumption of goods and services.

   While opportunity cost is an economic concept, it is not the term used to describe satisfaction from consumption. Totality, plaisir (french for pleasure), and hedonity are not correct.

9. Correct answer: e.

   Discussion: Statement b is correct because the ratio of the price of an ice cream cone/price of french fries is 2. Thus, the ratio of the marginal utility of an ice cream cone/marginal utility of french fries must be equal to 2. (See PET #3.) Statement d is also correct because, if the consumer buys 200 ice cream cones at a price of $1.50 per cone, he spends $300 and has $300 remaining to spend on french fries. At a price of $0.75 per bag of french fries, the consumer can by 400 bags of fries with the remaining $300 from his income.

   Statement a is not correct because the ratio is 2/1 not 1/2 (= 0.50). Statement c is not correct because the utility-maximizing rule only tells you about the ratio of the marginal utilities, not about the ratio at which ice cream cones and french fries would be eaten to maximize utility. For example, a 2/1 ratio of marginal utilities might correspond to 100 ice cream cones and 600 french fries, which is a ratio of 6 bags of, french fries/1 ice cream cone.

10. Correct answer: d.

    Discussion: Increased preferences for a good will shift the demand curve for it to the right.

    Statement a is true based on the Law of Demand. Statement b is true because more consumers increase the demand for a good. Statement c is true because a demand curve is representative of the market. Statement e is also true.

11. Correct answer: b.

    Discussion: Consumer surplus is measured using the formula for a triangle which is 1/2*base*height. In this case, the base is 200 units and the height is $10. Thus, the consumer surplus is 1/2*200units*$10/unit = $1,000.

Statement a is not correct; consumer surplus is measured by looking at the area above the price but below the demand curve. Area ABC is below the price. Statement c is not correct because consumer surplus increases when the price paid for the good decreases. (Draw in a lower price line). Statement d is not correct because you don't know what will happen to consumer surplus. On the one hand, the rightward shift will increase consumer surplus (draw a demand curve further to the right), but on the other hand, the price increase will decrease consumer surplus (draw in a higher price line). Statement e cannot be correct because a leftward shift in demand would decrease consumer surplus (draw a demand curve further to the left), as would a price increase (draw in a higher price line). Thus, consumer surplus would necessarily decrease.

VIII. ANSWER KEY: ESSAY QUESTIONS

12. Normal Good: When the price of a good drops, there are two effects: (1) the substitution effect and (2) the income effect. The substitution effect means that, as the price of a good drops, the opportunity, cost of purchasing it is now lower and so consumers are more inclined to buy more of the good. Thus, the price drop increases the quantity demanded (vice-versa for a price increase). The income effect occurs because, as the price of a good falls, a consumer is now able to purchase more of the good because his "real" income has increased. For example, if the price of a pair of shoes was $30 and they dropped to $15, a consumer could buy twice as many pairs of shoes as before, given the same nominal income. That is, the consumer's real income has increased. For a normal good, the price-drop induced increase in real income will increase the amount of the good that the consumer buys. The income effect also works in reverse. If the price increased rather than decreased, the consumer's real income would decline, and he would buy fewer units of the good.

    Inferior Good: The substitution effect described above for a normal good is also present for an inferior good. Thus, the substitution effect works exactly as explained above. However, the income effect works differently. For an inferior good, as the price of the good drops and the consumer's real income thus rises, the consumer will now buy less of the good because it is an inferior good. Generic soft drinks or toilet paper are good examples of inferior goods. If, instead, the price of the good increased, the substitution effect would act to reduce the purchases of the good by the consumer. However, the real income effect would, in this case, lead to an increase in the quantity demanded for the good by the consumer.

13. In order to decide how many books to buy, I would have to compute the marginal utility (addition to utility) I received from buying successively more and more books. I would also consider, in my mind, the opportunity cost of buying a book. The opportunity cost might be that I am able to buy fewer and fewer classical music CDs. I would then translate that opportunity cost into a loss of marginal utility. I would have to know what the marginal utility that I would lose would be of giving up the purchase of classical music CDs. I would also have to know what the price of a classical music CD was. For example, suppose I received 15 utils from the third book and, correspondingly, given that I purchased three books, I am able to purchase twenty classical music CDs where the twentieth classical music CD yields 10 utils. Further, suppose that the price of a classical music CD is $10. In this case, the marginal utility of the fifth book/price of book = 5 and the marginal utility of twentieth CD/price of CD = 1. Thus, I would benefit by buying more books and fewer CDs since I will receive a relatively bigger addition to utility (per unit price paid) from more books than I will lose from cutting back on my purchases of classical music CDs.

APPENDIX TO CHAPTER 7
CONSUMER CHOICE USING INDIFFERENCE CURVES

I.   OVERVIEW

In the appendix to Chapter 7, you will see a more graphical depiction of consumer choice. You will use budget lines and indifference curves which are just ways of representing income constraints for given prices of goods and services and preferences. You will also see how an individual demand curve is derived.

II.   CHECKLIST

By the end of this appendix, you should be able to:

- Draw a budget line assuming different prices for the goods under consideration.
- Define the slope of the budget line and explain why it is equal to the price of the good on the horizontal axis divided by the price of the good on the vertical axis.
- Define an indifference curve and explain the relationship of an indifference curve to one above it and one below it.
- Define the marginal rate of substitution.
- Explain why the indifference curve becomes flatter as you move down along the curve.
- Draw a graph of a budget line and indifference curve and find the utility-maximizing point.
- Explain why the utility-maximizing point is the point of tangency between the budget line and the indifference curve and why non-tangency points are not utility maximizing.
- Derive a demand curve by changing the slope of the budget line and finding new utility-maximizing points.

III.   KEY TERMS

Budget set: a set of points that includes all the combinations of two goods that a consumer can afford, given the consumer's income and the prices of the two goods.

Budget line: the line connecting all the combinations of two goods that exhaust a consumer's budget.

Indifference curve: the set of combinations of two goods that generate the same level of utility or satisfaction.

Marginal rate of substitution (MRS): the rate at which a consumer is willing to substitute one good for another.

IV.   PERFORMANCE ENHANCING TIPS (PETS)

PET # 1

The ratio of two variables can increase because the variable in the numerator gets bigger or because the variable in the denominator gets smaller. The ratio of two variables can decrease because the variable in the numerator gets smaller or because the variable in the denominator gets bigger.

For example, suppose the ratio of the marginal utility of good X to the marginal utility of good Y (MU_x/MU_y) is 4. Now, suppose a consumer consumes more of good X. Based on the law of diminishing marginal utility, the marginal utility of good X will decline. This means that the ratio, (MU_x/MU_y), will decrease from the value of 4. Suppose instead that the consumer consumes less of good Y. Based on the law of diminishing marginal utility (in reverse now because the consumer is consuming less, not more), the marginal utility of good Y will increase. This too, means that the ratio, (MU_x/MU_y), will decrease.

PET #2

The slope of the budget line is the ratio of the price of good X (good on the horizontal axis) to the price of good Y (good on the vertical axis. This is also equal to the ratio of the change in good Y divided by the change in good X.

Suppose the price of a single serving of pizza is $4 and the price of a deli sandwich is $2. Further, suppose a consumer has a budget/income of $200. If the consumer buys 20 pizzas, she will spend $80 and have $120 remaining to spend on sandwiches. Thus, she could buy 60 sandwiches. If the consumer decides to buy 30 pizzas, she will spend $120 and have $80 remaining to spend on sandwiches. Thus, she could buy 40 sandwiches. The change in the quantity of pizzas is +10 and the change in the quantity of deli sandwiches is -20.

Notice that the ratio of the price of a pizza to a sandwich is ($4/pizza)/($2/sandwich) = 2 sandwiches/1 pizza. Also, notice that, based on the numbers above, the change in the quantity of sandwiches divided by the change in the quantity of pizzas is 20/10 = 2 sandwiches/1 pizza (allowing for a negative sign since the consumer must trade-off sandwiches for pizzas).

V.   PRACTICE EXAM: MULTIPLE CHOICE QUESTIONS

1. Which one of the following is true of indifference curves?

   a. They represent the combination of two goods that generate the same level of income.
   b. Combinations of goods above the indifference curve generate more satisfaction.
   c. A lower point along an indifference curve yields less satisfaction than a higher point.
   d. The slope of the indifference curve gets bigger (steeper) as you move down the indifference curve.
   e. (b) and (c).

2. Which one of the following statements is true assuming the marginal rate of substitution between good G and good H is equal to 3?

   a. An increase in the consumption of good G and a decrease in the consumption of good H will increase the marginal rate of substitution.
   b. If the ratio of the price of good G to the price of good H is 4, then a consumer is maximizing his utility.
   c. An increase in the consumption of good G and an increase in the consumption of good H will increase the marginal rate of substitution.
   d. A decrease in the consumption of good G and an increase in the consumption of good H will increase the marginal rate of substitution.
   e. A decrease in income will reduce the marginal rate of substitution.

Use Figure 7-3 to answer the following question.

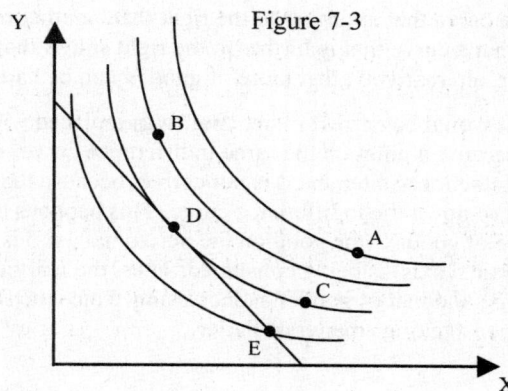

Figure 7-3

3. Which one of the points is associated with utility maximization?

   a. Point A.
   b. Point B.
   c. Point C.
   d. Point D.
   e. Point E.

4. Suppose you are given the following information:

Marginal utility of 1 cup coffee = 20 utils   Price of 1 cup of coffee = $1.00
Marginal utility of 1 can soft drink = 10 utils

What would the price of one soft drink have to be in order for the consumer to maximize his utility?

   a. $0.50.
   b. $2.00.
   c. $5.00.
   d. $200.
   e. Cannot be answered without information on consumer's income or budget.

VI.   PRACTICE EXAM: ESSAY QUESTION

5. Given the following information, draw a budget line for the consumer. Be sure to label the axes and provide a number for the vertical and horizontal intercepts.

Income = $2,000/month.   Price of 1 kilogram of steak = $8.00
Price of 1 kilogram of potatoes = $1.00

Now, draw several indifference curves into the picture, being sure to draw one that represents utility maximization. Describe what is true at the utility-maximizing point. Describe why points on the other indifference curves do not represent utility maximization.

VII.   ANSWER KEY: MULTIPLE CHOICE

1. Correct answer: b.

Discussion: An indifference curve that is further to the right than another represents a higher level of satisfaction. The reason is that a curve that is further to the right shows that more of good X can be had for every level of good Y or, alternatively, that more of good Y can be had for every level of good X.

Statement a is not correct; it would be correct if "income" was replaced with "utility" or "satisfaction." Statement c is not correct because a point on the same indifference curve, whether it is higher or lower, yields the same level of satisfaction. Statement d is not correct because the slope of the indifference curve gets flatter as you move down the indifference curve. This happens because, as you move down the indifference curve, more of good X (the good on the horizontal axis) is being consumed and less of good Y (the good on the vertical axis) is being consumed. Thus, the marginal utility (addition to utility) of good X is declining and that of good Y is increasing. Since the slope of the indifference curve is MU_x/MU_y, the slope is getting smaller or flatter.

2. Correct answer: d.

Discussion: A decrease in the consumption of good G will increase the marginal utility of good G (law of diminishing marginal utility in reverse because consumption of good G is decreasing, not increasing). An increase in the consumption of good H will decrease the marginal utility of good H. Since the question asks about MU_G/MU_H, this number will increase.

Statement a is not correct because the marginal rate of substitution would decrease. Statement b is not correct; for utility maximization the price ratio would have to be 3. Statement c is not correct because the marginal rate of substitution is defined with respect to trade-offs in consumption of one good relative to another. Statement c allows for an increase in the consumption of both goods. Statement e is not correct because income does not affect the marginal rate of substitution (which is the slope of the indifference curve).

3. Correct answer: c.

    Discussion: At point c, the indifference curve is tangent to the budget line. The tangency means that the marginal rate of substitution between good X and good Y is equal to the price ratio of good X to good Y.

    Points A, B, D, and E are not tangencies. Points A and B are unattainable given the current income of the consumer. Point D is on the same indifference curve as point C but is not the tangency point. Point E is on a lower indifference curve than point C and, thus, cannot be utility maximizing given the consumer's current income.

4. Correct answer: a.

    Discussion: The (marginal utility of 1 cup of coffee)/(marginal utility of 1 soft drink) is 2. Thus, the (price of 1 cup of coffee)/(price of 1 soft drink) must also be 2. Since the price of 1 cup of coffee is $1, a soft drink must cost $0.50 for utility maximization to prevail.

    Based on the above, statements b, c, and d cannot be correct. Statement e is not correct because you do not need information on the consumer's budget to determine the condition for utility maximization.

VIII. ANSWER KEY: ESSAY QUESTION

5. Our drawing (Figure 7-4) puts potatoes on the vertical axis and steak on the horizontal axis. With an income of $1,000, 2,000 kilograms of potatoes could be purchased in one month if no steak was purchased. With an income of $1000, 250 kilograms of steak could be purchased in one month if no potatoes were purchased. Thus, the vertical intercept is 2,000 kilograms of potatoes and the horizontal intercept is 250 kilograms of steak. The slope of the budget line is given by the ratio of the price of steak to the price of potatoes. Thus, the slope of the budget line is 8 kilograms of potatoes/1 steak. You can also figure out the slope of the budget line by taking two points (end points since you have information on them) and calculating the change in kilograms of potatoes consumed and kilograms of steak consumed. The change in kilograms of potatoes consumed is (2,000 - 0) and the change in kilograms of steak consumed is (250 - 0). Using the formula for a slope of rise/run, the slope of the budget line would be 8 kilograms of potatoes/1 kilogram of steak.

    The utility-maximizing point is found where the slope of the indifference curve is tangent to the budget line. This occurs at point A. At this point, the marginal utility of steak/marginal utility of potatoes = price of steak/price of potatoes. A consumer cannot get to a higher indifference curve, like point B, since his income does not allow him to afford that combination of goods. A point like point C is on a lower indifference curve than point A and, thus, not one that achieves the highest level of utility (satisfaction).

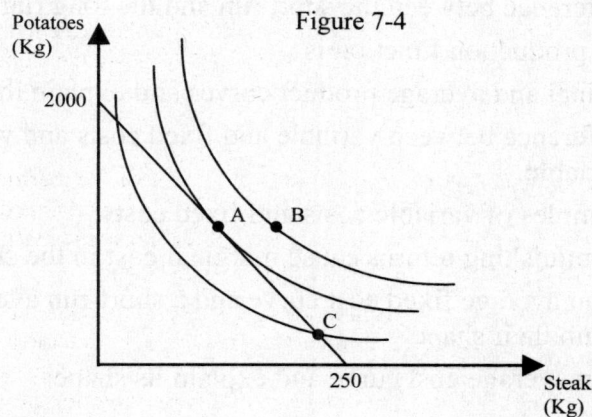

Figure 7-4

Chapter 7 Appendix

CHAPTER 8
A FIRM'S PRODUCTION AND COSTS: THE SHORT RUN AND THE LONG RUN

I.   OVERVIEW

In this chapter, you will learn about the link between the firm's decision to produce output and the costs associated with this decision. You will learn about labour productivity and the relationship between inputs and output in the short-run. You will learn about the costs a firm incurs when it produces output. You will learn that there are fixed costs and variable costs, and explicit and implicit costs of production. You will learn that a firm's marginal cost changes as it produces more and more (or less and less) output. You will also learn about a firm's short and long-run average costs. You will learn that the short and the long run are different time horizons that a firm considers when making decisions about how much to produce, whether to build another plant, hire more workers, or cut back production. You will re-encounter the concept of diminishing returns, which is a short-run concept. You will learn about economies and diseconomies of scale, which are long-run concepts.

II.   CHECKLIST

By the end of this chapter, you should be able to:
- Explain the difference between explicit and implicit costs.
- Give some examples of explicit costs and implicit costs.
- Explain the difference between accounting profit and economic profit.
- Explain the difference between the short run and the long run.
- Explain what a production function is.
- Draw the marginal and average product curves and explain their shape.
- Explain the difference between variable and fixed costs and why, in the long run, all costs are variable.
- Give some examples of variable costs and fixed costs.
- Explain why diminishing returns cause marginal cost in the short run to increase.
- Draw a short-run average fixed cost curve and a short-run average variable cost curve and explain their shape.
- Draw a long-run average cost curve and explain its shape.

- ❏ Draw a short-run marginal cost curve and explain its shape.
- ❏ Explain the relationship between marginal cost and the average cost curves.
- ❏ Explain what causes economies and diseconomies of scale.
- ❏ Define a firm's minimum efficient scale and represent it with a graph.

III.   KEY TERMS

Explicit costs: the firm's actual cash payments for its inputs.

Implicit costs: the opportunity costs of non-purchased inputs.

Economic cost: the sum of explicit and implicit costs.

Short run: a period of time over which one or more factors of production is fixed; in most cases, a period of time too short for a firm to modify an existing facility or build a new one.

Long run: a period of time long enough for a firm to change all the factors of production, meaning that a firm can modify its existing production facility or build a new one.

Production function: a relationship that links inputs to the production of outputs.

Fixed input: an input, usually capital, that is held constant.

Variable input: an input, usually labour, that can be varied to increase or decrease production.

Total product of labour: the amount of output produced by labour in a short-run production process.

Specialization: Concentration on a particular activity within a production process.

Average product of labour: the output divided by the labour input.

Marginal product of labour: The change in output resulting from a one-unit increase in the labour input while holding other inputs constant.

Short-run total cost (STC): the sum of all explicit and implicit costs of producing a particular level of output.

Fixed cost (FC): a cost that does not depend on the quantity produced.

Variable costs (VC): a cost that varies as the firm changes its output.

Sunk cost: a subset of fixed costs that are not recoverable if a firm goes out of business.

Short-run marginal cost (SMC): the change in total cost resulting from a one-unit increase in output.

Average fixed cost (AFC): fixed cost divided by the quantity produced.

Short-run average variable cost (SAVC): variable cost divided by the quantity produced.

Short-run average total cost (SATC): short-run total cost divided by the quantity produced.

Long-run average cost (LAC): total cost divided by the quantity of output when the firm can choose a production facility of any size.

Economies of scale: a situation in which an increase in the quantity produced decreases the long-run average cost of production.

Indivisible input: an input that cannot be scaled down to produce a small quantity of output.

Minimum efficient scale: the output at which the long-run average cost curve becomes horizontal.

Diseconomies of scale: a situation in which an increase in the quantity produced increases the long-run average cost of production.

IV. PERFORMANCE ENHANCING TIPS (PETS)

<u>PET # 1</u>

For any formula, if you are given two of three components, you can always figure out the third component. Likewise for three of four, four of five, and so on.

You encountered this PET in Chapter 5 where it was applied to the elasticity of demand. In this chapter, you can apply it to total, variable, and fixed costs, average total, average variable, and average fixed costs, and output. Let's see how.

Suppose you are told that the total cost of producing 100 units of output is $2,000. What is the average total cost? The average total cost (ATC) is computed using:

$$\text{ATC} = \frac{\text{Total Cost}}{\text{Output}}$$

Since you have two of the three components to the formula, you can figure out the third component. Thus, the average total cost would be $2,000/100 units = $20/unit.

Now, suppose you are told that the average total cost is $20/unit and that the output level is 100 units. What is the total cost (TC)? The formula above can be rearranged as below to figure out the total cost:

$$\text{TC} = \text{ATC} * \text{Output}$$

Thus, the total cost would be $20/unit * 100 units = $2,000.

Next, suppose you are told that the average total cost is $20/unit and that the total cost is $2,000. How many units of output (Q) must the firm be producing? The formulas above can be rearranged as below to figure out the output of the firm:

$$\text{Output} = Q = \frac{\text{Total Cost}}{\text{Average Total Cost}}$$

Thus, the firm must be producing $2,000/($20/unit) = 100 units.

The same is true for computing variable costs (total or average) and fixed costs (total or average).

You can also apply this PET to the relationship between short-run total cost, variable cost, and fixed cost, and to the relationship between short-run average total cost, average variable cost, and average fixed cost.

For example, suppose you are told that the variable cost of producing 100 units of output is $1,500 and the fixed cost of producing 100 units of output is $500. What is the short-run total cost?

The short-run total cost is the sum of the two:

Total Cost = variable cost + fixed cost

Thus, the total cost is $2,000.

Based on the information above, the average variable cost would be $1,500/100 units = $15/unit and the average fixed cost would be $500/100 units $5/unit. Thus, the average total cost would be:

Average total cost = average variable cost + average fixed cost

Thus, the average total cost would be $15/unit + $5/unit = $20/unit.

PET #2

Short-run marginal cost is computed by calculating the change in (or addition to) the short-run total cost as output increases by one unit. Since the short-run total cost is the sum of variable cost plus fixed cost, and since fixed costs do not change as the level of output changes, then marginal cost can also be computed by calculating the change in the short-run variable cost as output increases by one unit.

Suppose you are told that the variable cost of producing 10 units of output is $250 and that the fixed cost of producing 10 units of output is $100. Further, you are told that the variable cost of producing 11 units of output is $275. Since fixed costs are fixed, the fixed cost of producing 11 units of output remains at $100. What is the total cost of producing 10 units of output? Of 11 units of output? What is the marginal cost of the 11th unit of output?

Total cost of producing 10 units of output	$250 + $100 = $350.
Total cost of producing 11 units of output	$275 + $100 = $375.

The marginal cost (addition to cost) of producing one more unit of output, the 11th unit, is equal to the change in total cost which is also equal to the change in the variable cost. Let's see why:

Change in total cost	$375 - $350 = $25.
Change in variable cost	$275 - $250 = $25.
Change in fixed cost	$100 - $100 = $0.

Notice that the sum of the change in the variable cost plus the change in the fixed cost equals $25. This is because fixed costs do not change as output changes. That is, the marginal cost associated with fixed inputs is zero. Thus, in the short run, the marginal cost can also be computed as the change in the variable cost. Remember that in the long run, all costs are variable costs. There are no "fixed" costs.

PET #3

When marginal cost is less than average total (or average variable) cost, average total (or average variable) cost will decrease. When marginal cost is greater than average total (or average variable) cost, average total (or average variable) cost will increase. (This is also the case for average and marginal product of labour)

Suppose that you are told that the average total cost of producing 300 units of output is $60 and that the marginal cost of producing the 301st unit of output is $65. Will the average total cost of producing 301 units of output be greater or less than $60?

Since the marginal cost of increasing output by one unit to 301 units is greater than the average cost of producing the previous 300 units, then the average cost of producing 301 units will increase.

V.   PRACTICE EXAM: MULTIPLE CHOICE QUESTIONS

1. Which one of the following would be considered an implicit cost by a firm?
   a. Monthly electricity bill.
   b. Monthly rent for use of a warehouse.
   c. Weekly wages paid to workers.
   d. Foregone interest income because an entrepreneur must use her own money to start up a business.
   e. Payment for installation of a fax line.

2. In the long run, a firm can:
   a. alter the number of workers it hires.
   b. alter the amount of raw materials it uses.
   c. alter the size of the factory.
   d. open up new factories or close down factories.
   e. all of the above.

3. Which one of the following statements is true?

    a. Short-run total cost = variable cost - fixed cost.
    b. Short-run total cost = variable cost + fixed cost.
    c. Average total cost = average variable cost/average fixed cost.
    d. Fixed cost = average fixed cost/output.
    e. Average variable cost = variable cost * output.

4. Which one of the following explains why a firm's short-run marginal cost increases as it produces more and more output?

    a. Diminishing returns.
    b. Diseconomies of scale.
    c. Increasing returns to scale.
    d. Diminishing marginal utility.
    e. Diseconomies of scope.

5. Which one of the following statements is true?

    a. A firm's short-run average variable cost first increases and then decreases as output increases.
    b. A firm's short-run average total cost curve is shaped like a "W".
    c. A firm's average fixed cost always decreases as output increases.
    d. Average variable cost increases as output increases because each additional worker becomes less and less productive in the short run.
    e. (c) and (d).

Use the following information to answer the question below.

    Output = 250 units   Fixed cost = $1,000
    Average variable cost = $6 per unit   Average total cost = $10 per unit
    Marginal cost = $12

6. Which one of the following statements is true?

    a. Average fixed cost = $4 per unit and Total cost = $25,000.
    b. Variable cost = $1,500 and Average fixed cost = $4 per unit.
    c. Variable cost = $2,500 and Total cost = $1,500.
    d. Average fixed cost = $4 per unit and Total cost = $22.
    e. Total cost = $1,006 and Variable cost = $18.

Use the following information to answer the question below.

Output = 100 units

Short-run total cost = $800

Average fixed cost = $30 per unit

Marginal cost = $60

7. The firm's total variable cost must be:

   a. $500.00
   b. $770.00
   c. $77.00
   d. $7,700.00
   e. Cannot be calculated without more information.

Use Figure 8-1 to answer the following question.

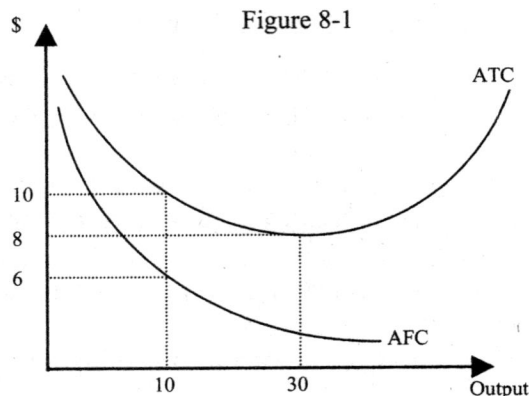

Figure 8-1

8. Which one of the following statements is true?

   a. The average variable cost of producing 10 units of output is $16 per unit.
   b. The total cost of producing 30 units of output is $8.
   c. The variable cost of producing 10 units of output is $40.
   d. The marginal cost of producing 30 units of output must be less than $8.
   e. None of the above is true.

9. Which one of the following defines the long-run average cost of production?

   a. Total cost divided by the quantity of output when the firm cannot alter the number of workers it hires.
   b. Total cost divided by the quantity of output when the firm can choose a production facility of any size.
   c. Total cost multiplied by the quantity of output when the firm can choose a production facility of any size.
   d. Total cost divided by the quantity of output when the firm cannot alter the size of its facilities.
   e. Total cost divided by the quantity of output when the firm cannot change the number of factories it operates.

A Firm's Production and Costs: The Short Run and the Long Run

10. Which one of the following is a reason for economies of scale?

    a. Specialization.
    b. Diminishing returns.
    c. Divisible inputs.
    d. Rising marginal costs.
    e. Comparative advantage.

11. Which one of the following is NOT an example of an indivisible input?

    a. An industrial mould for a giant bowl of Jell-O.
    b. A large cargo ship.
    c. "Clean rooms" used by a computer-chip maker.
    d. An expensive piece of medical equipment.
    e. All of the above are examples of indivisible inputs.

12. Which one of the following statements is NOT true?

    a. The minimum efficient scale for production is that output level where average costs are neither increasing nor decreasing, i.e., the long-run average cost curve is horizontal.
    b. Diseconomies of scale may arise from the use of indivisible inputs.
    c. Diseconomies of scale may occur because of co-ordination problems that arise as more and more output is produced.
    d. Diseconomies of scale may occur because input costs increase as a firm produces more and more output.
    e. In the long run, a firm does not encounter diminishing returns.

VI.   PRACTICE EXAM: ESSAY QUESTIONS

13. Explain why specialization can lead to economies of scale.

14. Distinguish diminishing returns from diseconomies of scale.

VII.   ANSWER KEY: MULTIPLE CHOICE QUESTIONS

1. Correct answer: d.

Discussion: An implicit cost is a cost for which there is not an explicit payment by cheque or money. Your textbook lists two types of implicit costs – the cost of a business owner's time and the cost of a business owner's use of his or her own funds (financial capital). Implicit costs should be included when calculating economic profit. However, they are not included when calculating accounting profit.

Statements a, b, c, and e are all examples of explicit costs.

2. Correct answer: e.

Discussion: The long run is defined as a period of time over which a firm is able to choose the combination of workers, raw materials, size of the factory, and number of factories to operate in order to produce output at the least per unit cost (average cost).

Statements a, b, c, and d are all factors of production that can be altered in the long run. In the short run, however, generally speaking, only the number of workers and the amount of raw material a firm uses can be altered. The size of the factory along with the number of factories currently in operation cannot simply be changed on short notice.

3. Correct answer: b.

Discussion: Short-run total cost is the sum of variable cost plus fixed cost. That's why it is referred to as "total."

Statement a is not correct because total cost is the sum of, not the difference between, variable cost and fixed cost. Statement c is not correct. It would have been correct if it had read "average total cost = average variable cost + average fixed cost." Statement d is not correct. It would have been correct if it had read "fixed cost = average fixed cost * output." Statement e is not correct. It would have been correct if it had read "average variable cost = variable cost/output." (See PET #1 for review.)

4. Correct answer: a.

Discussion: Diminishing returns means that each additional worker that is hired to produce more output is less productive than the workers hired before him. Thus, it becomes more costly to the firm to get that worker to produce the same level of output as the previous workers. A way to think about it is that that worker would have to work more hours than the other workers (and, therefore, be paid overtime) in order to produce the same amount of output as the other workers are producing.

Diseconomies of scale is a long-run concept. Increasing returns to scale is not a term you have encountered, nor is diseconomies of scope. Diminishing marginal utility is a concept related to consumer "satisfaction" not a firm's cost of production.

5. Correct answer: e.

Discussion: Statement c is correct because fixed costs do not change with the level of output. Since average fixed cost is calculated as fixed cost/output, as output increases, average fixed cost must decline. (The number in the denominator gets bigger but the number in the numerator does not change). Statement d is also correct. It is another way of stating that diminishing returns gives rise to increasing average variable cost (as well as increasing marginal cost).

Statement a is not correct because average total cost first decreases and then increases as output increases. Statement b is not correct; a firm's average total cost curve is shaped like a "U." Statements c and d are both correct, which is why statement e is the answer.

6. Correct answer: b.

Discussion: Variable cost is computed by multiplying average variable cost by the output level: $6 per unit * 250 units = $1,500. Average fixed cost is computed by dividing fixed cost by the output level: $1,000/250units = $4/unit.

Statement a is not correct because total cost is $2,500, not $25,000. Total cost can be computed from figuring out variable cost (as above), which is $1,500, and adding to it the fixed cost of $1,000. Statement c is not correct based on the discussion. Statement d is not correct because total cost is not $22. (Total cost is not the sum of marginal cost plus average total cost). Statement e is not correct because total cost is not $1,006 and variable cost is not $18.

7. Correct answer: a.

Discussion: To arrive at the correct answer, you must compute fixed cost using average fixed cost and output. Fixed cost = $3 per unit * 100 units = $300. Then, you can compute variable cost from the difference between total cost and fixed cost = $800 - $300 = $500.

Statements b, c, and d are not correct based on the above discussion. Statement e is not correct because there is enough information (i.e., you don't need to know average variable cost) to compute total variable cost.

8. Correct answer: c.

Discussion: Figure 8-1shows the average total cost and average fixed cost associated with different levels of production. Since the average total cost of 10 units of output is $10 per unit and the average fixed cost is $6 per unit, the average variable cost must be $4 per unit. Since the average variable cost is $4 per unit, the variable cost must be $4 per unit * 10 units = $70.

Statement a is not correct because the average variable cost is $4 per unit. Statement b is not correct. It would have been correct if it stated that the average total cost of production was $8. Statement d is not correct because average total cost is at its minimum point at 30 units of output. If the average cost is at its minimum, then the marginal cost must be equal to the average cost of $8, not less than $8. Statement e is not correct because statement c is correct.

9. Correct answer: b.

Discussion: Statement b is correct; it indicates a long-run concept since the production facility's size can be changed and because an average cost is computed by dividing a total cost by an output level.

Statements a, d, and e are not correct because they imply short-run concepts where the firm has some fixed factors of production that cannot be changed. Statement c is not correct because average cost is not computed by multiplying total cost by the output level.

10. Correct answer: a.

Discussion: When workers are able to specialize in the tasks that they do, they become more productive. They know how to do a task well and they don't have to spend time switching from task to task. Statement b is not correct; diminishing returns give rise to increasing marginal (and variable and total) costs of production. Statement c is not correct; indivisible inputs give rise to economies of scale, not divisible inputs. Statement d is not correct because, with economies of scale, marginal costs will be decreasing or not changing. Statement e is not a concept that is applied to economies of scale.

11. Correct answer: e.

Discussion: Indivisible inputs are those inputs that cannot be divided up to accommodate low levels of production. For example, a piece of medical equipment must be purchased by a hospital regardless of whether they will use it for one patient, two patients, twenty patients, or one thousand patients. The same is true of an industrial mould, a large cargo ship, and clean rooms used by a computer chip maker. Can you think of other examples?

12. Correct answer: b.

Discussion: Statement b is the only statement that is not true. Indivisible inputs give rise to economies of scale, not diseconomies of scale. All of the other statements are true.

VIII. ANSWER KEY: ESSAY QUESTIONS

13. Specialization is a long-run concept. In the long run, a firm is able to alter the amount of equipment each worker has to work with and the amount of space within which each worker works. Thus, in the long run, with more equipment and more space to work, workers can specialize at a task. This means that they can now spend more time on one task (rather than having to move between tasks). This makes workers more productive because time is not lost as workers move between tasks. Thus, each worker is able to produce more output per hour than before. Also, since workers spend more time on the same task, they learn to do the task more efficiently and, thus, can produce more output per hour than before. Since the workers are producing more output per hour and their wages have not changed, the average cost per unit of output will decline in the long run. Economies of scale is defined as a declining average cost as output increases.

14. Diminishing returns is a short-run concept and arises because one (or more) of the factors of production with which a firm produces output is fixed, i.e., the amount is not able to be changed in the short run. Typically, plant and equipment are considered the fixed factors of production. Since the amount of plant and equipment is fixed, if a firm wants to produce more output, it must hire more workers but cannot alter the amount of plant and equipment. Consequently, more and more workers are jammed into factory floor space and may have to waste time waiting for a piece of equipment to use to finish their task. What this means is that each additional worker that is hired by the firm will produce less output per hour than the previous worker. This is the definition of diminishing returns.

Diseconomies of scale is a long-run concept and arises because of coordination problems and increasing input costs when a firm gets bigger and bigger (produces more and more output). Diseconomies of scale is defined as an increase in long-run average cost as output increases. This is the reverse of economies of scale. Co-ordination problems can contribute to the average cost of production increasing as output increases. Co-ordination problems may arise because of layers of bureaucracy or management that a business decision must pass through before actually being executed and/or because of personnel problems. Also, as a firm produces more and more output, it increases its demand for inputs, which can put upward pressure on the price of inputs. This can thereby contribute to an increase in the average cost of production.

CHAPTER 9
PERFECT COMPETITION IN THE SHORT RUN

I.   OVERVIEW

In this chapter, you will learn about the four different types of market structure. However, in this chapter, you will focus on the perfectly competitive market structure and the characteristics that describe it. You will learn how a firm decides how much output to produce in a perfectly competitive market. You will use the cost concepts and cost curves that you learned about in the previous chapter together with a revenue and marginal revenue curve. You will re-encounter the marginal principle and apply it to determining the level of output that will maximize a firm's profit. You will learn about the factors that influence a firm's decision to either shut down its operation or to continue it even in the face of losses. You will learn what factors might contribute to entry to or exit from a perfectly competitive market. You will see how entry and exit affects the profit levels of the firms that are already operating in the market. You will also see how an industry supply curve is derived from individual firms' collective decisions about how much to produce at various prices. You will learn about producer surplus, which is analogous to the concept of consumer surplus that you learned about in Chapter 7. You will see that the interaction of supply and demand in a perfectly competitive market structure in which there is no spillover costs or benefits creates an efficient outcome.

II.   CHECKLIST

By the end of this chapter, you should be able to:

  □   List the characteristics of a perfectly competitive market structure.

  □   Give some real world examples of a perfectly competitive market structure.

  □   Define total and marginal revenue and represent them with a graph.

  □   Explain the difference between economic profits and accounting profit.

  □   Explain why marginal revenue equals price in a perfectly competitive market.

  □   Explain why the rule of picking an output level where price (marginal revenue) equals marginal cost maximizes a firm's profit.

  □   Use a graph to pick the profit-maximizing output level and represent profit on the graph.

  □   Explain when a firm would, in the short-run, decide to shut down its operation and when, in the long run, it would decide to shut down its operation.

- Explain what would happen in a perfectly competitive market to the typical firm earning zero economic profit when there is an increase in market demand (and vice-versa).
- Use graphs to show what would happen in a perfectly competitive market to the typical firm earning zero economic profit when there is an increase in market demand (and vice-versa).
- Define producer surplus and represent it with a graph.
- Use market demand and supply curve to explain market efficiency and to show why price ceilings and floors do not lead to efficiency.

III. KEY TERMS

Perfectly competitive market: a market with a very large number of firms, each of which produces the same standardized product and takes the market price as given.

Total revenue: the money the firm gets by selling its product; equal to the price times the quantity sold.

Economic profit: total revenue minus the total economic cost (the sum of explicit and implicit costs).

Marginal profit: the change in profit resulting from a one-unit increase in production.

Marginal revenue: the change in revenue resulting from a one-unit increase in production.

Breakeven price: the price associated with the minimum point on a short-run average total cost curve; at this price, a firm earns zero economic profit.

Shut-down price: the price at which the firm is indifferent between operating and shutting down.

Firm's short-run supply curve: a curve showing the relationship between price and the quantity of output supplied by a firm when technology and input prices are fixed.

Short-run market supply curve: a curve showing the relationship between price and the quantity of output supplied by an entire industry when technology, input prices, and the number of firms in the industry are held fixed.

Producer surplus: the difference between the market price of a product and the minimum amount a producer is willing to accept for that product; alternatively, the difference between the market price and the marginal cost of production.

Total value of a market: the sum of consumer surplus and producer surplus.

Deadweight loss: the loss in total value of the market because the market is not allowed to achieve its equilibrium price.

IV. PERFORMANCE ENHANCING TIPS (PETS)

PET # 1

Price and marginal revenue are the same number for a firm in a perfectly competitive market structure.

Let's explore why price and marginal revenue are the same number for a firm in a perfectly competitive market structure. In perfect competition, a firm is a price taker. This means that it does not have to lower the price of its product to sell more. It can sell all that it wants at the going price. This means that, as a firm sells more and more units of its output, it continues to get the same price for its output.

For example, suppose the price of output was $2 per unit. If a firm sells one unit, the total revenue it receives is $2. If a firm sells two units, the total revenue it receives is $4. If a firm sells three units, the total revenue it receives is $6, and so on. Now, what is the marginal revenue (or addition to revenue) from selling one more unit? When the firm sells two units instead of one, it adds $2 to its total revenue ($4 - $2). When the firm sells three units instead of two, it adds $2 to its total revenue ($6 - $4), and so on. Thus, marginal revenue and price are the same for a firm in a perfectly competitive market structure.

PET #2

The rule of picking an output level where price is equal to marginal cost in order to maximize profit can also be expressed as picking an output level where marginal revenue is equal to marginal cost. This happens because, in a perfectly competitive market structure, marginal revenue and price are the same number.

In the next few chapters, the rule for maximizing profits that you will encounter is to pick an output level where marginal revenue is equal to marginal cost (instead of where price is equal to marginal cost). It is really the same rule that you have learned in this chapter and the same rationale for why the rule maximizes a firm's profit applies. It may be better to remember the rule as marginal revenue = marginal cost instead of price = marginal cost. In the latter, it must be understood that price and marginal revenue are the same for a firm operating in a perfectly competitive market.

PET #3

Firms that earn zero economic profit can continue to operate. This is because a firm earning zero economic profit can be earning a positive accounting profit. The positive accounting profit is what a firm may use to fund projects that will allow it to continue to operate in the future.

V. PRACTICE EXAM: MULTIPLE CHOICE QUESTIONS

1. Which one of the following would be an example of a perfectly competitive industry?

   a. Restaurants.
   b. Hog farmers.
   c. Aircraft industry.
   d. Auto dealerships.
   e. Patented medical equipment industry.

2. Which one of the following is NOT a characteristic of a perfectly competitive market structure?

   a. Very large number of firms.
   b. Standardized (or homogeneous) product.
   c. Barriers to entry.
   d. No control over price.
   e. All of the above are characteristics of a perfectly competitive market structure.

   Use the information below to answer the following question.

   Quantity sold = 500,000 units   Price = $1.00 per unit
   Explicit costs = $400,000   Implicit costs = $150,000

3. Based on this information, the firm is:

   a. earning positive economic profit of $100,000.
   b. earning zero economic profit.
   c. earning positive accounting profit of $100,000.
   d. making an economic loss (negative economic profit) of $50,000.
   e. (c) and (d).

4. A firm can maximize its profits by picking an output level where:

   a. price > average variable costs.
   b. price > average total costs.
   c. marginal revenue = marginal cost.
   d. price = average variable cost.
   e. (b) and (c).

5. Which one of the following statements is always true of a firm in a perfectly competitive market?

   a. Price = marginal revenue.
   b. Price = marginal cost.
   c. Price = total revenue.
   d. Average total cost = average variable cost.
   e. Economic profit is positive.

6. Which one of the following statements is true?

   a. In the short run, if a firm shuts down, it will have zero revenue and zero costs.
   b. A firm should shut down if price is greater than average variable cost but less than average total cost.
   c. A firm can maximize its profits by producing an output level where price equals marginal revenue.
   d. In the short run, if a firm shuts down, it will have a loss equal to the amount of its sunk (or fixed) costs.
   e. None of the above.

Use Figure 9-1 to answer the following question.

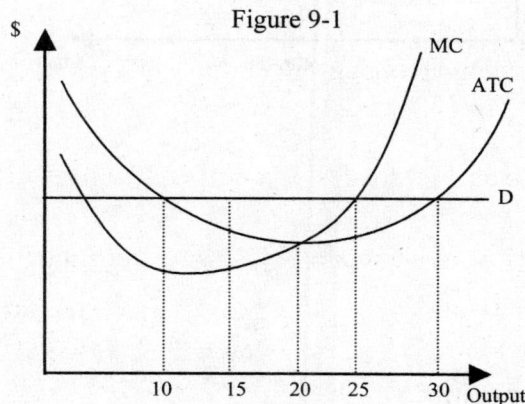

Figure 9-1

7. The output level that will maximize the firm's profit is:

   a. 10 units.
   b. 15 units.
   c. 20 units.
   d. 25 units.
   e. 30 units.

Use the information below to answer the following question.

Price = $5.00 per unit   Quantity = 200 units   Total variable cost = $400
Total fixed cost = $800   Marginal cost = $5.00

8. Which one of the following statements is correct?

   a. The firm is making a loss but should, in the short run, continue to operate.
   b. The firm is making a loss and should shut down its operation.
   c. The firm is making a profit of $600.
   d. The firm is making zero profit.
   e. Price is greater than average total cost.

Use Figure 9-2 to answer the following question.

Figure 9-2

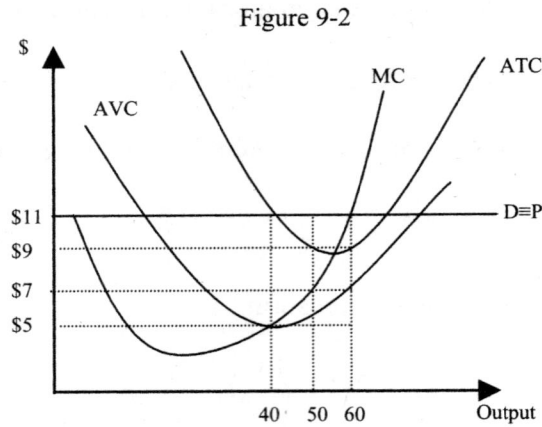

9. The firm's profit is:
   a. $0.
   b. $120.
   c. $240.
   d. $100.
   e. $80.

Use Figure 9-3 to answer the following question.

Figure 9-3

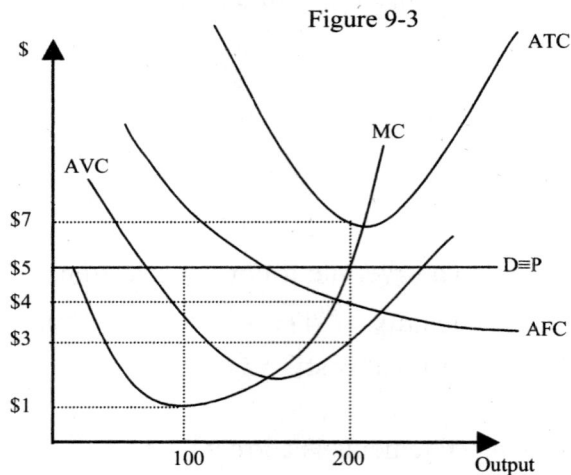

10. Which one of the following statements is correct?
   a. The firm is making a loss but should, in the short run, continue to operate.
   b. The firm is making a loss and should shut down its operation in the short run.
   c. The firm is making a profit of $400.
   d. The firm is making zero profit.
   e. Price is greater than average total cost.

Perfect Competition in the Short Run

Use Figure 9-4 to answer the following question.

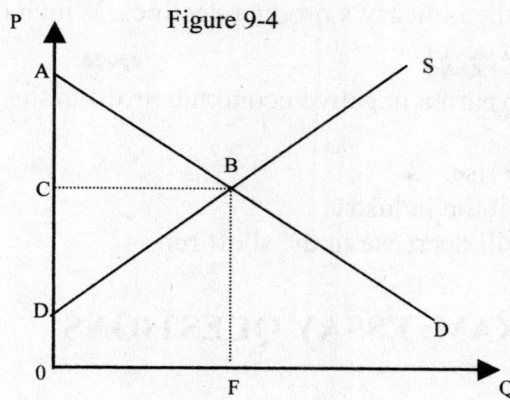

Figure 9-4

11. Producer surplus is measured by the area:

    a. ABC.
    b. ABD.
    c. CBD.
    d. OCBF.
    e. OBF.

Use Figure 9-5 to answer the following question.

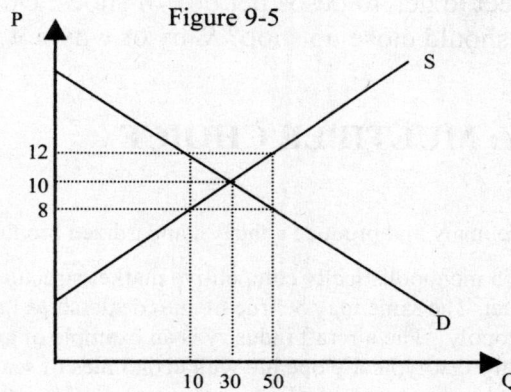

Figure 9-5

12. Which one of the following prices is the efficient price (the one that maximizes total market value)?

    a. 12.
    b. 10.
    c. 8.
    d. 30.
    e. 0.

13. Suppose all firms in a perfectly competitive industry are currently earning zero economic profit. Assume the price of output is $10 per unit. Now, suppose that consumer demand for the industry's product declines. Which one of the following would be least likely to occur?

    a. Firms may begin to earn a negative economic profit in the short run.
    b. Price will decline.
    c. Marginal costs will rise.
    d. Some firms will exit the industry.
    e. Producer surplus will decrease in the short run.

VI.　PRACTICE EXAM: ESSAY QUESTIONS

14. Briefly explain why it is profit maximizing for a firm to produce output up until the point at which marginal revenue equals marginal cost.

15. Suppose, after graduation, you take a job in a factory in Chile that produces faux leather shoes. One day, your boss comes in and says, "This factory isn't operating at a profit, and so we can minimize our losses by closing up shop." Yikes! You didn't think you'd lose your job that quickly. Your boss continues talking and states that the company is having to pay 300,000 pesos a month for rent, interest on debt, and other non-avoidable costs. He also says that it costs 150,000 pesos a month just to pay you and all the other workers, including paying for the raw materials, to produce the shoes. He states that, at current production of 5,000 boxes of shoes a month, the company can only expect to get 40 pesos per box of shoes. Do you agree with your boss that the company should close up shop? Why or why not?

VII.　ANSWER KEY: MULTIPLE CHOICE

1. Correct answer: b.

   Discussion: Hog farmers are many and produce a fairly standardized product, the hog.

   Pizzerias are an example of a monopolistically competitive market structure since they produce a slightly differentiated product. The same may be true of auto dealerships (although auto manufacturers are considered to be an oligopoly). The aircraft industry is an example of an oligopoly since there are few large firms in the industry that typically operate with economies of scale and there are some barriers to entry. A firm that has a patent typically has a monopoly. Thus, a patented medical equipment industry is an example of a monopoly.

2. Correct answer: c.

   Discussion: Barriers to entry characterize an oligopolistic and monopolist market structure.

   A perfectly competitive market structure is one in which there are a very large number of firms each producing a very small portion of overall industry output. The product produced is said to be "standardized" or "homogeneous," which means that consumers don't perceive very much of a difference in buying from one producer than any other. Since there are so many firms providing such a small portion of industry output, the firms have no control over price; the market forces of supply and demand dictate it. Firms are said to be "price takers."

3. Correct answer: e.

    Discussion: The total revenue that the firm is earning is $500,000 ($5 * 100,000 units). The economic cost is $550,000 ($400,000 + $150,000). Thus, economic profit is -$50,000. That is, the firm is earning a loss. The accounting profit that the firm is earning is equal to $100,000 ($500,000 - $400,000). Thus statements c and d are both correct. Statements a and b are not correct because the firm is making negative economic profit.

4. Correct answer: c.

    Discussion: The rule for maximizing profits is to pick an output level where marginal revenue equals marginal cost. There is only one output level where this is true. When a firm follows this principle, it may make positive profit, zero profit, or even a negative profit (in which case we'd say that the firm would be minimizing its losses) but this is the best the firm can do. To assure yourself that this condition will maximize a firm's profit, consider the two other possibilities: (1) marginal revenue > marginal cost and (2) marginal revenue < marginal cost. If condition (1) is true, then a firm could add more to its revenue than to its costs by producing one more unit of output. This means that the firm's profits would increase if it produced more output. Thus, the firm could not yet be maximizing profits. If condition (2) is true, then a firm is adding more to its costs than to its revenue by producing the additional output. By producing this output level, the firm would be cutting into its profits and would be better off reducing production.

    Statement a is not correct because there are a number of output levels where this would be true and, thus, the rule would offer no guidance about which output level to pick. The same is true of statement b. Statement d is not correct, but it is the condition that would say that a firm is indifferent between shutting down and remaining open in the short run. Statement e is not correct because statement b is not correct.

5. Correct answer: a.

    Discussion: For a perfectly competitive firm, which is a price taker, the firm's revenue from selling each additional unit of output, its marginal revenue, will always equal price.

    Statement b is not correct since firm's can in the short run earn positive or negative economic profit. Statement c is not correct; total revenue is equal to price * quantity. Statement d is not correct since a firm also has fixed costs. Statement e is not correct because a firm does not always earn positive economic profit.

6. Correct answer: d.

    Discussion: If a firm shuts down in the short run, it will have no revenue to offset the fixed costs that it must continue to pay. Thus, the firm will lose an amount equal to its fixed costs.

    Statement a is not correct because, if a firm shuts down in the short run, it will still have some costs to pay. Statement b is not correct. It would have been correct if it had said that a firm should remain open if price were greater than average variable cost but less than average total cost. Statement c is not correct because a perfectly competitive firm maximizes its profits by producing an output level where price (or marginal revenue) equals marginal cost. Statement e is not correct because statement d is correct.

7. Correct answer: d.

    Discussion: The output level that a profit-maximizing firm will choose is the output level is where marginal revenue (price) equals marginal cost. This occurs at an output level of 25 units (where the price and marginal cost curves intersect).

    Statements a, b, c, and e are all incorrect based on the above method for finding a firm's profit-maximizing level of output.

8. Correct answer: a.

The firm's total revenue from operating would be $1,000 ($5 * 200 units). The firm's total cost would be $400 + $800 = $1,200. If the firm operates, it will make a loss of $200. This is less than the firm would lose if it shut down its operation.

If the firm shut down its operation, it would not earn any revenue but would still have to pay for its fixed costs. Thus, the firm would lose $800. Thus, statement b is not correct. Statement c and d are not correct because the firm is not earning a profit. Statement e is not correct because average total cost is $1,200/200 units = $6. Thus, price is less than average total cost, which is why the firm is making a loss. Notice that, since price is equal to marginal cost, the firm is doing the best it can, i.e., minimizing its losses.

9. Correct answer: b.

Discussion: The profit is determined by first selecting the output level that a profit maximizing firm will choose. The profit-maximizing output level is where marginal revenue (price) equals marginal cost. This occurs at an output level of 60 units. Given that output level, the average total cost of 60 units of output is $9 and the price is $11. Thus, profit is equal to ($11 * 60) - ($9 * 60) = $120.

Statements a, c, d, and e are all incorrect based on the above method for finding and calculating a firm's profit.

10. Correct answer: a.

Discussion: To answer this question, you must first establish what the profit-maximizing output level of the firm is. It is found where price and marginal cost are equal (intersect) which is at an output level of 200 units. The average total cost of producing 200 units is $7. The average variable cost of producing 200 units is $3. The average fixed cost is $4. Since price exceeds average variable cost, the firm should continue to operate even though it will earn a loss of $400.

You could also calculate the total cost of producing 200 units of output as $1,400 and the revenue as $1,000. Thus, the firm will lose $400. Then, you could calculate how much the firm will lose if it shuts down. If it shuts down, it will have to pay its fixed costs. This can be read off the graph by taking the average fixed cost of $4 and multiplying it by the output level of 200 units. Thus, the firm's loss would be $800.

Therefore, statements b, c, d, and e are all incorrect based on the above discussion.

11. Correct answer: c.

Discussion: Producer surplus is measured as the area below the price line but above the supply curve out to the equilibrium level of output; CBD satisfies this area.

Statement a (area ABC) is a measure of consumer surplus. Statement b (area ABD) is a measure of total market value (consumer surplus + producer surplus). Statement d (area OCBF) measures price * quantity for the industry (market). Statement e area (OBF) does not correspond to anything.

12. Correct answer: b.

Discussion: The efficient price is the equilibrium price, which is $10. This is the price at which quantity demanded = quantity supplied. It is also the price that maximizes the sum of consumer + producer surplus.

None of the other prices are equilibrium prices, which means that transactions between buyers and sellers could be rearranged to make both parties better off. For example, at a price of $12, producers would be willing to sell 40 units of output. However, at price of $12, consumers would only be willing to buy 10 units. Since producers can only sell what consumers are willing to buy, producers would be able to sell 10 units of output. The marginal cost of production of the 10th unit is less than $12 but the marginal benefit of the 10til unit (read off the demand curve) is $12, society could be made better off. Producers will gain by selling more than 10 units (as long as the marginal cost of production is less than the price received for the good) and consumers will gain because they will be able to get more of the good at a lower price.

13. Correct answer: c.

Discussion: If demand declines, as you learned in Chapter 4, this would cause price to decline. Thus, statement b is likely to occur. As the price of the product declines, firms that were initially earning zero economic profit will see price drop below their average total cost. This will cause them to make a loss (negative economic profit) in the short run. Thus, statement a is likely to occur. As firms earn negative economic profit, there will be exit from the industry. Thus, statement d is likely to occur. As price declines, the profit-maximizing output level for firms will change – it will decrease. That is, firms will produce less output. Since both price and output have declined, producer surplus must necessarily decline. (The effect on consumer surplus would be ambiguous since the price decline would raise consumer surplus but the quantity decline would reduce it). Thus, statement e is likely to occur. Statement c is least likely to occur because, as a firm produces less output, its marginal cost of production will decline.

VIII. ANSWER KEY: ESSAY QUESTIONS

14. Note: P = price, MR = marginal revenue, MC = marginal cost.

When a firm produces output up to that level at which MR = MC, it is always adding more to revenue than it is to costs, and, thus, adding something (however small) to its profits. If a firm produced at an output level at which MR < MC, the firm is actually taking away from its profits because some of the output costs more to produce than it can be sold for. If a firm produces output where MR > MC, it could continue to expand production and though adding more to cost, could add even more to revenue, thereby adding to its profits. Thus, a firm maximizes profits where MR = MC.

15. Based on short-run analysis, you should disagree with your boss:

The costs of closing up shop in the short-run are 300,000 pesos (due to fixed costs). That is, 300,000 pesos must be paid regardless of whether the factory produces no shoes or some shoes. This is the loss the firm would sustain in the short-run if it were to close up shop. If the factory were to continue current operation, it could produce 5,000 boxes of shoes and earn revenue of 200,000 pesos, which could offset some of the fixed costs. However, by producing, the company would incur another cost – variable costs in the amount of 150,000 pesos. On net, there is a positive difference of 50,000 pesos between revenue and variable costs. This positive difference can help pay for fixed costs so that, if the firm continues to operate, its losses will be 250,000 pesos (Revenue - Fixed Costs - Variable Costs) instead of 300,000 (fixed costs).

You might also point out that, if the company is planning on closing the factory temporarily, it might make customers mad, which can have deleterious effects on future sales. Moreover, if the company temporarily lays off workers, they may go find work elsewhere and, thus, the company might face some retraining and re-hiring (or search) costs when they re-open the factory.

On the other hand, if the company is planning on closing the factory permanently, i.e., in the long run, perhaps because of a perceived permanent downturn in demand for faux leather shoes, then your advice may be different. You may advise the company to close the factory and sell its assets (to cover some of its fixed costs, like interest on debt). Also, by closing the factory, the company may be able to avoid fixed costs like rent as well.

CHAPTER 10
LONG-RUN SUPPLY AND MARKET DYNAMICS

I. OVERVIEW

In this chapter, you will revisit the distinction between the short and long run and learn how, in the long run, the quantity supplied is more responsive to changes in price than in the short-run. You will see that this occurs because, in the long run, firms can enter and exit the industry (in a perfectly competitive market structure) and alter the size of their production facilities. You will learn about how changes in demand affect the price of a product differently in the short-run than in the long run. You will also learn about increasing, decreasing, and constant cost industries which are determined by how productive inputs are as more firms enter (or exit) an industry and how the price of inputs changes as more firms enter (or exit) all industry. You will compare the slope of a short-run supply curve to the slope of a long-run supply curve and compute the elasticity of supply of each.

II. CHECKLIST

By the end of this chapter, you should be able to:
- ❑ Explain the difference between the short and the long run.
- ❑ Explain what causes firms to enter and exit an industry in a perfectly competitive market structure.
- ❑ Compare what happens to the quantity supplied as the price of the product increases (or decreases) in the short and the long run, and compare the difference.
- ❑ Explain what causes a supply curve to be positively sloped and explain what would cause it to be more steeply sloped.
- ❑ Explain the difference between increasing, decreasing, and constant cost industries and illustrate the difference using a graph of the long-run supply curve.
- ❑ Compute total and average costs of production for various output levels.
- ❑ Compute price elasticity of supply.

III.   KEY TERMS

Long-run supply curve: a curve showing the relationship between price and quantity supplied in the long run.

Increasing-cost industry: an industry in which the average cost of production increases as the industry grows, so the long-run supply curve is positively sloped.

Constant-cost industry: an industry in which the average cost of production is constant, so the long-run supply curve is horizontal.

Decreasing-cost industry: an industry in which the average cost of production decreases as the industry grows, so the long-run supply curve is negatively sloped.

IV.   PERFORMANCE ENHANCING TIPS (PETS)

<u>PET # 1</u>

The long-run supply curve is flatter than the short-run supply curve. This means that quantity supplied is more responsive to a given price change in the long run than is quantity supplied in the short run.

Compare the slope of supply curve (a) to supply curve (b) in Figure 10-1.

Figure 10-1

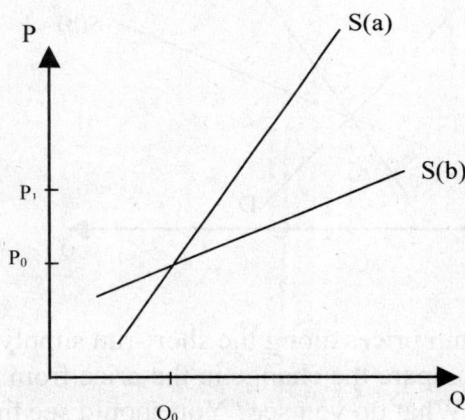

Supply curve (b) is flatter than supply curve (a). What does this mean in practical terms? Let's examine the response of quantity supplied to the same change in price along the two different supply curves. Draw a line from price P_0 across to the supply curves. Where the price line intersects the supply curves, draw a vertical line down to the quantity axis and mark this as the quantity supplied at price P_0 along S(a) and S(b). You will notice that, at this price, the quantity supplied in the short and long run is the same amount.

Now, draw a line from price P_1 across to the supply curves. Where the price line intersects the supply curves, draw vertical lines down to the quantity axis and mark these as the quantity supplied at price P_1 along lines S(a) and S(b). Compare the changes in the quantity supplied along supply curves S(a) and S(b). You will see that, as the price

Chapter 10

107

increases, the quantity supplied increases more along supply curve (b) than along supply curve (a). That means that quantity supplied is more responsive to price in the long run than in the short-run. Why does this occur? It occurs because, in the long run, as the price of a good increases, more firms enter the industry (attracted by profits due to the higher price) and existing firms may have expanded the size of their facility thus enabling them to produce more. Therefore, for any given price increase, more is willingly supplied by firms.

PET #2

An increase in demand raises the price of a good by less in the long run than in the short-run. A decrease in demand lowers the price of a good by less in the long run than in the short-run.

To see this, draw an increase in demand (rightward shift in the demand curve) in Figure 10-2.

Figure 10-2

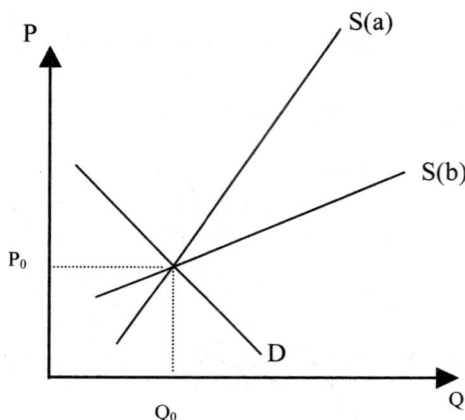

Now, mark the new equilibrium prices along the short-run supply curve (a) and along the long-run supply curve (b). Compare the change in the price from the initial price of P_0 along the two supply curves. What do you see? You should see that the price has increased by less along supply curve (b) –the flat, long-run supply curve than it has increased along supply curve (a).

Why does this occur? In the long run, remember that, in response to a price increase, more firms enter the industry and existing firms will expand the size of their facility; the higher price creates economic profits, which motivate entry and expansion in the industry. Thus, in the long run, the industry is better able to satisfy the increased demand for their product. Buyers do not have to bid as fiercely against each other for the ability to purchase the product and, thus, the price of the product does not rise by as much.

You should work through a decrease in demand on your own.

Long-Run Supply and Market Dynamics

V   PRACTICE EXAM: MULTIPLE CHOICE QUESTIONS

1. Which one of the following is the definition of the long run?

    a. A period of time over which the demand for a product can increase or decrease.
    b. A period of time over which firms can enter and exit an industry.
    c. A period of time over which firms can alter the size of their production facility.
    d. A period of time over which the price of inputs used by an industry remains constant.
    e. (b) and (c).

2. Suppose that the total cost to a typical firm of producing five-foot-high artificial Christmas trees is $3,000. Suppose the typical firm produces 500 artificial Christmas trees per season. Further, suppose that there are 600 firms in the industry. What is the average cost per Christmas tree and what is the total industry output?

    a. $6; 30,000.
    b. $3,000; 30,000.
    c. $6; 500.
    d. $6; 3,000.
    e. $0.10; 30,000.

3. Suppose the average cost of producing a set of golf clubs is $225. Suppose the price at which producers can sell a set of golf clubs is $230. Based on the information you are given, which one of the following best describes the industry response?

    a. Firms will exit the industry because the economic profit per set of golf clubs is so small.
    b. Firms will enter the industry because there are positive economic profits to be earned.
    c. The quantity of golf clubs supplied by the industry will remain unchanged.
    d. Demand for golf clubs will increase.
    e. The cost of graphite used in making golf clubs will increase.

4. Which one of the following explains why, in the long run, the average cost of production may increase as an industry expands (produces more output)?

    a. Rising input prices.
    b. Rising productivity of inputs.
    c. Falling input prices.
    d. Increasing fixed costs.
    e. (a) and (b).

5. Suppose that a typical farmer sells 10,000 bushels of peaches each season and that the total revenue he earns is $100,000. Further, suppose that the average cost of producing 10,000 bushels is $12 per bushel. Based on this information, which one of the following statements is correct?

   a. There are positive economic profits and farmers will enter the industry.
   b. There are negative economic profits and some farmers will leave the industry.
   c. The average cost of production is rising.
   d. The elasticity of supply is 1.2.
   e. Cannot be answered without information on price per bushel.

6. Which one of the following statements is NOT true?

   a. An increasing cost industry has a positively sloped long-run supply curve.
   b. The long-run average cost of production depends, in part, on how productive inputs are.
   c. A constant cost industry has a horizontal long-run supply curve.
   d. Diminishing returns explains why the average cost of production decreases in the long run.
   e. All of the above statements are true.

7. Consider the taxi industry that is assumed to be a constant cost industry. If the demand for taxi services decreases, in the short-run, the price for taxi services will _____ and, in the long run, the price for taxi services will _____.

   a. increase: decrease.
   b. decrease; decrease.
   c. decrease; remain unchanged.
   d. remain unchanged; decrease.
   e. none of the above.

Use the following information to answer the question below.

Initial equilibrium price = $10	Initial equilibrium quantity supplied (short and long-run) = 1,000 units
New equilibrium price = $15	
New equilibrium quantity supplied in short-run = 1,250	New equilibrium quantity supplied in long-run = 2,000 units

8. The short-run elasticity of supply is _____ and the long-run elasticity of supply is _____.

   a. 5/250; 5/1,000.
   b. 5.0; 20.
   c. 0.50; 2.0.
   d. 2.0; 0.50.
   e. 0.25; 0.20.

9. Economic profit is defined as:

   a. total revenue - implicit costs.
   b. total revenue - explicit costs.
   c. total revenue - implicit costs - explicit costs.
   d. total revenue + implicit costs + explicit costs.
   e. explicit costs - total revenue.

   Use Figure 10-3 to answer the following question.

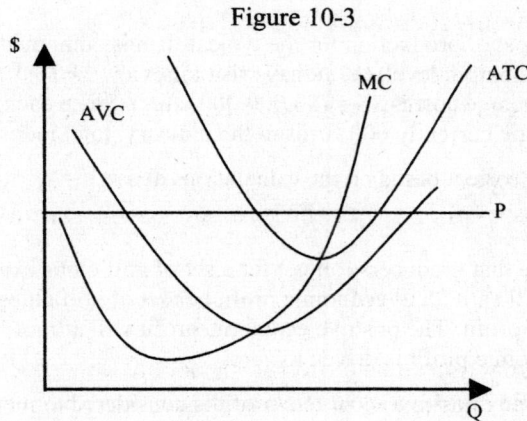

Figure 10-3

10. Suppose Figure 10-3 depicts the situation for a typical firm in a perfectly competitive market structure. Assume the industry is an increasing cost industry. What would be the most likely industry response?

   a. There will be entry into the industry.
   b. Existing firms will expand their production facilities.
   c. The prices of inputs will rise.
   d. The skill level of the workforce will decline.
   e. All of the above.

V.   PRACTICE EXAM: ESSAY QUESTIONS

11. Explain why the long-run supply curve is flatter than the short-run supply curve.

12. Consider the market for beef. Suppose that the demand for beef declines because of health concerns. Explain what will happen to the price and quantity of beef supplied in the short and long run assuming the industry is an increasing cost industry.

VII. ANSWER KEY: MULTIPLE CHOICE QUESTIONS

1. Correct answer: e.

    Discussion: The long run is a period of time over which new firms can enter the industry (to capture positive economic profits) or exit the industry (to cut their losses). Over a longer period of time, firms already in the industry can also alter the size of their production facilities. They may wish to expand their operation if economic profits increase, or they may wish to shut down some of their operation if they begin to incur losses.

    Statements a and d are not correct because the long run is not defined with respect to changes in demand or changes in input prices. Statements b and c are both correct, which is why statement e is the correct answer.

2. Correct answer: a.

    Discussion: The average cost of production for the typical firm is computed by dividing the total cost of production by the firm's output level. (You may wish to review PET #1 from Chapter 8 of the Study Guide). In this case, the average cost is $6 = ($3,000/500 units). Since each firm produces 500 Christmas trees and there are currently 600 firms in the industry, total industry output is 30,000 trees.

    Statements b - e cannot be correct based on the calculations above.

3. Correct answer: b.

    Discussion: Since the price that producers can get for a set of golf clubs exceeds the average cost of production by $5, firms will earn $5 of economic profit per set of golf clubs. That is, they will be earning positive economic profit. The positive economic profit will attract other firms into the industry. Entry will stop when economic profit is driven to zero.

    Statement a is not correct; any positive economic profit is considered to motivate entry into an industry. Statement c is not correct because the positive economic profit will prompt entry into the industry and, thus, leads to an increase in the quantity supplied. Statement d is not correct because there is nothing in the information given that gives a reason why the demand for golf clubs will increase. Statement e is not necessarily correct; it depends on whether the golf club industry is an increasing, decreasing or constant cost industry. If the industry is an increasing cost industry, then the price of graphite will likely increase. However, if the industry is a decreasing or constant cost industry, the price of graphite may actually decrease or not change at all as more golf club producers demand more graphite.

4. Correct answer: a.

    Discussion: As an industry expands (produces more output), the demand for inputs increases. This increase in demand for inputs can put upward pressure on the price of inputs and thereby lead to a rise in the cost of the price of inputs. This, in turn, would raise a firm's average cost of production.

    Statement b is not correct. Rising productivity would actually decrease the average cost of production, not increase it. Statement c is not correct since falling input prices would actually decrease the average cost of production. Statement d is not correct because, in the long run, there are no costs that are considered as fixed costs. Statement e is not correct because statement b is not correct.

5. Correct answer: b.

    Discussion: In this question, you must determine whether the typical farmer is making a positive, zero, or negative economic profit. You can determine the profit situation of the farmer by either calculating the price per bushel that the typical farmer receives for his peaches or the total cost of producing 10,000 bushels. Once you have made either one of these calculations, you can determine whether there is entry or exit into the industry. The price per bushel can be calculated by dividing total revenue by the number of bushels sold. Since the total revenue is $100,000 and the number of bushels sold is 10,000, the price per bushel is $10. With the average cost of production being $12, the typical farmer will lose $2 on every bushel sold. Alternatively, you could have calculated the total cost of producing 10,000 bushels as $120,000 ($12 * 10,000). In this case, the farmer will lose $20,000 for the lot of

10,000 bushels sold (i.e., $2 for every bushel sold). With either calculation, you should see that the farmer would not be making a positive economic profit. The long-run industry response to negative economic profits is for firms (farmers, in this case) to leave the industry.

Statement a is not correct based on the reasoning above. Statement c is not necessarily correct; it depends on whether the industry is an increasing, decreasing, or constant cost industry. If the industry is an increasing cost industry, as firms exit, there will be less demand for inputs and the price of inputs would drop. This would mean that the average cost of production would decrease. If the industry is a constant cost industry, the exit of firms will have no effect on the input prices and the average cost of production would remain constant. If the industry is a decreasing cost industry, as firms exit, the cost of inputs will rise which will raise the average cost of production. Statement d is not correct because you are not given enough information to calculate an elasticity of supply. In order to calculate elasticity, you would need changes in prices and quantity supplied from which you could compute percentage changes. Statement e is not correct because you are given enough information to answer the question.

6. Correct answer: d.

    Discussion: Statement d is correct because it is the only statement that is NOT true. Remember that diminishing returns is a short-run phenomenon. They arise because a firm, in the short-run, cannot alter the size of the capital stock (plant and equipment) that it uses to produce output. On the other hand, decreasing long-run average costs of production is a long-run phenomenon and is the result of entry/exit and alteration of plant size.

    Statements a, b, and c are all true. Since statement d is not true, statement e cannot be the correct answer.

7. Correct answer: c.

    Discussion: The key to answering this question correctly is to know what the shape of the long-run supply curve is when the industry is a constant cost industry. A constant cost industry has a horizontal supply curve. Thus, when demand decreases (shifts left) and moves along a horizontal supply curve, the price of the good will not change from its initial price. However, in the short-run, the supply curve is positively sloped. Thus, a decrease in demand will lead to a lower price for the good in the short-run.

    Statements a and d should be ruled out. From Chapters 4 and 5, you should know that a decrease in demand would lower the price of a good, not increase it or leave it unchanged. Statement b is not correct because, in the long run, the price of the good will remain unchanged, not decrease. Statement e is not correct because statement c is correct.

8. Correct answer: c.

    Discussion: The elasticity of supply is computed as the percentage change in the quantity supplied divided by the percentage change in the price. (You may wish to review Chapter 5 of the Study Guide). The percentage change in the quantity supplied in the short-run is [(1,250 - 1,000)/1,000] * 100 = 25%. The percentage change in the quantity supplied in the long run is [(2,000 - 1,000)/1,000] * 100 = 100%. The percentage change in the price is [($15 - $10)/$10] * 100 = 50%. Thus, the elasticity of supply in the short-run is 25%/50% = ½ = 0.50 and the elasticity of supply in the long run is 100%/50% = 10/5 = 2.

    Statements a, b, d. and e cannot be correct based on the calculations above.

9. Correct answer: c.

    Discussion: Economic profit considers implicit costs of production – that is, costs for which there is no direct or explicit outlay by the firm. An owner of a firm's cost of time is an opportunity cost for which there is no direct payment. Thus, it is an implicit cost and should be used in calculating a firm's economic profit. On the other hand, accounting profit, as you may recall from Chapter 8, is the difference between total revenue and explicit costs.

    Statement a is not correct because economic profit is calculated by considering both explicit and implicit costs, not just implicit costs. Statement b is not correct because it is a measure of accounting profit, not economic profit. Statement d is not correct because economic profit is the difference between total revenue and implicit and explicit costs, not the sum of these. Statement e is not correct because profit is calculated by subtracting costs from revenue, not vice-versa.

10. Correct answer: e.

Discussion: The graph for this question shows that the typical firm is earning positive economic profit. In order to determine this, you must first choose the profit-maximizing output level of the firm. Remember from Chapter 9 that the profit-maximizing rule is to produce at an output level where marginal revenue equals marginal cost. For a perfectly competitive firm, price and marginal revenue are identical numerically. Thus, the profit-maximizing output level is found where the price (marginal revenue) and marginal cost curves intersect. Find this point on the graph and then draw a vertical line down to the quantity axis. This quantity is the profit-maximizing output level. You may wish to label it q^*.

Now, you must determine whether the firm is earning a positive, zero, or negative economic profit. To do this, find the average cost of production of producing q^* and compare it to the price. The average cost of production is found by drawing a vertical line up from q^* to the average cost curve and then over to the $ axis. As you can see, the average cost is less than the price. This means that the typical firm is making positive economic profit.

Now that you have determined that the typical firm is making a positive economic profit, you should know that this will attract entry into the industry, lead to expansion of existing firms, put upward pressure on the price of inputs as more are demanded as the industry grows (in an increasing cost industry) and also lead to a decline in the skill level of workers. As the industry grows and produces more output, it will have to hire more workers. However, the firms will not be able to hire the cream of the crop as these workers are already employed in the industry. Thus, firms will end up hiring less skilled (and, therefore, less productive) workers.

Since statements a - d are all true of an increasing cost industry earning positive economic profit, statement e is the correct answer.

VIII. ANSWER KEY: ESSAY QUESTIONS

11. The long-run supply curve and the short-run supply curve both show the relationship between the price of a good and the quantity supplied. However, the time period considered for the relationship is different. In the short-run, the number of firms producing for the industry is fixed, as is the current size of each firm's facility. In the long run, the number of firms producing for the industry can change as firms enter or exit the industry and the size of the facilities of existing firms can be altered. This means that in the long run, the total industry output can be much more responsive to a price change than in the short-run. For example, when the price of a good increases (because of an increase in demand), the short-run output response of the industry is constrained by how many firms are already producing for the industry and the current size of their operation. A given number of firms with a given plant size can only produce so much more in response to a higher price for the output they produce. However, in the long run, a higher price may lure more firms into the ind0ustry as well as motivate some firms to alter the size of their operation. Thus, a higher price may elicit a bigger increase in output in the long run than in the short-run. Graphically, this would be represented by a supply curve that is flatter for the long-run (and, thus, steeper for the short-run). You may want to take a look at PET #1 of this chapter to inspect the difference between the long and short-run supply curves.

12. An increasing cost industry has a long-run supply curve that is positively sloped. Of course, the short-run supply curve is also positively sloped. However, the long-run supply curve is flatter (more elastic) than the short-run supply curve as Figure 10-4 illustrates. A decline in the demand for beef would be represented by a leftward shift in the demand curve (D_0 shifts to D_1). The reduced demand for beef will, in the short and long run, lead to a lower price of beef as shown in Figure 10-4. However, in the short-run, the price drop will be bigger than in the long run. Figure 10-4 also shows that the equilibrium quantity of beef will decline. It will decline by more in the long run than in the short-run.

Figure 10-4

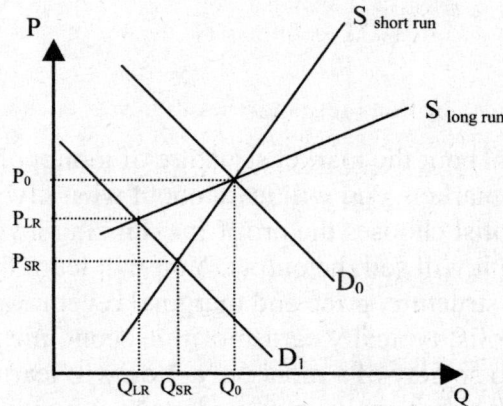

The drop in demand for beef will, in the short-run, cause some firms to shut down their operation altogether. Other firms will continue to operate, but they cannot change the size of the capital stock (and, thus, their fixed costs) that they operate with. In the long run, some firms will make a decision to exit the industry as they sustain losses, whereas other firms that remain will likely reduce the size of their operation (lay off workers, shut down some factories, etc). In the long run, the number of firms in the industry will decline and the size of their facility will likely decrease.

CHAPTER 11
MONOPOLY AND PRICE DISCRIMINATION

I.   OVERVIEW

In this chapter, you will learn about the market structure of monopoly in which there is a single supplier of output to a market. You will learn about what gives rise to a monopoly. You will learn how a monopolist chooses the profit-maximizing level of output and determines the price at which it will sell the output. You will learn that, in contrast to a perfectly competitive market structure, price and marginal revenue are different for a monopolist and that a monopolist typically earns positive economic profit. You will learn about the costs and benefits to society of a monopoly. You will learn about the behaviour of price discrimination, which a monopolist may undertake. You will learn that price discrimination is the practice of charging different prices to different groups of customers for the same product and that the elasticity of demand can be used to decide which group of customers should be charged a higher price.

II.   CHECKLIST

By the end of this chapter, you should be able to:
- Describe the characteristics of a monopoly.
- List factors that would give rise to a monopoly.
- List some real world examples of a monopoly.
- Explain why marginal revenue is less than price for a monopolist but equal to price for a perfectly competitive firm.
- Use a graph to depict the profit-maximizing output level a monopolist would produce, the price that would be charged for the product, and the profit the monopolist would earn.
- Discuss and compare the relationship of price, marginal revenue, marginal cost, and average cost for a profit-maximizing monopolist.
- Compare the price and output decisions of a monopolist to a perfectly competitive firm.
- Explain rent seeking.
- Discuss the trade-offs that occur when a patent is granted to a firm that gives the firm monopoly power.
- Describe the conditions that make it possible for a firm to price discriminate.

❏ Describe how a price discrimination scheme works and which group of customers would be charged a higher price.

III. KEY TERMS

Monopoly: a market that is served by a single firm.

Price discrimination: the process under which a firm divides consumers into two or more groups and picks a different price for each group.

Patent: the exclusive right to sell a particular good for some period of time.

Franchise or licensing scheme: a policy under which the governing body picks a single firm to sell a particular good.

Natural monopoly: a market in which there are large economies of scale, so a single firm will be profitable but a pair of firms would lose money.

Rent seeking: the process by which firms spend money to protect their monopoly profits or to break an existing monopoly so that they can share the profits.

Dumping: a firm's practice of charging a lower price in a foreign market.

IV. PERFORMANCE ENHANCING TIPS (PETS)

<u>PET #1</u>

The profit-maximizing rule for a monopolist (as for any firm) is to produce an output level where marginal revenue equals marginal cost.

Remember that marginal revenue is the addition to revenue from selling one more unit of output and marginal cost is the addition to cost from producing one more unit of output. As long as the addition to revenue (marginal revenue) exceeds the addition to cost (marginal cost), the monopolist will add to its profits. Thus, the monopolist will maximize its profits by continuing to produce and sell output until marginal revenue is just equal to marginal cost. Beyond that output level, profits will actually be smaller (not maximized).

<u>PET #2</u>

For a profit-maximizing monopolist, the price of its output will be greater than the marginal cost.

This performance enhancing tip is based on two principles: (1) the addition to revenue (marginal revenue) that a monopolist earns from selling one more unit of output is less than the price it receives for selling that one more unit of output, (see your textbook for a good explanation); and (2) a profit-maximizing firm produces an output level where marginal revenue equals marginal cost. Statement (1) says that price > marginal revenue. Statement (2) says that marginal revenue equals marginal cost.

Thus, it must be the case that, for a monopolist, price > marginal cost.

<u>PET #3</u>

A monopolist produces an output level that is less than a perfectly competitive industry would produce and charges a price that is higher than would prevail under perfect competition.

Under perfect competition, a profit-maximizing firm produces an output level where marginal revenue equals marginal cost, just as does a monopolist. However, for a perfectly competitive firm, marginal revenue and price are identical. This means that a profit-maximizing firm in a perfectly competitive market also ends up producing an output level where price is equal to marginal cost. This is not true of a monopolist as PET #2 discusses. This is the reason that a monopolist will produce a lower output level and charge a higher price for its output than it would if it were a perfectly competitive firm.

To see this, look at the Figure 11-1.

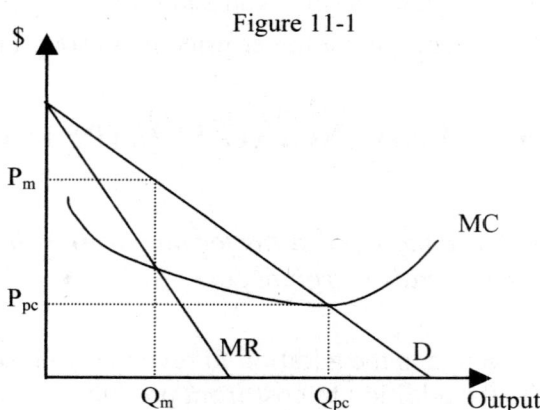

Figure 11-1

The monopolist will produce output level Q_m, which is where marginal revenue and marginal cost are equal. The monopolist will decide on a price for output level Q_m by using the demand curve. At output level Q_m, the demand curve dictates that the price be P_m. Now, suppose the monopolist were to behave as a perfectly competitive firm. It would produce an output level where price equals marginal cost and charge a price dictated by the demand curve for that output level. Price equals marginal cost where the demand and marginal cost curves intersect. The output level in this case would be Q_{pc}. The price charged would be read off the demand curve corresponding to output level Q_{pc}, which is P_{pc}. As Figure 11-1 shows, the monopolist's price exceeds what would be charged by a perfectly competitive firm and produces an output level that is less than would be produced under perfect competition.

V. PRACTICE EXAM: MULTIPLE CHOICE QUESTIONS

1. Which one of the following characteristics is true of a monopoly?

   a. There are a large number of firms in the industry.
   b. There are barriers to entry into the industry.
   c. The firm acts as a price taker.
   d. Price equals marginal revenue.
   e. All of the above.

2. Which one of the following would NOT be an example of a monopoly?

   a. A patent granted to a computer company.
   b. A franchise awarded to a food service on campus.
   c. The Canadian Medical Association.
   d. Major League Baseball.
   e. All of the above.

3. A monopolist maximizes profit by picking the output level where:

   a. marginal revenue = marginal cost.
   b. price = marginal revenue.
   c. price = marginal cost.
   d. price > average cost.
   e. price = average cost.

4. Which one of the following is true for a monopolist?

   a. Freedom of entry.
   b. Price > marginal revenue.
   c. Produces a socially efficient output level.
   d. Is unable to price discriminate.
   e. Earns zero economic profit in the long run.

5. Suppose the price at which a monopolist is selling its output is $12 and the marginal revenue associated with selling the last unit of output is $9. Further, suppose the marginal cost of the last unit of output sold is $10. Which one of the following best describes what the monopolist should do?

   a. Increase output and raise price.
   b. Increase output and lower price.
   c. Decrease output and lower price.
   d. Decrease output and raise price.
   e. Shut down.

Use Figure 11-2 to answer the following question.

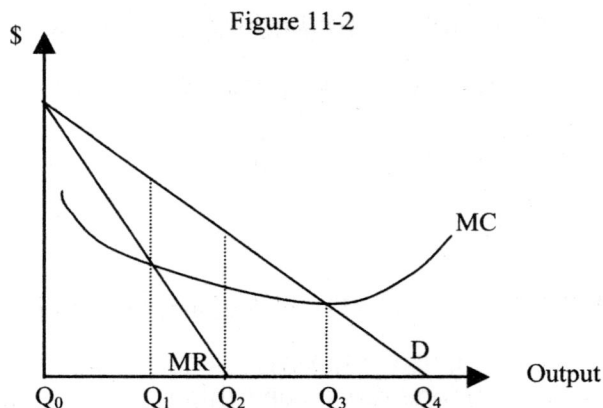

Figure 11-2

6. The profit-maximizing output level for the monopolist shown in Figure 11-2 is:

   a. Q_0
   b. Q_1
   c. Q_2
   d. Q_3
   e. Q_4

7. If the average cost curve is horizontal, say at $2 per unit of output, then:

   a. marginal cost = $2.
   b. marginal cost = $0.
   c. marginal cost > $2.
   d. marginal cost = $1.
   e. cannot be determined with information given.

8. Which one of the following is a cost of a monopoly?

   a. The price consumers pay is higher than they would under perfect competition.
   b. Output is less than under perfect competition.
   c. Rent seeking leads to loss in output in other industries.
   d. Consumer surplus is less than under perfect competition.
   e. All of the above.

9. Which one of the following is a benefit to consumers of a patent-generated monopoly?

   a. Rent seeking.
   b. Innovation.
   c. Deadweight loss.
   d. Monopoly profits.
   e. Price discrimination.

10. Which one of the following would NOT be a good example of price discrimination?

   a. Mail in rebates on combined purchases of washer and dryers.
   b. No-fee chequing to bank customers that keep $500 or more in their chequing accounts.
   c. Restaurant discounts to early bird (before 5:00 pm) diners.
   d. Coupons for dry-cleaning.
   e. Senior citizen discounts for popcorn at the movies.

11. The practice of price discrimination:

   a. occurs when a monopolist sells a product below the marginal cost of production.
   b. increases a monopolist's revenue.
   c. will always increase a monopolist's profit.
   d. does not require that a firm have control over the price at which it sells its output.
   e. is to charge a higher price to the high elasticity demand group of customers and a lower price to the low elasticity demand group of customers.

VI.   PRACTICE EXAM: ESSAY QUESTIONS

12. Discuss the costs and benefits to society of a monopoly that is created because a patent is granted for the product the firm produces.

13. Explain whether a monopoly could increase its revenue *and* its profits by charging different prices to different groups of customers. You may wish to give a numerical example to illustrate your point.

VII.   ANSWER KEY: MULTIPLE CHOICE QUESTIONS

1.   Correct answer: b.

   Discussion: Barriers to entry characterize a monopolistic market structure -- some barriers are artificial (or government created) and others arise naturally (as will be discussed in Chapter 12).

   Statements a, c, and d are all characteristics of a perfectly competitive market structure.

2.   Correct answer: e.

   Discussion: Patents are one way that monopolies are created. Franchise and licensing schemes, industrial, sports, and other associations that restrict the number of firms in the market also create a monopolistic market.

3.   Correct answer: a.

   Discussion: A monopolist (or any type of firm) will maximize profits by producing an output level where marginal revenue = marginal cost (see PET #1 of this chapter for review).

   Statement b describes the relationship between price and marginal revenue for a perfectly competitive firm. Statement c is another version of the profit-maximizing condition for a perfectly competitive firm. Statement d would ensure profit greater than zero but not necessarily the biggest (maximized) profit. Statement e would ensure zero economic profit.

4. Correct answer: b.

Discussion: A monopolist (unlike a perfectly competitive firm) must lower the price of its output to all of its customers in order to sell more to a few more customers. This means that the price the monopolist receives from selling the last unit of output is not simply the price received from selling the last unit of output. The marginal revenue from selling the last unit will be less than the price the firm receives on that last unit because while the firm gets paid $X for the last unit of output, it loses revenue from lowering the price to the previous customers who were paying the higher price. The sum of these two effects makes the marginal revenue earned on the last unit of output sold less than the price received on the last unit of output sold.

Statement a is not correct because a monopolist does not face freedom of entry, but rather barriers to entry. Statement c is not correct because a monopolist produces a socially inefficient output level (it produces too little output). Statement d is not correct because a monopolist may be able to price discriminate. Statement e is not correct because a monopolist earns positive economic profit in the long run.

5. Correct answer: d.

Discussion: Since marginal cost > marginal revenue, the monopolist is not maximizing its profits and, in fact, is producing too much output. If the monopolist is producing too much output, then, based on the demand curve, he is charging a price below the profit-maximizing price. Thus, the monopolist should reduce his output level until marginal revenue = marginal cost. By reducing the output level, the monopolist moves back along the demand curve to a higher price for his output.

Statements a and b are not correct because, if the monopolist increased his output level, he would continue adding more to his costs than to his revenue and profits would decline. Statement c is not correct because the monopolist should not lower but raise price. Statement e is not correct because there is no information that tells you whether the monopolist should shut down.

6. Correct answer: b.

Discussion: A profit-maximizing monopolist picks an output level where marginal revenue equals marginal cost (which occurs where these two curves intersect). The output level at the intersection of these two curves is Q_1.

Statements a, b, c, and e are all output levels corresponding to other intersection points. The output level where the demand and marginal cost curves intersect is the output level that would be set if price equal to marginal cost was the rule the monopolist followed. This would be a socially efficient output level.

7. Correct answer: a.

Discussion: When the average cost curve is horizontal, it means that the average cost per unit of output is not changing as more and more output is produced. If the average cost is not changing, it must be the case that the marginal cost is equal to the average cost. (Your book gives an example using your GPA, which is an average of the grades you made in the courses you've already taken. If your GPA is 3.0 and you get a B (= 3.0) on a course you take in the summer (the marginal course), your GPA (average) will remain at 3.0).

Statements b and d are for a marginal cost that is less than the average cost. If this were the case, then the average cost of production would decline and, thus, not remain constant. Statement c is for a marginal cost that exceeds the average cost; in this case, the average cost would be "pulled up" or increase and, thus, not remain constant. Statement e is not correct because you are given enough information to get an answer.

8. Correct answer: e.

Discussion: A monopolist charges a higher price and produces less output than would arise under perfect competition. This is costly to consumers (see your textbook, PET #3, and essay #1 for further discussion). This also means that consumer surplus (a measure of the benefits to consumers from their purchases) is smaller under a monopolistic market structure than a perfectly competitive one.

Monopoly and Price Discrimination

Monopolies, which often arise as a result of rent seeking undertaken by lobbyists, also entail an opportunity cost to society in that the lobbyists could be employed elsewhere, thereby adding to output in other industries which consumers could, in turn, purchase.

9. Correct answer: b.

    Discussion: The awarding of a patent to a firm grants the firm monopoly status (at least for 20 years). The monopoly status means the firm is more likely to make positive economic profits. The profit incentive then motivates the firm to actually produce and market the product, thereby making it available to consumers. Without the assurance of profit, the firm may not undertake production of the product and, thus, consumers would lose out on innovative new products.

    Statements a and c are costs of a monopoly. Statement d is a benefit to the monopolist but not to consumers. Statement e is not necessarily a benefit to consumers: price discrimination by a monopolist might lead the monopolist to charge some groups of customers a higher price than other groups.

10. Correct answer: e.

    Discussion: One of the conditions necessary for price discrimination to work is that it not be possible for customers to resell (or buy for others) the product that is being discounted. In the case of senior citizen discounts for popcorn at movie theatres, the senior citizen can easily purchase the popcorn and then, once inside the movie theatre, share it or give it to his or her companion(s) who may not be senior citizens.

    Statements a - d are all examples of price discrimination that are practiced. Your book also lists similar examples.

11. Correct answer: b.

    Discussion: Price discrimination is the practice of charging different customers different prices for the same product with the intent of increasing a firm's revenue.

    Statement .a is not correct because it is not the definition of price discrimination. Statement c is not correct because a monopolist's profits will not necessarily increase with price discrimination if the cost of serving two or more different customer groups increases. Thus, while price discrimination would raise revenue, it may also raise a monopolist's costs and, thus, lead to lower, not higher, profit.

    Statement d is not correct because price discrimination requires that a firm have some control over the price at which it sells its output. Statement e is not correct; it is actually the reverse. A higher price should be charged to the low elasticity of demand customers and a lower price to the high elasticity of demand customers.

VIII. ANSWER KEY: ESSAY QUESTIONS

12. The cost to society of a monopoly is that consumers are charged a higher price for the product than they would if entry into the industry could occur as in perfect competition. Also, the industry output under a monopolist is less than would occur if the industry operated as a perfectly competitive one.

    Thus, society loses on two accounts -- customers pay a higher price for the output and there are some customers who don't get to purchase the output because not enough is produced. This means that consumer surplus is lower under a monopolistic market structure than under a perfectly competitive market structure. Also, rent-seeking behaviour is likely to occur and this entails an opportunity cost to society. Rent seeking occurs because, in general, firms prefer to be protected from competition so that they can thereby earn positive economic profits indefinitely. Thus, a firm might hire lobbyists to go to Ottawa in the hopes that the lobbyists will be able to get the firm some form of protection from competition, i.e., status as a monopoly. The time and effort of the lobbyists, however, entails an opportunity cost in that the lobbyists could be employed in other industries, thereby increasing output elsewhere that consumers could purchase.

    Of course, there are benefits to the monopolist (a member of society, too). The monopolist earns positive economic profit (at least for the life of the patent). Also, with patent-generated monopolies, a society at least gets the benefit that new products will be produced instead of none at all. That is, innovation benefits society. For example, a new drug that benefits cancer patients may not be produced unless a patent, which ensures the innovating firm positive economic profits, is granted. That is, a firm with the technology to produce a new drug may choose not to if they know that, as soon as they produce it, other firms will enter the market and drive economic profits to zero.

The problem with patent granting is that the government does not always know which products will be produced even without a patent. Thus, the government may inadvertently grant monopoly status and, thus, monopoly profits to a firm that does not otherwise truly need the assurance of monopoly profits to produce the product. In this way, society loses for the reasons mentioned above.

13. A monopolist that charges different prices to different customers is practicing price discrimination. First, consider the revenue from a monopolist that is not practicing price discrimination. Suppose the monopolist charges a price of $10 per unit of output and sells 2,000 units. The total revenue earned by the monopolist is $20,000. Price discrimination by the monopolist will be possible if three conditions are met: (1) the firm has some control over the price at which it sells its output; (2) different groups of customers must be willing to pay a different price for the same product; (3) resale is not possible. Assuming these conditions are met, a monopolist may wish to split its customer base into two groups (although more than two is also an option). The two groups are established based on the differences in the responsiveness to price changes. Assume one group is very price conscious. That is, a lower price will induce them to buy substantially more and a higher price will induce them to buy substantially less. This is just a way of saying that, for this group, the elasticity of demand is high (exceeds 1). The second group is not as price conscious. While a lower price will induce them to buy more, they will not be inclined to buy much more and, while a higher price will induce them to buy less, they will not be inclined to cut back their purchases very much. This is just a way of saying that, for this group, the elasticity of demand is not very high (is less than 1).

Suppose the elasticity of demand for the price sensitive group is 2 and for the "price insensitive" group is 0.4. Based on the differences in the elasticity of demand, the firm's total revenue could actually be greater than $20,000 using the following pricing scheme: charge a price higher than $10 (say, 10% higher) to the low elasticity demand group and charge a price lower than $10 (say, 10% lower) to the high elasticity demand group. What will happen is the following:

For the group charged the 10% higher price, the quantity sold will, using the elasticity of demand of 0.4, decline by 4%. However, total revenue will still increase because the increase in price in percentage terms exceeds the decrease in quantity demanded in percentage terms. (See Chapter 5 for review.)

For the group charged the 10% lower price, the quantity sold will, using the elasticity of demand of 2, increase by 20%. However, total revenue will increase because the increase in the quantity sold in percentage terms exceeds the decrease in the price in percentage terms. (See Chapter 5 for review.)

Since both price changes lead to an increase in total revenue, the firm will see its total revenue increase above $20,000.

While the example I used assumed that the monopolist raised price to the low elasticity demand group by the same percentage as it lowered price to the high elasticity demand group, a monopolist could raise and lower the price to the different groups of customers by different percentages and still see its profits increase.

One thing to mention is that, while the price discrimination scheme increased the total revenue of the firm, we cannot be sure what happens to the profits of the firm without knowing how or if the total cost of serving two different groups of customers has changed. If the cost does not change, then the price discrimination scheme will increase total revenue and profits. However, it may be possible that the costs increase by more than the revenue increases and, thus, the firm could end up making less in profit, but more in revenue.

CHAPTER 12
ENTRY DECISIONS: NATURAL MONOPOLY AND MONOPOLISTIC COMPETITION

I.   OVERVIEW

In this chapter, you will learn about what a firm considers before deciding to enter a particular industry. You will learn that, in the case of industries with very high fixed costs of start up, often only one firm will enter the industry. This is the case of a natural monopoly. You will learn that in the case of industries with low fixed costs of start up, there is often a great deal of entry and, thus, competition amongst firms. This is the case of monopolistic competition. You will learn how firms already in an industry are affected by the entry of new firms into the industry. You will learn why the government typically regulates natural monopolies. You will learn that the government regulation comes in the form of an "average cost pricing policy" which is aimed at achieving a more socially efficient outcome than would arise under an unregulated situation. You will learn that an average cost pricing policy ensures a natural monopoly a guaranteed profit but reduces the incentive for the monopoly to keep its costs of production low.

II.   CHECKLIST

By the end of this chapter, you should be able to:
- [ ] Explain what gives rise to a natural monopoly.
- [ ] List some real world examples of natural monopolies.
- [ ] Explain why natural monopolies are often regulated.
- [ ] Explain a natural monopoly's reaction to regulation.
- [ ] Describe the objective and policy used in regulating natural monopolies.
- [ ] Use a graph to show how an average cost pricing policy works.
- [ ] List the characteristics of a monopolistically competitive market structure.
- [ ] List some real world examples of firms that operate under monopolistic competition.
- [ ] Explain the profit-maximizing rule for a monopolistically competitive firm and depict it with a graph for both the short and the long run.
- [ ] Discuss the relationship between price, marginal revenue, marginal cost, and average cost of a firm in a monopolistically competitive market structure.

- ❑ Discuss the costs and benefits to a monopolistically competitive market structure.
- ❑ Explain what motivates firms to enter a monopolistically competitive market structure.
- ❑ Describe what happens to the price, output, and profits of firms in a monopolistically competitive market structure in the long run.

III. KEY TERMS

Entrepreneur: a person who has an idea for a business and then coordinates the production and sale of goods and services, taking risks in the process.

Natural monopoly: a market in which the entry of a second firm would make price less than average cost, so a single firm serves the entire market.

Average-cost pricing policy: a regulatory policy under which the government picks the point on the demand curve at which price equals average cost.

Monopolistic competition: a situation in which each firm has a *monopoly* in selling its own differentiated product, but *competes* with other firms selling similar products.

IV. PERFORMANCE ENHANCING TIPS (PETS)

PET #1

The profit-maximizing rule for a natural monopoly is to produce an output level where marginal revenue is equal to marginal cost.

This is just PET #1 from Chapter 11 restated for a natural monopoly, You may want to review PET #1 from Chapter 11 since it provides a more detailed explanation of the PET. You may also want to review PET #2 and PET #3 from Chapter 11 since they also apply to a natural monopoly.

PET #2

An average cost pricing policy lowers the price that consumers would pay compared to an unregulated situation and increases the output produced compared to an unregulated situation.

An unregulated natural monopoly would produce an output level where marginal revenue equals marginal cost and charge a price based on what the demand curve would support for that output level. In Figure 12-1, the unregulated natural monopoly would produce an output level Q_m and charge a price P_m.

An average cost pricing policy dictates that the price of output equal the average cost to produce it. This occurs at the intersection of the demand (price) and average cost curves. Figure 12-1 shows that the output level corresponding to price = average cost is Q_{ac}. Of course, the price associated with this output level (read off of the demand curve) is P_{ac}.

Entry Decisions: Natural Monopoly and Monopolistic Competition

Figure 12-1

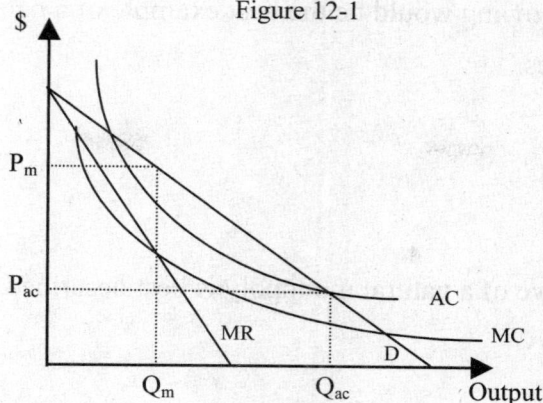

Since $P_{ac} < P_m$ and $Q_{ac} > Q_m$, the average cost pricing policy moves closer to a socially efficient outcome (where MC intersects the demand curve).

PET #3

A monopolistically competitive firm maximizes its profit by producing at an output level where marginal revenue equals marginal cost.

The same reasoning discussed in PET #1 of Chapter 11 applies to a monopolistically competitive firm as well. You may want to review it if you are not comfortable with the principle.

PET #4

The entry of firms into a monopolistically competitive market structure causes the demand curves of all firms to shift to the left since each firm now gets a smaller piece of the consumer market. Since the demand curves shift to the left, the marginal revenue curves also shift to the left.

Since the demand and marginal revenue curves of monopolistically competitive firms shift as entry occurs in the industry, the profit-maximizing output level and corresponding price the firms will charge will also change.

V   PRACTICE EXAM: MULTIPLE CHOICE QUESTIONS

1. Which one of the following gives rise to a natural monopoly?

    a. Patents.
    b. Increasing average costs of production.
    c. Economies of scale.
    d. Inelastic market demand.
    e. Competition.

2. Which one of the following would be the best example of a natural monopoly?

    a. Video rental stores.
    b. Wheat farming.
    c. Oil refineries.
    d. Sewage treatment.
    e. Auto dealerships.

3. The average cost curve of a natural monopoly is best described as:

    a. L-shaped.
    b. J-shaped.
    c. U-shaped.
    d. W-shaped.
    e. S-shaped.

Use Figure 12-2 to answer the following question.

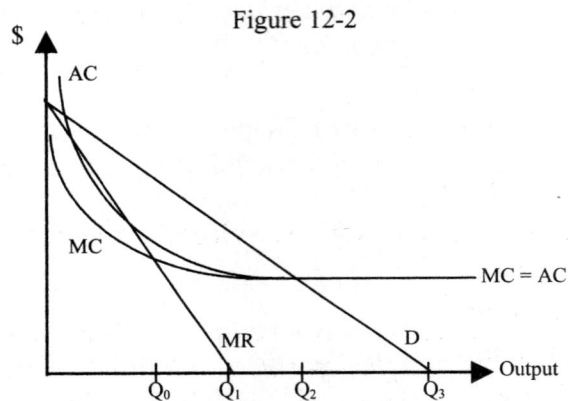

Figure 12-2

4. The output level a profit-maximizing natural monopoly would produce is _____ and the output level a regulated natural monopoly would produce is _____.

    a. Q_0; Q_1.
    b. Q_1; Q_2.
    c. Q_0; Q_2.
    d. Q_1; Q_3.
    e. Q_2; Q_3.

5. Which one of the following statements is NOT true of an average-cost-pricing policy?

    a. It will create zero economic profit.
    b. It is established where the demand curve intersects the average cost curve.
    c. It creates little incentive for the monopolist to control costs.
    d. It leads to a higher price than would be charged by an unregulated monopolist.
    e. It leads to more output being produced than would arise if the monopoly was not regulated.

Use Figure 12-3 to answer the following question.

Figure 12-3

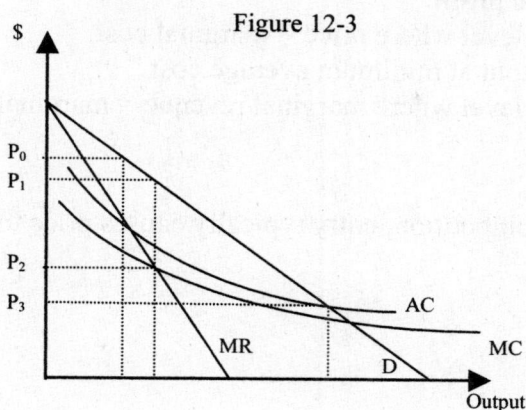

6. The price a profit-maximizing natural monopoly would charge for its output is _____ and the price a regulated natural monopoly would charge is _____.

a. P_0; P_1
b. P_1; P_2.
c. P_0; P_2.
d. P_1; P_3.
e. P_2; P_3.

7. Which one of the following would NOT be a characteristic of a monopolistically competitive market structure?

a. Homogeneous product.
b. Many firms in the industry.
c. Slight control over price.
d. No artificial barriers to entry.
e. All of the above are characteristics of a monopolistically competitive market structure.

8. Which one of the following would NOT differentiate one product from another under monopolistic competition?

a. Location.
b. Special services that go along with the purchase of a product.
c. Economies of scale.
d. Physical characteristics.
e. Product image.

9. In the long run, firms in a monopolistically competitive market structure:

    a. earn zero economic profit.
    b. produce an output level where price = marginal cost.
    c. do not produce output at minimum average cost.
    d. produce an output level where marginal revenue = marginal cost.
    e. a, c, and d are true.

10. Under monopolistic competition, entry typically causes price to _____ and profits to _____.

    a. decrease; decrease.
    b. decrease; increase.
    c. increase; increase.
    d. increase; decrease.
    e. decrease; remain unchanged.

11. Government elimination of artificial barriers to entry can be expected to:

    a. lead to more competition.
    b. lead to improved service.
    c. lead to a lower price for output.
    d. lead to lower profits.
    e. all of the above.

12. Which one of the following would be the best example of a monopolistically competitive firm?

    a. A sugar farmer.
    b. A railway transportation firm.
    c. An Italian restaurant.
    d. A drug company.
    e. A food service at a national park.

VI. PRACTICE EXAM: ESSAY QUESTIONS

13. Public utilities such as electricity are referred to as natural monopolies and are often subject to regulation by a Provincial authority. Explain why a public utility, such as electricity is referred to as a "natural monopoly." Explain how and why an average cost pricing policy is applied to public utility. Discuss the effects of the policy on the price and output the utility sells at and produces. Discuss how the policy affects the utility's profits and costs.

14. Consider a small city's dry-cleaning market that is monopolistically competitive. Currently, the typical drycleaner is charging $5 an item. The average cost of dry-cleaning is $2. The typical drycleaner cleans 1,000 items per week. (Each customer

drops off approximately 4 items). Suppose a new drycleaner was to enter the market. Explain what would happen to the price, average cost, output, and profit of a typical drycleaner. Discuss the costs and benefits to consumers of having a dry-cleaning market that is monopolistically competitive.

VII.   ANSWER KEY: MULTIPLE CHOICE QUESTIONS

1.   Correct answer: c.

Discussion: Economies of scale (average cost declining over large ranges of output) arise because the fixed costs of starting up a business are very high. This typically occurs if the business requires the use of indivisible inputs.

Statement a is not correct because a patent creates an unnatural or artificial monopoly. Statement b is not correct; decreasing average costs over a large range of output characterize a natural monopoly. Statement d is not correct because demand has nothing to do with market structure. Statement e is not correct: monopolies are characterized by barriers to entry and, hence, the absence of competition.

2.   Correct answer: d.

Discussion: Natural monopolies typically arise because of the use of indivisible inputs and high fixed costs of start up. A natural monopoly is where there is a single supplier of a good or service. Sewage treatment is a good example of a natural monopoly.

Since there are typically more than one video rental store per town and because the costs of start up are low, video rental stores are best characterized as monopolistically competitive firms. Wheat farmers produce a homogeneous product and serve a very small portion of the overall market. They also have little control over the price at which they can sell their wheat. Wheat farmers are thus best characterized as perfectly competitive firms. Auto dealerships have a lot in common with video rental stores and are thus characterized as monopolistically competitive firms. While oil refineries may have high fixed start-up costs and require the use of indivisible inputs, there is typically several oil refining companies that service a country. In Chapter 13, you will see that an oil refinery is best characterized as an oligopoly.

3.   Correct answer: a.

Discussion: The average cost of production of a natural monopoly is very high at low levels of output. As output expands, average costs drop and continue to decline over large ranges of output. In fact, average costs typically are constant over large ranges of output. Thus, an average cost curve would be L-shaped.

A J-shaped average cost curve would indicate that average costs of production are low at low levels of output and then increase as output expands. A U-shaped average cost curve is typical of short-run analysis. W- and S-shaped cost curves have not been addressed in your textbook.

4.   Correct answer: a.

Discussion: An unregulated natural monopoly produces where marginal revenue = marginal cost (the two curves intersect). This occurs at output level Q_0. A regulated natural monopoly produces where price = average cost (demand and average cost curves intersect). This occurs at output level Q_1. Thus, statement a is the only correct answer.

5.   Correct answer: d.

Discussion: One of the aims of an average-cost-pricing policy is to lower the price that customers must pay for the product or service. Thus, an average-cost-pricing policy leads to a lower price, not a higher price than would be charged by an unregulated monopolist.

Statements a, b, c, and e are all true of an average-cost-pricing policy. Since the policy sets price = average cost, the monopoly earns zero economic profit. This price-setting policy can be depicted where demand and the average cost curves intersect. Since the regulated monopolist's price will always be set equal to average costs, it has no incentive to hold down its costs. The monopolist knows that, whatever costs they incur, they will always be covered by the pricing policy. Another aim of the average cost pricing policy is to force the monopolist to serve as many customers as possible. Thus, the policy will increase the output of the monopolist.

6. Correct answer: d.

Discussion: To arrive at the correct answer, you must first establish at what output level a profit-maximizing natural monopoly will produce. Once you have determined that output level, you read up to the demand curve and over to the price line to establish the price the natural monopolist would charge, In this case, the profit-maximizing output level occurs where marginal revenue = marginal cost (they intersect) and the price is P_1. For a regulated natural monopoly, price is set equal to average cost. This occurs where the demand and average cost curves intersect. At this point, read over to the vertical axis and that will be the price the regulator sets. In this case, it is P_3. Thus, statement d is the only correct option.

7. Correct answer: a.

Discussion: A monopolistically competitive market structure is characterized by product differentiation, real or perceived. A homogeneous product is virtually identical (sugar, wheat, etc.) and is characteristic of a perfectly competitive market structure.

In a monopolistically competitive market structure, there is still a lot of competition and, hence, there are many firms in the industry. However, the firm does have some control over the price it sets. Furthermore, there are no artificial barriers to entry, which is why there is a lot of competition.

8. Correct answer: c.

Discussion: Economies of scale typically characterize monopolies, particularly natural monopolies.

Statements a, b, d, and e are all factors that can cause similar products to be differentiated from one another.

9. Correct answer: e.

Discussion: In the long run, competition in the monopolistically competitive market leads to entry up until the point at which it is no longer desirable. This occurs where the firms in the industry are earning zero economic profits. Monopolistically competitive firms do not produce at minimum average cost because they serve a small portion of the market and because their profit-maximizing strategy is to set marginal revenue = marginal cost. As just mentioned, the profit-maximizing strategy of any firm is to set marginal revenue = marginal cost. Thus, statements a, c, and d are true of a monopolistically competitive market structure.

Statement b describes a version of the profit-maximizing rule that a perfectly competitive firm could use.

10. Correct answer: a.

Discussion: Competition in a monopolistically competitive market will lead to a lower price for the firms' output. This acts to reduce firms' profits. Also, the average cost of production typically rises for monopolistically competitive firms. This too acts to reduce firms' profits. Thus, statement a is the only correct option.

11. Correct answer: e.

Discussion: Studies have shown that, when the government steps in to remove artificial barriers to entry and thereby promote competition amongst firms that all of the above will result.

12. Correct answer: c.

Discussion: Statement c is the best example because there are many Italian restaurants each with their own characteristics that differentiate them from each other. Furthermore, entry into the restaurant business is very open.

Entry Decisions: Natural Monopoly and Monopolistic Competition

A sugar farmer is an example of a perfectly competitive firm. Railway transportation is an example of a natural monopoly. A drug company is an example of a patent-generated monopoly. Food service at a national park is an example of a licence-generated monopoly.

VIII. ANSWER KEY: ESSAY QUESTIONS

13. A public utility, such as electricity, is an example of a natural monopoly. A natural monopoly occurs when there is a single supplier of the output to the market because any more than one firm in the industry would not be profitable. The reason that more than one firm would not be profitable is that a natural monopoly is characterized by very high fixed start-up costs and, thus, very high average costs at low levels of output. This means that, with more than one firm in the market, each firm would have only a portion of the overall market and, thus, would produce for a smaller portion of the market.

   However, since average costs of production are very high at low levels of output and, since each firm is producing for only a portion of the market, each firm will face a very high average cost of production. The firms may not be able to extract a price from their customers that is high enough to cover the costs of providing a service to them and, thus, each firm will earn negative economic profit. Faced with this prospect, firms typically choose not to enter an industry with high fixed start-up costs where one firm is already present. In other words, the market supports only one firm in the industry. Since this type of monopoly arises naturally, i.e., without the government offering franchises, patents, etc., it is referred to as a natural monopoly.

   An average cost pricing policy is often used in the interest of creating a more socially efficient outcome – that is, where price is lower and output higher than would arise if the monopolist were unregulated. Under an average cost pricing policy, the regulatory commission effectively sets a price equal to the monopolist's average cost of production and requires that the electric company serve all customers willing to pay the price. In terms of a graph, the regulatory commission forces the utility to produce an output level where the demand and average cost curves intersect. Since price is set equal to average cost, the electric company earns zero economic profit (but positive accounting profit). The average cost pricing policy creates a disincentive for the utility to minimize its costs of production. The reason the disincentive is created is that the utility knows that the regulated price will be set based on the utility's average cost of production: the utility's average cost of production will always be covered, so the utility is always assured of at least zero economic profit, no less. Thus, the utility does not have an incentive to keep costs of production low, as would an unregulated firm that desires to maximize profits.

14. In a monopolistically competitive market, there is ease of entry. The ease of entry, however, means that there will be a lot of competition for customers amongst the firms. Thus, firms that are currently making positive economic profit face the threat of entry by entrepreneurs who believe that they, too, could make a profit in the industry. In fact, entry in a monopolistically competitive market structure typically occurs up until the point at which firms are making zero economic profit. At this point, there is no incentive for more entry into the market.

   In the case of the dry-cleaning business of the small city, the typical drycleaner is making $2,000 in profit per week based on the approximately 250 customers served (1,000 items per week/4 items dropped off per customer). If a new drycleaner enters the market, there will be some competition from him. This means several things. First, the existing drycleaners may have to lower the price of their service in order to hold on to their customer base. Since the new drycleaner will likely take away customers from the existing drycleaners, their demand curves (and marginal revenue curves) will shift to the left. However, the lower price charged by the drycleaners will mean that they may not lose as many customers as anticipated. Second, be, cause the existing drycleaners will be serving fewer customers (less output), the average cost of serving each customer will rise. (Remember that average costs decline as output increases and vice-versa, i.e., average cost increases as output declines). Third, since the drycleaners will be charging a lower price for their service and incurring a higher average cost of production, the drycleaners' profits will be reduced. In the end, entry into the small city's dry-cleaning business will stop when economic profits are driven to zero.

There are costs and benefits to the dry-cleaning business operating under a monopolistically competitive market structure. With ease of entry, there will be a lot of drycleaners serving the market, each with their own level of customer service, location, etc. Thus, in a monopolistically competitive market structure, customers get the benefits of being able to select from a variety of slightly differentiated products and services. Also, customers will likely see that the travel time to the drycleaner they patronize will decrease since more drycleaners in the city means more locations being serviced. The customers also benefit in that competition typically leads to a lower price for the product or service being purchased. The cost to society of a monopolistically competitive market is that the average cost of production is higher. From an efficiency standpoint, this is a cost to society since it would be better off if the drycleaners could produce where average cost is minimized and, correspondingly, the price paid by consumers would be the lowest possible. Of course, competition leads to price being reduced to some degree.

Entry Decisions: Natural Monopoly and Monopolistic Competition

134

CHAPTER 13
OLIGOPOLY AND COMPETITION POLICY

I.   OVERVIEW

In this chapter, you will learn about the market structure of oligopoly. You will learn about the characteristics of an oligopoly and what gives rise to an oligopoly. You will also learn how firms in an oligopoly make pricing decisions. You will learn that firms within an oligopoly act strategically, anticipating the actions of their competitors in response to their own pricing decisions. You will learn that firms within an oligopoly may enter into price-fixing schemes, price-matching schemes, price leadership, mergers, or practice entry deterrence in an attempt to avoid the consequences of competition. You will use a game tree to analyze the choices and probable strategic outcomes faced by firms. You will learn about contestable markets. You will also learn about an "insecure" monopolist and the steps they may take to deter entry by other firms. You will learn what role competition policy as well as trade policy play in regulating the behaviour of an oligopoly so that they do not enter into anti-competitive agreements. You will also learn how deregulation has affected some oligopolies.

II.   CHECKLIST

By the end of this chapter you should be able to:
- Describe the characteristics of an oligopoly.
- Explain what gives rise to an oligopoly.
- List some real world examples of an industry that could be characterized as an oligopoly.
- Discuss the duopolists' (2-firm oligopoly) dilemma.
- Discuss and explain the rationale for price-fixing schemes, price-matching schemes, price leadership, predatory pricing, and mergers and trusts. Discuss why such schemes are often likely to break down.
- Use a game tree to determine what the likely pricing outcome will be between two firms (a duopoly).
- Explain the behaviour of an insecure monopolist.
- Define a concentration ratio and discuss how it might be used to establish whether an oligopoly exists.
- List some of the major pieces of Canadian competition policy legislation and explain their purpose.

III.   KEY TERMS

Oligopoly: a market served by a few firms.

Four-firm concentration ratio (CR4): a measurement of the percentage of sales revenues commanded by the top four firms in an industry.

Herfindahl-Hirschman index (HHI): an index based on the square of the percentage of sales revenues realized by all firms in an industry.

Market power measure: a comparison of the slope of a firm's demand curve with the slope of the market demand curve.

Price mark-up value: a comparison of a product's price with its marginal cost.

Cartel: a group of firms that coordinate their pricing and/or output decisions.

Price fixing: an arrangement in which two or more firms explicitly coordinate their pricing decisions.

Game tree: a visual representation of the consequences of different strategies.

Dominant strategy: an action that is the best choice under all circumstances.

Duopolists' dilemma: a situation in which both firms would be better off if they chose the high price, but each chooses the low price.

Guaranteed price matching: a firm's guarantee that it will match a competitor's lower price.

Grim-trigger: a strategy under which a firm responds to underpricing by choosing a price so low that each firm makes significantly lower economic profit for a sustained period.

Tit-for-tat: a strategy under which the one firm starts out with the cartel price and then chooses whatever price the other firm picked in the preceding period.

Price leadership: an arrangement under which one firm sets a price and other firms in the market match the leader's price.

Entry Deterrence: a scheme under which a firm increases its output and accepts a lower price to deter other firms from entering the market.

Secure monopolist: a monopoly that faces little possibility of entry from a competing firm.

Insecure monopolist: a monopoly faced the possibility that a second firm will enter the market.

Contestable market: a market in which the costs of entering and leaving are very low, so the firms in the market are constantly threatened by the entry of new firms.

Conspiracy: formal – usually secret – agreements between firms to reduce competition.

False or misleading advertising: a firm's use of advertising that deliberately fools the public in an attempt to increase sales.

Abuse of dominant position: a dominant firm's use of position to further reduce competition.

Merger: a process in which two or more firms combine their operations to operate as one firm.

Deregulation: a process in which government-imposed barriers to entry in a particular industry are removed.

IV.   PERFORMANCE ENHANCING TIPS

PET # 1

The oligopolists' (or duopolists') dilemma is that each firm knows that by choosing to sell its output at a high price, the competition will sell at a lower price and, thus, undercut the high-priced firm's profits. Thus, each firm chooses to sell at the low price but in so doing, each firm ends up with a profit below what they could earn if they collectively agreed to the high price.

The dilemma thus creates an incentive for the oligopolists to collude – devise pricing schemes that lead to the high price outcome for all firms. However, such schemes are often illegal under competition policy.

PET #2

Cartels and other price-fixing schemes create the incentive for one or more of the participating firms to cheat (undercut the agreed upon price). The cheater is tempted to cheat because his firm's profits will increase at the expense of the other cartel members.

Because of the temptation to cheat, cartels and other price-fixing schemes are often hard to sustain unless there is some enforcement mechanism or punishment that deters the cheater(s) from cheating.

V.   PRACTICE EXAM: MULTIPLE CHOICE QUESTIONS

1. Which one of the following is an example of an oligopolistic industry?

    a. Aircraft and parts.
    b. Video rental stores.
    c. Apple growers.
    d. Sewage and water treatment.
    e. Clothing stores.

2. Which one of the following would NOT be true of an oligopolistic market structure?

    a. Each firm sells a similar product or service.
    b. Each firm is a price taker.
    c. There are economies of scale in production.
    d. A firm may carry out a big advertising campaign.
    e. A few firms serve the market.

3. A cartel is:

   a. an industrial association in which research and development is shared.
   b. the firm in the industry that sets the going price.
   c. a policy designed to prevent mergers that produce a concentration ratio greater than 40%.
   d. a group of firms that coordinate their pricing decisions, often by charging the same price.
   e. an industry watchdog group that monitors the price of output to ensure that consumers are not being ripped off.

4. Which one of the following statements is true?

   a. Cartels and price fixing are legal in the Canada
   b. A four-firm concentration ratio is the percentage of industry profits earned by the four biggest firms.
   c. A tit-for-tat strategy will promote price undercutting.
   d. A grim-trigger strategy is when a firm prices its output so low that the competition makes losses and, thus, is driven out of the market.
   e. Free-trade policy promotes competition.

Use the information in Table 13-1 to answer the following question.

Table 13-1		
Two-Firm Oligopoly (duopoly).		
Firm A will earn $5,000 in profit if it charges a price of $10	AND	Firm B charges a price of $10: Firm B will earn $5,000 in profit.
Firm A will earn $2,000 in profit if it charges a price of $10	AND	Firm B charges a price of $7: Firm B will earn $6,000 in profit.
Firm A will earn $6,000 in profit if it charges a price of $7	AND	Firm B charges a price of $10: Firm B will earn $2,000 in profit.
Firm A will earn $3,000 in profit if it charges a price of $7	AND	Firm B charges a price of $7: Firm B will earn $2,000 in profit.

5. If Firm A must pick the price at which it sells its output without knowing what price Firm B will pick and Firm B must pick the price at which it sells its output without knowing what price Firm A will pick, at what price combination will Firms A and B ultimately sell?

   a. $10; $10.
   b. $10; $7.
   c. $7; $10.
   d. $7; $7.
   e. Cannot be determined without further information.

6. The rational outcome of a guaranteed price matching or "meet-the-competition" policy is that:

    a. both firms will sell at the low price.
    b. one firm will sell at a high price until the competition sells at a low price: then it will sell at the low price.
    c. both firms will sell at the high price.
    d. consumers are fooled into thinking the price matching scheme will protect them from high prices.
    e. (c) and (d).

7. Which one of the following is NOT a retaliation strategy that firms would apply to one that cheated on a price-fixing scheme by selling at a price below the agreed-upon fixed price?

    a. All other firms sell at the same low price as the cheating firm.
    b. All other firms sell at a price that ensures zero economic profit for all firms.
    c. Each period, all other firms sell at the price picked by the cheater in the previous period.
    d. All other firms collect a penalty fee from the cheater.
    e. All of the above are retaliation schemes used by oligopolists.

8. Which one of the following statements is NOT true?

    a. A firm that chooses to cheat on a price-fixing scheme should consider the short-term gain in profits from cheating versus the long-term loss in profits from being punished.
    b. The duopoly-pricing strategy leads to negative economic profits.
    c. Cartels may break down because of the incentive to cheat.
    d. Price leadership arrangements are an implicit price-fixing scheme.
    e. All of the above are true statements.

9. Which one of the following statements is NOT true?

    a. A monopolist may act like a firm in a market with many firms, picking a low price and earning a small profit so as to deter entry and thereby guarantee profits for the longer term.
    b. A contestable market is one in which firms can enter and leave the market without incurring large costs.
    c. A firm can increase its share of the market by merging with other firms.
    d. Predatory pricing forces the predator and the prey to incur losses.
    e. Mergers are illegal under Canadian competition policy.

10. The purpose of competition policy is to:

    a. promote competition.
    b. reduce the price that consumers pay for output.
    c. protect domestic firms from foreign trade.
    d. ensure that firms do not avoid paying income taxes.
    e. (a) and (b).

V.   PRACTICE EXAM: ESSAY QUESTIONS

11. Explain why the duopolists' dilemma often leads to price-fixing schemes. Be sure to discuss a number of different price-fixing schemes and what may cause them to break down. Also discuss the enforcement mechanisms that the duopolists might undertake to ensure that a price-fixing scheme does not break down.

12. Suppose you ran the only bakery in town and were currently very profitable. What things might you consider if you wanted to ensure that you continued to enjoy the same success in the future?

VII.   ANSWER KEY: MULTIPLE CHOICE QUESTIONS

1. Correct answer: a.

    Discussion: Aircraft and parts are examples of oligopolistic market structures. Video rental stores and clothing stores are examples of monopolistically competitive market structures. Apple growers are an example of a perfectly competitive market structure and sewage and water treatment is an example of a natural monopoly.

2. Correct answer: b.

    Discussion: In an oligopolistic market structure, firms have some control over price and act strategically in setting price. That means that each firm considers the reaction of the other firms to the price that it may choose to sell its output. Firms are price takers in a perfectly competitive market structure.

    Statements a, c, d, and e are all true of an oligopolistic market structure.

3. Correct answer: d.

    Discussion: A cartel is a group of firms that get together to agree to fix the price at which they sell their output. The purpose of the agreement is to ensure higher profits for all firms than if they acted independently.

    Statements a, b, c, and e are all incorrect. Statement b is the definition of a price leader.

4. Correct answer: e.

    Discussion: Free trade is a policy that does not prohibit foreign firms from selling in the domestic market. As such, free-trade policy promotes competition and works to achieve some of the same objectives as competition policy.

    Statement a is not correct. Price-fixing agreements are illegal in Canada. Statement b is not correct. A four-firm concentration ratio is the percentage of industry sales that the four biggest firms in the industry produce. Statement c is not correct. A tit-for-tat pricing strategy actually promotes cartel pricing by penalizing any firm that tries to undercut the price of other firms in the cartel. Statement d is not correct because a grim-trigger strategy is not designed to lead to losses for firms but rather zero economic profits.

5. Correct answer: d.

    Discussion: The duopolist's dilemma means that the two firms end up both choosing the low price even though it is not the price at which each firm's profits would be maximized. The reasoning is as follows: Firm A knows that, if it picks the high price, Firm B will pick the low price since that way, Firm B will get bigger profits. Thus, Firm A does not have the incentive to pick the high price. For the same reasoning, Firm B knows that, if it picks the high price, Firm A will pick the low price since, that way, Firm A will get bigger profits. Thus, Firm B will not choose the high price. So, if both firms have to pick the price at which they will sell output without knowledge of what price the other has selected, they will both end up picking the low price. Furthermore, we see that both firms have a dominant strategy to pick the low price. You should always remember that, if you have a dominant strategy, you should use it!

6. Correct answer: e.

    Discussion: A guaranteed price-matching strategy never actually has to be enacted by the firm that sets the policy. This is because both firms will end up selling at the high price. Thus, consumers may think that they are being protected when in fact the protection is just an "empty promise." The reason the policy leads to a high price by both firms is that, once the competitor sees the other firm selling at the high price (albeit with the price-matching policy), the other firm is now able to select the price that will guarantee it the biggest profit. That price is the higher price, so both firms end up being able to sell at the higher price.

7. Correct answer: d.

    Discussion: Statement d is not correct. The book does not discuss any scenario in which firms are able to impose and effectively collect penalties from the cheater.

    Statement a is the definition of a duopoly price retaliation strategy. Statement b is the definition of the grim-trigger retaliation strategy. Statement c is the definition of a tit-for-tat pricing strategy. Statement e cannot be correct because statement d is not correct.

8. Correct answer: b.

    Discussion: A duopoly-price strategy leads to smaller profits than would arise under a price-fixing agreement. Predatory pricing, on the other hand, leads to negative economic profits.

    Statements a, c, and d are all true.

9. Correct answer: e.

    Discussion: Only those mergers that would substantially reduce competition are disallowed under the provisions of the Competition Act. Mergers can be a reviewed by the government under the Canadian Competition Policy.

    Statements a, b, c, and d are all true. You may wish to look at the answer to essay #2 for a detailed discussion related to statement a. Contestable markets are market structures that may populated by only one or a few firms yet the behaviour of the firms is more like the industry is populated by many firms. The threat of entry is what characterizes a contestable market. A merger creates a group of firms who make the decisions as a single entity. In this way, the same pricing decisions can be ensured across companies. This effectively works to fix prices. Predatory pricing is a very aggressive pricing strategy that put the predator's profits on the line for the ultimate goal of securing monopoly status.

10. Correct answer: e.

    Discussion: Competition policies are designed to promote competition. Remember that a perfectly competitive market ensures a socially efficient outcome and that the other market structures lead to prices that would be higher than under perfect competition and output levels that would be lower than under perfect competition. Thus, consumers benefit the more competition there is. Of course, competition policy cannot create perfectly competitive markets out of other market types, but they are aimed at achieving markets in which freedom of entry is easier.

VIII. ANSWER KEY: ESSAY QUESTIONS

11. The duopolists' dilemma is that each firm, fearful that its competitor will undercut its profits, ends up charging a price lower than they would otherwise want to. Thus, each firm makes a smaller profit than they could if they each charged a higher price. Given this dilemma, there is an incentive for the duopolists to get together and agree to a higher price at which they will both sell their output. That way, they can both be guaranteed profits that are more attractive than when they don't agree to fix the price. While such explicit price-fixing schemes are illegal in Canada, some firms still engage in price-fixing schemes because the fines and legal fees they might have to pay if they are found guilty of price fixing are less than the profits they anticipate earning over the time the price-fixing scheme is in operation.

    There are a number of different types of price-fixing schemes. Firms can form a cartel and agree to all sell at a fixed price or agree that some firms can sell at price X while others sell at price Y. A price-matching scheme is another pricing strategy. It is not explicitly illegal. In this strategy, a firm announces (through the media) that it will match the prices of its competitor. It is important that the firm be credible in its policy. Since the competitor believes that any low price it tries to sell at will be matched, and, thus, that their profits will be competed for, they will choose to sell at the same high price, too. Thus, the firm announcing the price-matching policy is able to continue selling at the high price. In this way, both firms enjoy higher profits than if there was no matching policy. Price leadership is another form of price fixing albeit an implicit agreement. In this context, the firm that is the price leader sets the price and all other firms simply follow suit. That way, there is no price competition and, implicitly, the price at which firms sell is fixed.

    Price-fixing agreements, whether explicit or implicit, carry a temptation to cheat. The temptation exists because, once the price is fixed, the cheaters know that, if they sell at below the fixed price, they will get a larger share of the market and thereby reap increased profits. However, cheaters should think about the long-term consequences of cheating since the other firms that are selling at the fixed price might punish the cheaters (and, incidentally, themselves as well) by all selling at a lower price, perhaps the one at which the cheaters were selling ("the duopoly price") or even one low enough that all firms earn zero economic profit (the grim-trigger strategy). The threat of retaliation, which arises in a repeated game sequence, may curtail, to some degree, the temptation to cheat.

12. If I ran the only bakery in town and it was very profitable, I would be worried that other entrepreneurs, seeing how profitable I was, would be motivated to open up other bakeries in town. Thus, I would be, in the terms of the textbook, an "insecure monopolist." My insecurity would be that the future success (read profitability) of my bakery might be threatened by the entry of other bakeries into the town. So, what to do? I would consider lowering the price I charge for the array of baked goods I provide to my customers. Of course, I would realize that the lower price might lead to lower economic profits (if my revenue didn't increase and my costs remained the same or even if, at the lower price, my revenue increased, but my costs increased by more). The lower price and presumably lower economic profits would make it less attractive for other firms to enter the business and, thus, I may be able to secure my monopoly status and the long-term prospect of at least positive economic profits.

    On the other hand, if I do nothing to deter entry and it occurs, I will likely see my profits reduced. However, if they do not fall by as much as my "low price deterrence strategy," then it would make sense for me to do nothing.

CHAPTER 14
PUBLIC GOODS, TAXES, AND PUBLIC CHOICE

I.   OVERVIEW

In this chapter, you will learn about public goods – goods that benefit society but are so expensive to pay for that no individual can pay for it by him- or herself. You will learn that government policy, including the tax system, can be used to ensure that worthwhile public goods are provided to society. You will also learn that sometimes the government is unable to make informed decisions about which public goods to provide. You will learn what distinguishes public goods from private goods and learn of the special challenges that public goods create in a market economy. You will revisit the spillover principle that was discussed in Chapter 3 of your textbook. You will learn about a branch of economics called "public choice" which studies the way in which governments operate and how they make decisions.

II. CHECKLIST

By the end of this chapter, you should be able to:
- Define a public good and the characteristics of a public good.
- Compare and contrast public and private goods.
- List some real world examples of public goods.
- Explain what spillover benefits (external benefits) are and give some examples.
- Explain how in the presence of spillover benefits, the market equilibrium determined by demand and supply is not efficient.
- Explain how a subsidy by a government might lead to a more efficient outcome in the case of spillover benefits.
- Discuss the three reasons for government inefficiency.
- Explain the free-rider problem and why voluntary contributions will generally not lead to the provision of a public good.
- Discuss some ways in which organizations can increase the voluntary contributions that they receive.
- Use supply and demand analysis to analyze the effects of taxes.
- Explain the forward and backward shifting effects of a tax on a good.
- Predict who will bear the bulk of the tax burden.

- ❑ Explain the three views on how the government operates.
- ❑ Explain the median-voter rule.

III. KEY TERMS

Public good: a good that is available for everyone to consume, regardless of who pays and who doesn't.

Private good: a good that is consumed by the single person or household who pays for it.

Spillover benefit: the benefit from a good experienced by people who do not decide how much of the good to produce or consume.

Positive externality: another term for spillover benefit; some of the benefits are external to the decision-maker.

Government failure: a situation in which the government fails to make an efficient choice in providing public goods or subsidies.

Free-rider problem: each person's attempt to receive the benefit of a public good without paying for it, trying to get a free ride at the expense of others.

Excess burden: the difference between the total burden of a tax and the amount of revenue collected by the government.

Public choice: a field of economics that explores how governments actually operate.

Median-voter rule: a rule suggesting that the choices made by government will reflect the preferences of the median voter.

IV. PERFORMANCE ENHANCING TIPS

<u>PET # 1</u>

The market demand and supply curves of goods with spillover benefits or spillover costs do not depict the efficient equilibrium outcome.

This means that, in the presence of spillover benefits or costs, the equilibrium price and quantity represented by the intersection of market demand and supply curves is not "efficient." This means that the price and quantity outcome does not take into account those consumers (or producers) that receive benefits or incur costs but are not directly using the good. Your book gives a good example using education as the good.

<u>PET #2</u>

A subsidy is a transfer of money from the government to private citizens; a tax is a transfer of money from private citizens to the government.

Since a subsidy is the reverse of a tax, it is sometimes referred to as a "negative tax." It should be pointed out, however, that the ability of the government to extend subsidies to certain private citizens or groups of private citizens comes from the taxes that private citizens (households and businesses) pay to the government. Thus, your tax dollars are used to pay for government subsidies. Thereby, indirectly, your tax dollars are transferred to other citizens in society.

PET #3

Shifting the supply curve to the left represents a tax on a good or service. The vertical distance between the two supply curves is determined by the size of the tax. The rise in the equilibrium price depends on how flat or steep (elastic or inelastic) the demand curve is.

To see this, look at Figure 14-1 below.

Figure 14-1

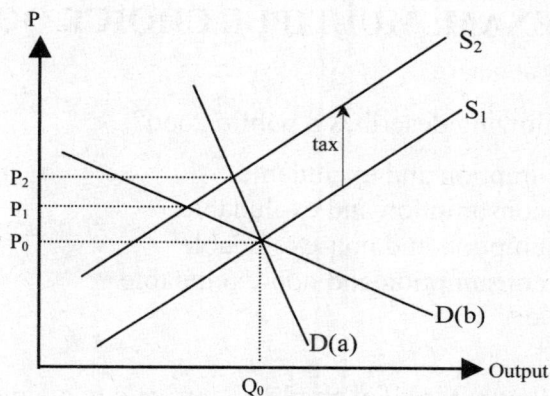

The steeper demand curve, D(a), is the less elastic demand curve; the flatter demand curve, D(b), is the more elastic demand curve. The shift in the supply curve from S_1 to S_2 is caused by a per-unit tax on the good. As you can see, the equilibrium price rises by more along the less elastic demand curve (P_0 to P_2), and rises by less along the more elastic demand curve (P_0 to P_1). Thus, more of the tax is shifted forward to consumers with a less elastic demand curve than with a more elastic demand curve. Consequently, when demand is less elastic the price rises more to consumers so that more of the tax is paid for by them, less of the tax is shifted backward to input suppliers. This means that, with a less elastic demand curve, input suppliers bear less of the burden of the tax than when demand is more elastic.

PET #4

A tax on the supply of a good shifts the supply of the good to the left, reduces the equilibrium quantity: sold, and, thus, reduces the demand for inputs used in producing the good and. thus, the price of inputs.

You should know from Chapter 4 of your textbook and the Study Guide that a leftward shift in the supply of good X reduces the equilibrium quantity (and raises the price of the good) of good X. From this, you should be able to logically infer that, if industry X is

Chapter 14

selling fewer units of output, it will need fewer units of inputs. In economics terms, this means that the demand for inputs will decline. You should also know from Chapter 4 of your textbook and the Study Guide that a decrease in the demand for any good (represented by a leftward shift in demand) will reduce the equilibrium price (and reduce the equilibrium quantity) of the good. In this case, the good is an input into good X.

One input into the production of most goods is labour. Thus, a tax on good X may not only raise the price of good X, it may also reduce the demand for labour (and other inputs) used in making good X. When the demand for labour declines, the equilibrium price (in this case, the wage) of labour and the equilibrium quantity will decline (that is, some workers will lose their jobs). You may want to review the Application on Luxury Taxes in Chapter 14 of your textbook.

V.   PRACTICE EXAM: MULTIPLE CHOICE QUESTIONS

1.   Which one of the following describes a public good?

   a.   It is rival in consumption and excludable.
   b.   It is non-rival in consumption and excludable.
   c.   It is rival in consumption and non-excludable.
   d.   It is non-rival in consumption and non-excludable.
   e.   None of the above.

2.   Which pair of the following is an example of a private good and a public good?

   a.   Preservation of endangered species/space exploration.
   b.   Public housing/free concert in a city park.
   c.   Highways/ice cream.
   d.   Newspapers/golf courses.
   e.   Law enforcement/national defence.

3.   Which one of the following statements is NOT true?

   a.   The government spends money only on public goods, not private goods.
   b.   Public and private goods can both generate spillover benefits.
   c.   The interaction of market demand and supply will not necessarily lead to an efficient outcome if a good generates spillover benefits or costs.
   d.   Education is likely to generate a workplace spillover.
   e.   A government subsidy for a good with a spillover (external) benefit can lead to a more efficient outcome.

4. Which one of the following statements is NOT true of a subsidy?

   a. Subsidies are often given in the case of private goods that carry spillover (external) benefits.
   b. Subsidies internalize a spillover (external) benefit.
   c. Taxpayers ultimately pay for subsidies.
   d. A subsidy for education might come in the form of government grants for financial aid.
   e. All of the above are true of subsidies.

5. Which one of the following is NOT an example of a private good with a spillover benefit?

   a. Education.
   b. On-the-job training.
   c. The space program.
   d. Preventative health care.
   e. Research at private universities.

6. Which one of the following explains why the government may not always make good choices about which goods to provide and which goods to subsidize?

   a. Inadequate information on the true benefits and costs of a particular good.
   b. A tax system that cannot always impose higher taxes on those who would use more of a public good than others.
   c. Special interest groups lobby for their own interests and policymakers often give in to them.
   d. People do not always reveal the true amount of benefits they would receive from certain government projects and programs.
   e. All of the above.

7. Which one of the following explains why voluntary contributions typically do not work as a way of funding public goods and goods with spillover benefits?

   a. The free-rider problem.
   b. The chump problem
   c. The anonymity problem.
   d. The no-free-lunch problem.
   e. X-gifting.

8. Which one of the following is NOT true of voluntary contributions as a way of funding public goods and goods with spillover benefits?

   a. Some citizens will not contribute at all.
   b. Some citizens will contribute an amount that is small relative to the benefits they receive from the good.
   c. Voluntary contributions work better than taxes at ensuring that a project is funded.
   d. Voluntary contributions may increase through programs like "matching contributions" and giving coffee mugs, etc., to contributors.
   e. Public radio and TV has been very successful at overcoming the free-rider problem.

9. Suppose the government imposes a tax on the sale of new refrigerators. The government collects the tax from appliance centres and other outlets that sell the refrigerators. Who pays for the tax, assuming market demand is negatively sloped and supply is a horizontal?

   a. Consumers.
   b. Consumers and refrigerator input suppliers.
   c. Appliance centres and other outlets.
   d. Consumers and appliance centres.
   e. Refrigerator input suppliers.

10. Which one of the following statements is true of a tax that is collected from producers in a perfectly competitive market?

    a. It shifts the demand curve to the left.
    b. The demand for inputs will decline and so will the price of inputs.
    c. In the long run, producers' profits will decline.
    d. The price of output will decline.
    e. It shifts the supply curve to the right.

11. Consider the market for yachts. A tax on yachts collected by the government from yacht producers will:

    a. Shift more of the tax forward to consumers if demand is inelastic than if it is inelastic.
    b. Put the tax burden on consumers and yacht input suppliers, including workers in the yachting industry.
    c. Reduce the price of yacht inputs by more if input supply is inelastic rather than elastic.
    d. Reduce the equilibrium quantity of yachts sold.
    e. All of the above.

Use Figure 14-2 to answer the following question.

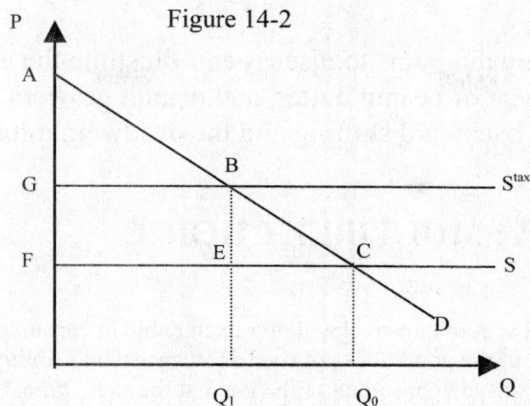

Figure 14-2

12. The deadweight loss (excess burden) of a tax placed on gasoline is given by:

    a. area ABG.
    b. area BCE.
    c. area GBCF.
    d. area GBFE.
    e. area ABC.

13. The median-voter rule:

    a. is that people vote with their feet, i.e., move to communities where their median preferences are reflected.
    b. may not be true if people cannot vote on individual issues but must instead vote on packages.
    c. suggests that the decisions made by elected officials may not always be the most efficient.
    d. implies that candidates for office will take extreme positions.
    e. (a) and (c).

14. Public choice economics suggests that government decisions are made based on:

    a. the government's desire to make the economy operate more efficiently.
    b. the median voter.
    c. the self-interest of politicians.
    d. people voting with their feet.
    e. all of the above.

VI.   PRACTICE EXAM: ESSAY QUESTIONS

15. Suppose that you are the head of a government agency that oversees retraining programs for the unemployed. Discuss whether the service that your agency delivers is a public or private good. Will the private market of demand and supply lead to an

efficient outcome? Why or why not? Discuss how your agency is funded. How well do you think a voluntary contribution scheme would work in funding your program?

16. Use demand and supply diagrams to discuss and illustrate the effects of a tax on peanut butter, consumers of peanut butter, and peanut growers. Be sure to discuss the extent of forward and backward shifting and the deadweight loss caused by the tax.

VII.   ANSWER KEY: MULTIPLE CHOICE

1.   Correct answer: d.

Discussion: A public good is both non-rival and non-excludable in consumption. Non-rival means that one person's consumption of the good does not rival another person's ability to consume/use the good. That is, more than one person can consume/use the good at the same time. Non-excludable means that people who do not pay for the good cannot be excluded from using and receiving the benefits of the good. Thus, even if one person were to pay for the good, others could use it without having to pay for it.

Statement a describes a private good. A private good can only be consumed and, thus, enjoyed by the consumer. That is, it is rival in consumption. A private good can also only be consumed/used by the person paying for it. That is, a private good is excludable. Reading a book, attending a movie, going to a private school, buying a house, and eating an ice cream cone are some examples.

As an aside, you should remember that a private good could have spillover benefits as can a public good.

2.   Correct answer: b.

Discussion: Public housing is both rival and excludable in consumption even though it is a government-provided good. A free concert in a city park is non-rival and non-excludable. More than one person can enjoy it and people can enjoy it regardless of whether they pay for it. Of course, citizens who live around the park who may not prefer the noise of the concert will experience a spillover (external) cost.

Statement a is an example of two public goods. Statement c is an example of a public good/private good (instead of vice-versa). Statement d is an example of two private goods. Statement e is an example of two public goods.

3.   Correct answer: a.

Discussion: Statement a is not true because a government spends money on public goods like highways, law enforcement, and the armed forces as well as on education (a private good with spillover benefits), housing, and food (a private good).

Statement b is true because a public good like the space program can generate spillover benefits -- high-tech companies may learn new and improved ways to do things from the space program. Private goods like education, health care, and even deodorant create spillover benefits. Statement c is true because, when a private good has spillovers, not all of the benefits and costs of the good are revealed in the demand and supply curves. That is, not all of the consumers or even producers are represented in the demand and supply curves. Statement d is true -- education generates not only workplace but also civic spillovers. Statement e is true because the government, by subsidizing particular goods, is attempting to achieve a more desirable (truthful) market outcome.

4.   Correct answer: e.

Discussion: All of the above are true of a subsidy. While statement a is true, it does not mean that the government provides subsidies to any and every private good that carries a spillover benefit. Statement b means that a subsidy forces an external benefit to be reflected in the market demand curve. Statement d suggests that there are many ways in which the government can give money back to citizens for the purchase of a private good. Statement c is also true, as discussed in PET #2.

5. Correct answer: c.

Discussion: Statement c is an example of a public good, not a private good, which has spillover benefits. All of the other examples are examples of private goods with spillover benefits.

6. Correct answer: e.

Discussion: The government does not always end up funding projects and programs that are efficient from an economic perspective. Statements a-d all provide reasons why this may happen. Statements a and d are related in that the government will have inadequate information on the true costs and benefits of a particular program if people are not truthful in revealing how much they would really benefit (and presumably pay) for a good.

7. Correct answer: a.

Discussion: The free-rider problem is that people who benefit from a program may not be willing to pay for it because they figure that other people who benefit from it will contribute to it. Thus, the free rider will get to use the program without having to pay for it. The problem is that, when everyone behaves this way, the program does not receive enough funds to be funded and, thus, the program is not started up and nobody gets to use it.

8. Correct answer: c.

Discussion: Statement c is not true; taxes work better at ensuring that a project is funded than do voluntary contributions. In effect, a tax ensures that everybody pays for the project, not just those willing to contribute.

Statements a and b reflect a common problem with voluntary contributions. Statement d suggests that there are ways (that are costly to somebody, however) to increase voluntary contributions to a specific project. Statement e is true. In fact, public radio and television in the United States have used some of the tactics listed in statement d as a way of increasing voluntary contributions.

9. Correct answer: b.

Discussion: A tax leads to "forward shifting" – i.e., consumers pay some of the tax and "backward shifting" – i.e., input suppliers pay some of the tax (in the form of receiving a lower price for the inputs they provide). While the appliance centre may write and send the check to the government, the tax dollars paid by the appliance centre are, in effect, collected from the consumers and input suppliers. As an aside, if the demand for refrigerators were vertical (perfectly inelastic), consumers would pay for the entire tax.

10. Correct answer: b.

Discussion: shifting the supply curve to the left represents a tax collected from producers. Thus, statements a and e are not true. As the supply curve shifts to the left, the price of output will rise. Thus, statement d is not true. Statement c is not true because, as your textbook points out, producers' profits remain at zero in the long run. Statement b is true because, when the supply curve shifts to the left, not only does the price rise, but also the equilibrium quantity falls. Suppose the good in question is furniture. As the equilibrium quantity of furniture sold declines, the demand for inputs used in making furniture, like labour and wood, will decline. As the demand for these inputs declines, the price of the inputs declines. (See PET #4 for review.)

11. Correct answer: e.

Discussion: A tax on yachts will shift the supply of yachts to the left. If demand for yachts is inelastic (steeper), the price paid by consumers will increase by more than if the demand for a yacht was elastic (see PET #3 for review). As just discussed in the answer to question (10), consumers and input suppliers of yachts both bear the burden of the tax. Since the demand for inputs will decline, there will be a drop in the price of yacht inputs. The price drop will be bigger the more inelastic is the supply of the inputs.

Chapter 14

12. Correct answer: b.

Discussion: The deadweight loss is the loss in the area of consumer surplus that is not covered by the gain in tax revenue collected by the government. In this case, the initial consumer surplus area is area ACF. After the tax, when the price goes up, the consumer surplus area is ABG. The loss in consumer surplus is thus GBCF. However, the gain in tax revenue is the amount of the tax times the equilibrium quantity. The area GBEF measures this. Thus, the deadweight loss is the difference between the area GBCF and area GBEF, which is area BCE.

13. Correct answer: e.

Discussion: The median-voter rule is that government decisions made by elected officials represent the preferences of the median voter, which is the voter whose preferences are exactly midway between the preferences of all of the voters. However, the median-voter rule is best applied to government decisions that are made on an individual basis rather than as part of a package. That is, the median-voter rule may not be correct if voters vote "yes" or "no" on a package of programs rather than "yes" or "no" on each item in the package. Also, the median-voter rule means that the most efficient outcomes are not necessarily guaranteed. Since the median voter's preferences do not necessarily reflect the most efficient outcomes for society, there is no guarantee that the median-voter rule will lead to the most efficient government decisions.

Statement a is not the definition of the median-voter rule. Statement d is not true of the median-voter rule; in fact, the median-voter rule implies that candidates will come closer and closer in their positions on issues as Election Day approaches.

14. Correct answer: e.

Discussion: There are many views in public choice economics on how the government actually arrives at the decisions that it makes. All of the above are possible and not necessarily mutually exclusive.

VIII. ANSWER KEY: ESSAY QUESTIONS

15. The worker-retraining program is a private good with spillover benefits. It is a private good because only those enrolled in the retraining program are able to use it. Furthermore, only companies that pay for the program, also supported by subsidies from the government, are able to use it. However, there are spillover benefits to the retraining program. Not only do the unemployed and the companies using the program benefit, but society benefits as well. People who are employed pay taxes and are less likely to get involved in illegal activities. Since the retraining program has spillover benefits, the market demand and supply curves will not lead to an efficient outcome, i.e., not enough retraining will be provided by the private market on its own. This is why the government subsidizes the worker retraining programs. This gets the private market to "internalize" the external benefits. While my agency is funded through subsidies provided by the government and also through companies paying into the program for its use, the government subsidies ultimately come from tax-paying citizens.

A voluntary contribution scheme would probably not lead to the level of support currently provided because of the free-rider problem. What typically happens under a voluntary contribution scheme is that some people who use the program will not contribute anything at all while others will contribute but not in accordance with the actual benefits they receive. Thus, a voluntary contribution scheme would likely lead to an under-funded program which may not be able to continue to run. Of course, I might suggest that our agency's fundraising efforts include matching contributions and free gifts. However, somebody will have to pay for these.

16. A tax on peanut butter is represented by a leftward shift in the supply curve in Figure 14-3. The supply curve of peanut butter is drawn to reflect the short run. Thus, the leftward shift in the supply curve also appears as an upward shift showing: that, at every quantity supplied the price at which suppliers would now be willing to produce would be higher. This is because part of the money they receive on the sales of peanut butter will have to be paid in taxes to the government. The leftward shift in the supply curve does two things: (1) the equilibrium price of peanut butter rises; and (2) the equilibrium quantity of peanut butter falls.

Public Goods, Taxes, and Public Choice

Figure 14-3

P

S^{tax}

S

$4.25 G   H

$4.00

$3.75 J   K   I

D

Q

5000   5500

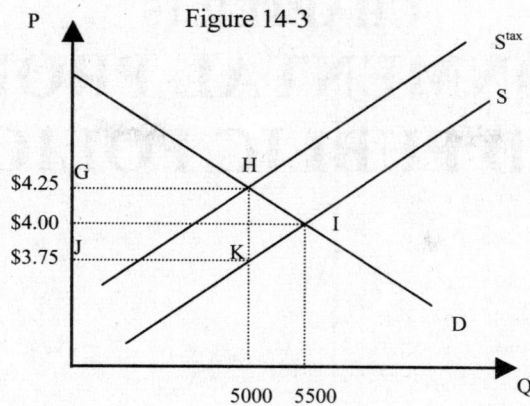

The rise in the price of peanut butter means that consumers will now pay more for peanut butter. That is, some of the tax is shifted forward to consumers. The equilibrium price rises but not by the full $0.50. The extent of the price increase to consumers depends on how elastic the demand for peanut butter is. If the demand for peanut butter is very elastic (perhaps because there are a lot of close substitutes like cream cheese, butter, jelly, etc.), the price rise will not be very great – certainly not the full $0.50. Suppose the equilibrium price increases from $4.00 a jar to $4.25. Suppliers must still pay $0.50 per jar in taxes to the government, which means the supplier will be left with $3.75. The price that they receive per jar of peanut butter has effectively dropped from $4.00 to $3.75. Will their profits decrease?

Perhaps in the short run, but in the long run the costs of peanut butter production may fall so that in the end the producer may still be earning $4.00 per jar of peanut butter. The reason the cost of peanut butter production will fall is that the equilibrium quantity of peanut butter sold drops. Peanut butter producers thus need less peanut butter to bring to the market. This, in turn, means that peanut butter producers will not need to buy as many peanuts. So, the demand for peanuts will decrease and this will bring down the price of peanuts, an input into the production of peanut butter. Thus, peanut growers in effect bear some of the burden of the tax because they receive a lower price for their output. This is the backward-shifting nature of the tax. In the long run, with a tax of $0.50, peanut growers will receive $0.25 less for their peanuts, which means that the cost of production to the peanut butter producers will decline. That's why the peanut butter producer is still, in a way, receiving $4.00 per jar of peanut butter. Or, you could say the profit per jar of peanut butter will be unchanged before and after the tax.

As for the tax revenue, the government collects $0.50 per jar of peanut butter. The new equilibrium quantity (let's say it is 5,000 jars per week) times the tax per jar gives the government $2,500 in tax revenue per week.

As for consumers, they pay a higher price for peanut butter and purchase a smaller equilibrium quantity so their consumer surplus declines. Figure 14-3 shows that the decline in consumer and producer surplus (area GHIJK) exceeds the gain in tax revenue (area GHKJ) so that, on net, there is a deadweight loss to society equal to area HIK.

Chapter 14

153

CHAPTER 15
ENVIRONMENTAL PROBLEMS AND PUBLIC POLICY

I.   OVERVIEW

In this chapter, you will learn about the economic consequences and policy surrounding environmental problems. You will learn how a public policy, such as a tax on polluters, both leads to firms taking steps to cut the pollution that they create when they produce output and reduces the amount of output that polluters produce. You will also learn that the government can use regulation to reduce the amount of pollution that producers may be generating. You will learn about the traditional or compliance-based form of pollution regulation and the market-based incentive form of pollution regulation. You will learn which policy is most efficient from an economic standpoint. You will learn about global warming, ozone depletion, acid rain, and urban smog and how public policy has been devised to address these problems.

II.   CHECKLIST

By the end of this chapter, you should be able to:
- Explain the two ways in which a pollution tax reduces the level of pollution.
- Explain the effects of a tax on pollution using demand and supply.
- Use the marginal principle to determine how much abatement a firm would undertake in response to a pollution tax.
- Discuss how command and control regulations work to reduce pollution.
- Compare the efficiency of command and control regulations to a tax.
- Explain the effects of pollution regulation using demand and supply.
- Discuss how market-based pollution permits work to reduce pollution.
- Compare the efficiency of pollution permits to a tax and regulations.
- Explain when pollution permits will be traded – who will buy and who will sell them.
- Compare the effects of marketable versus non-marketable permits in reducing the amount of pollution.
- Discuss some of the shortcomings of pollution permits.
- Explain some of the economic effects of global warming on agriculture.
- Discuss the economic effects of a carbon tax on reducing global warming.

- ❑ Discuss the economic effects of a ban on CFCs aimed at reducing ozone depletion.
- ❑ Discuss the type of regulation currently used to control urban smog and suggest some alternative policies.
- ❑ Explain how common-pool resources generate problems similar to pollution.
- ❑ Discuss how individual transferable quotas work to reduce over-fishing.

III.   KEY TERMS

Pollution tax: a tax or charge equal to the spillover cost per unit of waste.

Spillover cost: the cost from a good that is experienced by people who did not decide how much of the good to produce or consume.

Negative externality: another term for a spillover cost; some of the costs are external to the decision-maker.

Command and control policy: a pollution-control policy under which the government *commands* each firm to produce no more than a certain volume of pollution and *controls* the firm's production process by forcing the firm to use a particular pollution-control technology.

Marketable pollution permits system: a system under which the government picks a target pollution level for a particular area, issues just enough pollution permits to meet the pollution target, and allows firms to buy and sell the permits.

Carbon tax: a tax based on a fuel's carbon content.

Common-pool resources: resources for which it is costly to exclude users, so costs are, in part, shared by all users.

Individual transferable quotas (ITQs): tradable quotas that limit holders to a certain percentage of the year's total allowable catch in a particular fishery.

IV.   PERFORMANCE ENHANCING TIPS (PETS)

<u>PET #1</u>

A spillover cost of production (such as pollution) is a cost that producers do not explicitly pay for unless they are forced to by the government.

Consider a firm that produces chemicals. A by-product of the production process is that some emissions are released into the air. The emissions create pollution, which creates health hazards for which people ultimately pay. The chemical producer generates a spillover cost by polluting the air and creating costs for other members of society. Because air is free, the chemical producer does not have to explicitly pay for the "use of the air." A tax on the chemical producer, in effect, forces it to pay for the cost of the air (and indirectly, assuming the tax revenues are used to help clean up the air) for the health costs that spill over to society.

PET #2

"Abatement" is the term economist's use for "pollution clean-up" or "pollution reduction".

When a firm undertakes an abatement project, it is cleaning up (or at least reducing) the amount of pollution that it creates.

You should also know that the marginal cost of pollution reduction increases as the firm attempts to lower the level of pollution. That is, the cost of *reducing* pollution by one unit, and then by one more, and then by one more, increases. For example, Table 15-1 in Chapter 15 of your textbook shows that, as waste-per-tonne of output is reduced from 5 litres of waste-per-tonne to 0 litres of waste-per-tonne, the production cost of one tonne of output increases. This means, in effect, that the cost of doing more and more clean up for the same one tonne of output increases. Using the numbers from Table 15-1, the clean-up costs increase from $60 to $116. The marginal cost of eliminating a litre of waste from 5 litres to 4 litres is $1 ($61-$60), and the marginal cost of eliminating a litre of waste from 4 litres to 3 litres is $3 ($64-$61), and so on. Thus, the marginal cost increases.

PET #3

A tax imposed on a polluter increases their cost of production and, hence, the price at which they sell their output. This is represented by a leftward shift in the supply curve. The equilibrium quantity of output the producer sells will decline. The tax works to reduce the amount of pollution by (1) reducing the amount of production the firm undertakes (and consequently the pollution that results), and (2) by motivating the firm to devise abatement methods so as to avoid having to pay the tax. Thus, new and improved methods of abatement may emerge.

PET #4

A sale of a pollution permit from one firm to another will occur if two conditions are satisfied: (1) the seller receives more money from the sale of the permit than is his marginal cost of having to abate, and the buyer pays less for the permit than is his marginal cost of having to abate; and (2) the buyer is willing to pay an amount to the seller which is equal to or more than the seller is willing to sell the permit for.

Condition (1) can be explained in the following way. A seller of a permit gives up some of his right to pollute. Without the right to pollute, the seller must abate (do pollution clean up). If the seller can receive, say, $500,000 for his permit but must pay $400,000 to devise a clean-up method, the seller will sell the permit. A buyer of a permit thereby obtains the right to pollute more than he is currently polluting. With the right, the seller doesn't have to clean up as much, so the cost of abatement (pollution clean-up) declines. If the buyer can pay, say $500,000 for a permit to pollute and, thus, avoids $600,000 in abatement costs, the buyer will purchase the permit. The overall pollution reduction designed by the permit system is achieved by the firms for which it is least costly to do so. This is just an application of the marginal principle.

Condition (2) is just a way of saying that the buyer's willingness to pay is greater than or equal to the seller's willingness to accept. To put it in more practical terms, suppose you would like to buy a used TV for your apartment or dorm room and the amount you would be willing to pay is $100. If the seller is willing to accept $75, then a deal could be struck. You may buy the TV for $85. In the example above, if the seller of the permit was willing to sell at $500,000 and the buyer was willing to pay at $600,000, a deal could be struck.

V.   PRACTICE EXAM: MULTIPLE CHOICE QUESTIONS

1.   Which one of the following is NOT a public policy for reducing pollution?

    a.   A tax on polluters.
    b.   Marketable permits for pollution.
    c.   Non-marketable permits for pollution.
    d.   Government regulation.
    e.   Subsidies to polluters.

2.   In economics, pollution:

    a.   is a spillover (external) cost.
    b.   is a private good.
    c.   generates diminishing returns.
    d.   is really a cost of production.
    e.   (a) and (d).

3.   Which one of the following is an effect of a pollution tax on paper production?

    a.   The price of paper will decline.
    b.   Paper producers will have an incentive to abate.
    c.   The quantity of paper produced will rise.
    d.   The marginal cost of paper production will decline.
    e.   None of the above.

4.   Which one of the following is true of traditional pollution regulation (command and control policy)?

    a.   The policy imposes that a single abatement technology (method of clean-up) be used.
    b.   It creates an incentive to pollute.
    c.   It encourages innovation in new and less costly methods of abatement.
    d.   It is less costly than imposing a tax on polluters.
    e.   All of the above are true.

Use the Table 15-1 to answer the following question.

Table 15-1		
Waste-per-tonne	**Clean-up Cost (per tonne)**	**Tax Cost (per tonne)**
20 litres	$100	$60
19 litres	$102	$57
18 litres	$106	$54
17 litres	$112	$51
16 litres	$120	$48

5. What is the optimal amount of waste-per-tonne that a firm will decide to emit?

   a. 20 litres.
   b. 19 litres.
   c. 18 litres.
   d. 17 litres.
   e. 16 litres.

6. Which one of the following is true of a comparison between a pollution tax and traditional pollution regulation?

   a. Regulation raises the price of the output of the polluter more than would a pollution tax.
   b. Firms produce and sell less output under regulation than a tax.
   c. Pollution is reduced by less with a regulation than with a tax.
   d. Regulation does not produce any tax revenue that can be used to fund other clean-up projects.
   e. All of the above.

7. Marketable pollution permits:

   a. make it hard to predict how much pollution abatement will actually take place.
   b. can only be bought and sold by polluters.
   c. may lead to severe pollution in some areas.
   d. lead to the high-abatement-cost firms selling the permits and the low-abatement-cost firms buying the permits.
   e. are not as effective as non-marketable permits at reducing the amount of pollution.

8. Which one of the following would explain why a firm might not sell its marketable pollution permit?

    a. The cost to the firm of reducing pollution is greater than the price the firm will get for selling the permit.

    b. The cost to the firm of reducing pollution is less than the price the firm will get for selling the permit.

    c. The cost to the firm of increasing pollution is greater than the price the firm will get for selling tine permit.

    d. The cost to the firm of increasing pollution is less than the price the firm will get for selling the permit.

    e. None of the above.

9. Which one of the following is NOT true of global warming?

    a. It is due to an accumulation of carbon dioxide in the atmosphere.

    b. There is uncertainty about how much the earth's temperature will actually rise.

    c. Total rainfall is expected to decrease.

    d. A carbon tax (a tax on the burning of fossil fuels like oil, coal, and gasoline) is one solution aimed at reducing the pace of global warming.

    e. Sea levels are expected to increase.

10. Which one of the following is NOT expected to be an effect of the ban on production of CFCs (chlorofluorocarbons)?

    a. A slower pace of ozone depletion.

    b. Innovation of products that achieve the same purpose as CFCs.

    c. Short-run increase in the price of refrigerators.

    d. Innovation in products that have previously used CFCs.

    e. All of the above.

11. Which one of the following statements is true?

    a. A recent study of global warming suggests that crop production may fall substantially.

    b. Acid rain in Canada is controlled through regulation and pollution taxes.

    c. A ban on the production of CFCs has been in place since 1985.

    d. The government currently uses non-marketable permits to control the amount of urban smog.

    e. All of the above are true.

VI.   PRACTICE EXAM: ESSAY QUESTIONS

12. Explain how a tax on polluters works to help reduce the amount of pollution.

13. Explain how a system of marketable permits to pollute works to reduce the amount of pollution. Be sure to discuss who will buy and sell the permits and why some communities do not like the system.

VII.   ANSWER KEY: MULTIPLE CHOICE QUESTIONS

1.   Correct answer: e.

   Discussion: A subsidy to a polluter may not discourage them from polluting. All of the other public policies are discussed in your textbook as ways in which the government attempts to reduce the amount of pollution.

2.   Correct answer: e.

   Discussion: Pollution is a spillover cost of production because it imposes costs on other segments of society that bear the costs of pollution such as health costs, inability to use a river to fish or a lake to swim, etc. Pollution should also rightly be considered a cost of production because a firm that pollutes a river or the air is using the river or the air in the production process. Thus, it should be treated as a cost just like the use of labour and raw materials is considered a cost of production.

   Statement b is not correct because pollution is a public good (that is, in fact, bad). Statement c is not correct because the reduction of pollution entails increasing marginal costs.

3.   Correct answer: b.

   Discussion: A tax forces the polluting firm to bear some of the cost of polluting in production. Since the tax imposes a cost on the firm, the firm has an incentive to avoid it by finding methods of abatement.

   Statement a is not correct because the price of paper will rise. Statement c is not correct because the quantity of paper produced will decline. Statement d is not correct because the marginal cost of abatement will increase. Statement e cannot be correct because statement b is true.

4.   Correct answer: a.

   Discussion: A command and control pollution policy imposed by regulators forces all firms in the same industry to use the same method of abatement.

   Statement b is not true; regulation does not create the incentive to pollute but rather forces the polluter not to pollute. Statement c is not true because the policy discourages innovation in pollution abatement by dictating that all firms use the same method of clean up. Statement d is not true because command and control regulation is more costly to polluters than a tax. Statement e is not true because statement a is true.

5.   Correct answer: b.

   Discussion: The marginal cost of reducing pollution from 20 litres to 19 litres per tonne is $2 whereas, if the polluter did not clean up, the tax cost would be $3. (The government forces the polluter to pay $3 more to pollute 20 litres instead of 19 litres). Thus, the marginal cost of abatement is less than the tax cost, so the firm should abate.

   The marginal cost of reducing pollution from 19 litres to 18 litres per tonne is $4 whereas, if the polluter did not clean up that one more litre of waste, the tax cost would be $3. Since the tax cost of polluting by one more litre is less than the cost of cleaning up, the polluter will not clean up but will instead pay the tax cost. The same reasoning applies to the 17th and 16th litres.

6.   Correct answer: e.

Discussion: A pollution tax is more efficient than traditional pollution regulation. All of the statements above are reasons why it is more efficient.

7.   Correct answer: c.

Discussion: Marketable pollution permits mean that a firm that buys the permit has the right to pollute more than the target level set by the government. Thus, some firms with high costs of abatement will buy up a lot of permits and pollute a lot. If the firm resides in your community, your community will experience a lot of pollution.

Statement a is not true because marketable pollution permits make it easy to predict how much pollution will be emitted by firms, collectively. While the government cannot predict how much each firm will emit individually, the government can predict how much firms will in total (collectively) emit. Statement b is not true because environmental groups can purchase marketable pollution permits, as well. Statement d is not true; it is the reverse – low-abatement-cost firms sell their permits to high-abatement-cost firms. Statement e is not true because marketable permits are more effective than non-marketable permits in reducing the amount of pollution.

8.   Correct answer: a.

Discussion: If the firm sells its permit, it will not have the right to pollute as much and, thus, will have to do more clean up. This implies that the firm will incur additional clean up costs. If the cost of clean up is more than the firm can receive from the sale of its permit, it will choose to hold on to the permit and thereby avoid the cost of clean up. If it chose to sell its permit, it would not receive enough money to cover the clean-up costs that it would incur as a result of not having a permit to pollute. Thus, based on the marginal principle, it makes sense not to sell the permit.

Based on the above reasoning, statements b, c, d and e cannot be true. In fact, statement b suggests that the firm would sell the permit. This is because the price the firm would receive from selling the permit is greater than the costs of clean up it will incur without having the permit.

9.   Correct answer: c.

Discussion: Global warming is expected to increase, not decrease, the amount of rainfall. All of the other statements are true.

10. Correct answer: e.

Discussion: The ban on CFCs has been established for the purpose of reducing the pace of ozone depletion (and, thus, the amount, too). The ban on CFCs will inspire innovation in products that previously used CFCs as well as in finding a replacement for CFCs. Because refrigerators (air conditioners, hairspray, etc.) used CFCs in the past and must now find another technology that achieves the same purpose as CFCs, the cost of producing a refrigerator will rise, at least in the short run.

11. Correct answer: b.

Discussion: Currently, Canada has chosen to rely on command and control policies to control the amount of emissions (SO_x, NO_x, and VOCs) that eventually lead to acid rain. As stated in your textbook, Canada has experimented with marketable pollution permits, but has yet to implement such a scheme.

A recent study of global warming suggests that crop production may not fall by as much as previously predicted, in part because farmers will find new ways of growing crops just as efficiently as before in a "globally-warmed" climate. The ban on CFCs has been in place since 1996 (although Canada did not sign onto the ban until 1998). The government currently uses a traditional command and control regulatory policy to control urban smog.

Chapter 15

VIII. ANSWER KEY: ESSAY QUESTIONS

12. A tax on polluters implicitly raises their cost of production as they must pay for the tax or adopt methods of abatement to avoid the tax. Abatement, of course, is a cost to the firm. However, since the tax creates the incentive to adopt methods of abatement, pollution will be reduced by the abatement actions of the firms. Secondly, a pollution tax raises the cost of output that the polluter produces. (This is represented by a leftward shift in supply). A higher cost of production is, in part, passed on to consumers through a higher consumer price. The higher price reduces the equilibrium quantity of the output demanded. Firms respond by producing less of the output, which means they, in turn, end up polluting less. It may also happen that firms invent a similar product that has a manufacturing process that does not pollute or pollutes by much less.

13. A system of marketable permits is a new form of regulation aimed at reducing the amount of pollution. Under such a system, the government sets a target limit of pollution that they desire to achieve. They then give firms permits to pollute, but only by a specified amount. The innovation is that firms can buy and sell the permits so that they are not constrained to pollute only up to the amount allotted in the permit. However, in total, the target amount of pollution desired by the government is maintained. For example, suppose there are only two firms that pollute and the government issues permits to each of them allowing them to emit 30 tonnes of waste per year. The government's target level of pollution is thus 60 tonnes of waste per year. If one firm sells its permit to the other, the selling firm can no longer emit any waste (it must completely abate) and the buying firm is now permitted to emit up to 60 tonnes of waste per year. Thus, the target level of waste per year is achieved while each individual firm's emission level may vary.

    A firm for which it is very expensive to abate (clean up) will be a buyer of a permit if the price they have to pay for the permit (the right to pollute) is less costly than having to clean up. A firm for which it is not very expensive to abate will be a seller of a permit if the price it can sell their permit for is greater than the cost of having to clean up. In this case, the money it receives for the permit would pay for the firm's clean up and leave it with extra money that it could use elsewhere. For a deal to be struck, the buyer's willingness to pay must be equal to or greater than the seller's willingness to accept. For example, if the buyer was willing to pay $200,000 for a permit and the seller was willing to accept $175,000, then the two could likely reach a price at which an exchange of the permit for money would take place.

    Some citizens do not like the system of marketable permits because they may end up getting a lot more pollution in their community, especially if they have a high-cost-of-abatement firm in their town. The high-cost-of-abatement firm is much more likely to be a buyer of permits and, thus, will acquire the right to pollute more rather than less under the policy.

CHAPTER 16
IMPERFECT INFORMATION AND DISAPPEARING MARKETS

I.   OVERVIEW

In this chapter, you will learn about the effect of imperfect information on buyers and sellers and the price at which they strike deals. You will learn that markets with imperfect information are typically "mixed markets" meaning that the quality of a good sold in a particular market is not uniform and that it is difficult for buyers to know whether the good that they are purchasing is of high or low quality. That is, there is a chance that a buyer will purchase a high quality good and a chance that a buyer will end up purchasing a low quality version of the same good. You will learn that imperfect information arises when one side of the market (either buyers or sellers) has more information about the good in question than the other side of the market. You will learn that this situation is referred to as an information asymmetry and that it arises most commonly in the market for used goods and insurance. You will learn about the adverse-selection problem. You will also learn what a thin market is and why it occurs. You will use probabilities to compute expected amounts that uninformed buyers may be willing to pay. You will learn about some methods used to overcome the asymmetric information problem. You will also learn about applications of asymmetric information to the market for used cars, baseball pitchers, and auto insurance.

II.   CHECKLIST

By the end of this chapter, you should be able to:
- ❑ Define asymmetric information.
- ❑ Explain the effects of asymmetric information on the price, quality, and volume of a good sold in a market.
- ❑ Apply the asymmetric information problem to a market for used goods or insurance.
- ❑ Explain why asymmetric information typically raises the cost of insurance and lowers the price of used goods.
- ❑ Explain why the actual probability of a buyer purchasing a lemon (low quality good) in a used market is greater than the probability that may be casually assumed.
- ❑ Define the adverse-selection problem and explain what gives rise to it.
- ❑ Define a thin market and explain what gives rise to it.

- ❑ Define the moral hazard problem and explain what gives rise to it.
- ❑ Use probabilities to compute expected prices.

III. KEY TERMS

Asymmetric information: one side of the market – either buyers or sellers – has better information than the other about a good or service.

Adverse-selection problem: the uninformed side of the market must choose from an undesirable or adverse selection of goods.

Thin market: a market in which some high quality goods or services are sold, but fewer than would be sold in a market with perfect information.

Moral hazard: a situation where one party to an agreement may be able to act in a way that benefits him- or herself at the expense of the other party.

IV. PERFORMANCE ENHANCING TIPS (PETS)

<u>PET # 1</u>

The expected (or average) amount that a buyer is willing to pay for a good of unknown quality is computed using the probabilities associated with whether the good is high or low quality (we'll assume only two categories of qualities) and what the corresponding prices would be for a good of a certain quality.

Let's suppose that you are considering buying a used computer. You are aware that more lemon computers are likely to be sold in the used market than not. Suppose the probability of getting a faulty computer is 75% and the probability of buying a good computer is 25%. If the going price for a good used computer were $1,000 and the going price for a faulty used computer were $200, what is the expected price at which used computers will sell in the mixed market of good and faulty computers?

To answer the question, use the following formula:

$$\left(\frac{\text{probability of high quality good}}{100}\right) * \left(\text{price of high quality good}\right) + \left(\frac{\text{probability of low quality good}}{100}\right) * \left(\text{price of low quality good}\right)$$

Thus, your answer to the question should be:

$$\left(\frac{25}{100}\right) * (\$1000) + \left(\frac{75}{100}\right) * (200) = \$400$$

The probability of a low (or high) quality good in the market can be determined by dividing the observations of a low (or high) quality good by the total number of goods (i.e., sum of low plus high quality goods).

Suppose you have done some research on the market for used evening gowns and determined that in your city, 30 used evening gowns are typically for sale each month. Further, you've determined that typically, 20 of the used evening gowns are very high quality and that 10 of the evening gowns are low quality. What is the probability in any given month that you or somebody that you may give advice to will buy a low quality evening gown?

The probability of purchasing a low quality evening gown is (10/30) * 100 = 33.3%

Thus, the probability of buying a high quality evening gown must be 66.7% (100% - 33.3%).

V.   PRACTICE EXAM: MULTIPLE CHOICE QUESTIONS

1. A mixed market is one in which:

    a. consumers can be buyers and sellers and producers can be sellers and buyers.
    b. there are different qualities of a good being sold in the market and there is imperfect information about the quality of each good.
    c. a seller of a good requires that the purchase of one good be tied to the purchase of another.
    d. demand is positively sloped and supply is negatively sloped.
    e. none of the above.

2. In a market for used goods,

    a. the seller has more information than the buyer about the quality of the good.
    b. the buyer has more information than the seller about the quality of the good.
    c. there are no high quality used goods for sale.
    d. low quality used goods will be underpriced.
    e. the quality of used goods sold in the market will typically rise over time.

3. Which one of the following is an example of asymmetric information?

    a. A grocery store selling cookies that are stale.
    b. A builder building a house with 4" instead of 6" studs.
    c. A company hiring an employee that has an addiction to sleeping pills.
    d. A seller at a flea market selling stolen goods.
    e. All of the above.

4. Which one of the following is true of a used market, e.g., used market for cars?

   a. A consumer typically overestimates the probability of getting a lemon (low quality car).
   b. The more pessimistic buyers become, their chance of buying a high quality car is high and the lower will be the price of all (low and high quality) used cars.
   c. There is an adverse-information problem.
   d. The willingness to pay and the willingness to accept are equal.
   e. (b) and (d).

5. The adverse-selection problem is that:

   a. the informed side of the market pays more for a good than the less informed side of the market.
   b. a seller does not inform a buyer of all of the add-on fees that will be incurred upon the purchase of a good.
   c. product differentiation makes it difficult to decide which product to buy.
   d. the uninformed side of the market must choose from an undesirable selection of goods.
   e. all of the above.

6. Which one of the following is an equilibrium?

   a. Buyers assume a 40% chance of getting a lemon and 8 lemons and 2 plums are supplied.
   b. Buyers assume a 60% chance of getting a lemon and 6 lemons and 4 plums are supplied.
   c. Buyers assume a 40% chance of getting a lemon and 4 lemons and 4 plums are supplied.
   d. Buyers assume an 80% chance of getting a lemon and 2 lemons and 8 plums are supplied.
   e. Buyers assume a 75% chance of getting a lemon and 7 lemons and 3 plums are supplied.

7. Which one of the following is NOT true of a thin market?

   a. It may be caused by asymmetric information.
   b. There are relatively few high quality goods sold.
   c. In a thin market, there may be some sellers of high quality goods because of extenuating circumstances (moving out of the country, increased family size, etc.)
   d. The price of a high quality good will be higher than if the market was thick.
   e. All of the above.

8. A mixed market is:

   a. dominated by low quality goods.
   b. one in which there is asymmetric information.
   c. one where buyers encounter an adverse-selection problem.
   d. typical of used goods and insurance.
   e. all of the above.

   Use the following information to answer the following question.

Average cost of settling a car accident of a careful driver	$6,000.
Average cost of settling a car accident of a reckless driver	$36,000.
Probability that a careful driver will want additional collision insurance	25%
Probability that a reckless driver will want additional collision insurance	75%

9. Assuming insurance companies cannot distinguish between careful and reckless drivers, an insurance company will charge $_____ for the additional car insurance and a careful driver would be inclined to _____ insurance.

   a. $28,500; not buy.
   b. $21,000; not buy.
   c. $36,000; not buy.
   d. $21,000; buy.
   e. $42,000; not buy.

VI.   PRACTICE EXAM: ESSAY QUESTIONS

10. Suppose you are a university admissions director and every year you receive 5,000 applications for admission to your school while your school only has 1,000 slots open. Your school is prestigious and has a reputation for producing some of the best and brightest graduates on the national market. What problems might you encounter as the admissions director? How might you handle them?

11. Explain the effects of asymmetric information on the price, quality, and volume of used computers sold in a market.

VII. ANSWER KEY: MULTIPLE CHOICE QUESTIONS

1. Correct answer: b.

    Discussion: In a mixed market, there are different qualities of a good being sold and unfortunately the buyer or seller of the good may not know for sure (has imperfect information) what the quality of the good is. The market for used goods is typically a mixed market as is the market for insurance.

    All of the other statements are bogus.

2. Correct answer: a.

    Discussion: A market for used goods is a market for which there is asymmetric information – in this case the information is asymmetric because the seller knows more about the true quality of the good than does the buyer.

    Based on the above, statement b is not true. Statement c is generally not true (only in extreme cases would no high quality used goods be for sale) because a market for used goods is also one that is "mixed" – high and low quality versions of the same good will be offered for sale. Statement d is not true because the price of low quality used goods is based on the price at which a high and low quality version of the good would be priced. This leads to a higher price for a low quality good than reflects its true value. Statement e is not true because there is a tendency for the quality of goods sold in a market for used goods to decrease over time.

3. Correct answer: e.

    Discussion: While asymmetric information typically arises in a market for used goods, it can occur elsewhere. All of the above examples are cases in which one party (the buyer or the seller) has more information about the product than the other party.

4. Correct answer: b.

    Discussion: When buyers become more pessimistic that their chance of buying a high quality car is high, they will attach a lower probability to the price they would be willing to pay for a high quality car and a higher probability to the price they would be willing to pay for a low quality car. This necessarily lowers the price that a buyer would be willing to pay for a car about which they have no information as to its quality.

    You may wish to review PET #1 and attach different probabilities to that, associated with buying a good computer and a faulty one and then see what happens to the expected price of the computer.

    Statement a is not true; consumers typically underestimate the probability of purchasing a lemon. Statement c is not correct because the term is "adverse selection" not "adverse information." Statement d is not true because there are typically differences in the willingness to pay and accept (which is why buyers and sellers bargain with each other). Statement e is not true because statement d is not true.

5. Correct answer: d.

    Discussion: The adverse-selection problem arises in a mixed market because the buyer does not know the quality of every good being sold in a particular market. That is, the uninformed side of the market must choose which good to buy knowing that some of the selection is of poor quality but not knowing which of the goods are poor quality.

6. Correct answer: b.

    Discussion: Equilibrium will be reached in the market when the assumed (or perceived) chance of purchasing a lemon is equal to the actual chance. In statement b, the actual chance is $(6/10) * 100 = 60\%$. (See PET #2 for review).

    Statement a is not correct because the actual chance is 80%. Statement c is not true because the actual chance is 50%. Statement d is not true because the actual chance of getting a lemon is 20%. Statement e is not true because the actual chance of getting a lemon is 70%.

Imperfect Information and Disappearing Markets

7. Correct answer: d.

    Discussion: A thin market is a market in which there are relatively few high quality goods but an abundance of low quality goods being offered for sale. This drives down, not up, the price of the good in a thin market. If the market were thicker, the price of the good would be higher than in a thin market. Thus, in a thin market, where both qualities of good are being sold at the same price, it will generally be the case that low quality goods are overpriced (relative to their true value) and high quality goods underpriced (relative to their true value).

    A thin market, in part, exists because of asymmetric information. Asymmetric information leads to a lower price for the high quality good and, thus, induces many of the sellers of the high quality good not to sell. However, there will be some high quality goods being sold perhaps because sellers find themselves in extenuating circumstances where they are forced to sell their good.

8. Correct answer: e.

    Discussion: Your textbook stresses that all of the above are true of a mixed market and hopefully so, too, will your instructor because then you'll be prepared for a question like this!

9. Correct answer: c.

    Discussion: In this example, insurance companies face an adverse-selection problem about car drivers because they do not have as much information about how careful or reckless a driver is while the driver knows more about him- or herself than the insurance company. Faced with the adverse-selection problem, insurance companies protect themselves against it by charging a price that is equal to the average settlement that the reckless driver pays. In this example, that price is $36,000. However, since careful drivers know that they are careful and that their average settlement is $6,000, they find it less costly to settle than to pay for additional collision insurance. Thus, careful drivers will not buy the insurance.

    Based on the above reasoning, statements a, b, d, and e are not correct.

VIII. ANSWER KEY: ESSAY QUESTIONS

10. As the admissions director, and having read Chapter 16 of the textbook, I would recognize that I am facing an adverse-selection problem that arises because of asymmetric information. There is asymmetric information because the students (the sellers of their talents and aptitude) have more information about themselves (the product they are selling) than I might have about their true abilities. Students vary a good deal in quality, and their high school academic record may not always be the best reflection of the quality of a student. That is, some students may have shining academic records but .in fact, be very poor students. In the language of the used car market, some students are "lemons." In fact, the pool of students applying to the school represents a mixed market – there are high quality and low quality students in the pool together. As the admissions director, I would like to avoid the problem of admitting lemons, particularly because the admittance of such students could ultimately harm the prestigious reputation of the University.

    So, as admissions director, I may not only use high school transcripts to determine who should be admitted, but also require a written essay, personal interviews, letters of reference, and evidence of extracurricular activity involvement. The additional information may help reduce the probability that I will admit lemons to my University. In a way, you could say that essays, interviews, and the like are the school's form of insurance against admitting a poor student.

11. In a market with asymmetric information, the price of a used good is typically lower than it would otherwise be. The reason is that a used market is a mixed market where high and low quality goods are being sold without obvious information on which of the goods are high quality, and which are low quality. In such a market, the seller has more information about the quality of the good being sold than the buyer has. Thus, buyers attach a probability to the possibility that they will end up buying (unbeknownst to them) a low quality good rather than a high quality good. Since buyers are not willing to pay very much for a low quality good, the probability that they will end up buying one is factored

into the price that they will offer to pay. This means that high quality used goods will also have to be sold at a lower price. For example, a buyer may be willing to pay $1,000 for a high quality used computer but only $200 for a low quality used computer. Thus, the price they will be willing to offer will range between $200 and $1,000 and will depend on how likely the buyer thinks they are to end up getting a low quality computer. That is, the equilibrium price for used computers (regardless of their quality) will range between $200 and $1,000. The higher the probability that buyers attach to getting a low quality computer, the lower will be the equilibrium price at which used computers sell.

Since the equilibrium price of used computers (both high and low quality) will be lower than otherwise, the quality of used computers offered for sale will be lower than otherwise, too. This is because sellers with high quality computers will not, unless extraordinary circumstances dictate, be willing to part with their computers for such a low price. This means that, in the used market for computers, there will be a lot more low quality computers for sale than one might expect had they not taken account of how the price feeds into determining the quality of used computers offered for sale. The market may also end up being a "thin" market in the sense that there will be fewer high quality computers for sale in because the sellers of tile high quality computers have elected not to sell at the low price.

CHAPTER 17
THE LABOUR MARKET

I. OVERVIEW

In this chapter, you will learn about the labour market using demand and supply analysis where the price of labour is the wage rate. You will learn that demand for labour is a derived demand since the demand for labour is derived from the demand for the output that labour produces. You will learn what will cause the wage rate and employment to change. You will learn why the wage rate differs for different occupations and for different groups of people. You will analyze the effects of various public policies aimed at the labour market: a minimum wage law, pay equity, and occupational licensing. You will learn about labour unions. You will learn about the labour market in a setting where the employee has more information than the employer about how productive he or she will be on the job. You will learn that "efficiency wages" may be paid by an employer to reduce the problems that may arise with the information asymmetry. Finally, you will learn about monopsony power in the labour market and its effect on the wage rate.

II. CHECKLIST

By the end of this chapter, you should be able to:
- ❑ Explain why the supply of labour is positively sloped.
- ❑ Explain why the demand for labour is negatively sloped.
- ❑ Explain what will cause the demand for and supply of labour to shift and analyze the effects on the equilibrium wage and employment.
- ❑ Explain why the short-run labour supply curve is more steeply sloped than the long-run supply curve.
- ❑ Use the marginal principle to determine whether a firm would benefit by hiring one more worker.
- ❑ Discuss a firm's short-run demand for labour and relate it to diminishing returns.
- ❑ List four explanations for why wages differ across different occupations.
- ❑ Explain why women and minorities on average earn less for an hour of work than do white males.
- ❑ Discuss the learning and signalling effect to explain why university graduates typically earn more than high school graduates.
- ❑ Discuss the trade-offs associated with a minimum wage law.
- ❑ Define employment equity policies and describe their effects on wages and employment.

- ❑ Discuss occupational licensing and its effect on wages and employment.
- ❑ List some examples of craft unions and industrial unions.
- ❑ Discuss three ways in which a labour union attempts to raise the wage of the union members.
- ❑ Discuss whether unions can create more productive workers.
- ❑ Explain efficiency wages and why a firm may pay them.
- ❑ Explain what monopsony power is and how it can affect wages and employment.

III.   KEY TERMS

Market supply curve for labour: a curve showing the relationship between the wage and the quantity of labour supplied.

Derived demand: the demand for an input such as labour that is derived from the demand for the final product.

Long-run demand curve for labour: a curve showing the relationship between the wage and the quantity of labour demanded in the long run.

Output effect: the change in the quantity of labour demanded resulting from a change in the quantity of output.

Input substitution effect: the change in the quantity of labour demanded resulting from a change in the relative cost of labour.

Marginal product of labour: the change in output resulting from a one-unit increase in the labour input, while holding other inputs constant.

Marginal revenue product of labour (MRP): the extra revenue generated from one more unit of labour; equal to price of output times the marginal product of labour.

Short-run demand curve for labour: a curve showing the relationship between the wage and the quantity of labour demanded in the short run.

Learning effect: the increase in a person's wage because he or she has acquired skills required for certain occupations.

Signalling or screening effect: the increase in a person's wage because his or her educational background has signalled that he or she has a particular skill level.

Earnings gap: the percentage gap between two groups' annual earnings; one minus the ratio between two groups' annual earnings.

Wage gap: the percentage gap between two groups' hourly wages; one minus the ratio between two groups' hourly wages.

Pay equity legislation: legislation designed to remove wage gaps that exist due to both systemic and individual discrimination.

Piece-rate wage: a wage rate that is based on the number of units a person produces rather than the number of hours a person works.

Labour union: an organized group of workers with the main objective of improving working conditions, wages, and fringe benefits.

Craft union: a labour organization that includes workers from a particular occupation, for example, musicians, bricklayers, or doctors.

Industrial union: a labour organization that includes all types of workers from a single industry, for example, steelworkers or autoworkers.

Union density: the percentage of a country's workforce that belongs to a union.

Efficiency wage: a higher wage offered by a firm as a method of screening employees in order o decrease shirking and increase average productivity.

Monopsony: a market in which there is a single buyer of an input.

IV.   PERFORMANCE ENHANCING TIPS (PETS)

PET # 1

The wage rate is the price of labour.

Since the wage rate is the price of the commodity labour, demand and supply analysis can be used to examine what happens to the price of labour (wage rate) when the demand or supply of labour change.

PET #2

Factors, other than a change in the wage rate, that are relevant to the labour market may cause the demand and supply curves for labour to shift. Changes in the wage rate cause a movement along the demand and supply curves.

For review, you may wish to review PET #1 of Chapter 1 of the Study Guide as well as PET #1-5 of Chapter 4 of the Study Guide.

PET #3

A higher wage rate will cause some workers to work more (quantity of labour supplied increases) and will cause some workers to work less (quantity of labour supplied decreases).

For workers that work more hours when the wage rate rises, they are behaving according to the law of supply. That is, for these workers, the supply of labour is positively sloped. These workers will reduce the amount of leisure time they take (because the opportunity cost of leisure time has increased since the wage rate has increased) and, therefore, work more hours. We could say that these workers substitute work for leisure time.

For workers that work fewer hours when the wage rate rises, they are not behaving according to the law of supply since they increase the amount of leisure time they take and, thus, work fewer hours. That is, for these workers, the supply of labour is negatively sloped. Workers may choose to respond this way to a higher wage rate because they recognize that they can now work fewer hours (more leisure time) and still maintain the same income. We could say that these workers substitute leisure time for work.

You should be aware that Chapter 17 of the text points out some other reasons why the supply curve will be positively sloped.

PET #4

When the firm is operating in a perfectly competitive output market, the marginal revenue product of labour is equal to the price at which a firm sells its output multiplied by the marginal product (productivity) of labour.

To see this, recall that the price of output (P) is measured as $ per unit of output and the marginal product of labour is measured as the addition to output produced by one more worker (or from one more hour of work). That is, (additional output/one unit of labour). When the marginal product of labour multiplies price, the result is:

$$P * \left(\frac{\text{additional output}}{\text{one unit of labour}} \right) = \left(\frac{P * \text{additional output}}{\text{one unit of labour}} \right) \qquad where\ P * \text{additional output} = \text{Marginal revenue}$$

Thus, the marginal revenue product of labour is the addition to revenue that one more worker generates for the firm.

PET #5

Factors that cause an increase in the demand for output that labour produces will lead to an increase in the demand for labour and, thus, an increase in the equilibrium wage.

A firm's demand for labour is a derived demand for labour. It is derived from the demand for the output that labour helps to produce. An increase in the demand for output leads to an increase in the price of output. The increase in the price of output means that each worker's work effort (productivity) will add more to the revenue of the firm than before the price increase. That is, the marginal revenue product of labour increases. Using the marginal principle, the marginal benefit to the firm of additional workers has increased. If the wage rate (marginal cost of an additional worker) is unchanged, the firm will find it profitable to hire more workers.

PET #6

A minimum wage policy is like a minimum price (or price floor, price support).

Remember from Chapter 6 that a minimum price is a price below which the price may not fall. For a minimum price policy to be effective, it must be set above the equilibrium price. In the case of minimum wage policy, a minimum wage that is set above the equilibrium wage will create a surplus of labour (quantity of labour supplied will exceed quantity of labour demanded). If the minimum wage is set below the equilibrium wage, the policy is ineffective since there is no tendency for the equilibrium wage to fall below the minimum wage. You may want to review PET #3 from Chapter 6 of the Study Guide.

An efficiency wage is a wage that is paid by a firm that is above the equilibrium wage (or going market-rate) for a particular job or occupation.

An efficiency wage may be paid by a firm in order to attract high quality, productive workers, to reduce the worker's incentive to shirk (i.e., make them work harder), and to reduce absenteeism and turnover. The higher wages paid by the firm may not necessarily mean that the firm's profits will suffer. The workers may be more productive than their counterparts working for other firms in the same industry, who are not being paid an efficiency wage. Thus, even though the firm's wage cost may be higher with efficiency wages, the cost of production may not rise because the productivity increase acts to offset the higher labour costs.

V.   PRACTICE EXAM: MULTIPLE CHOICE QUESTIONS

1. If an increase in the wage rate causes workers to reduce the amount of hours they work and increase the amount of leisure time they take, then:

    a. the labour supply curve for these workers is positively sloped.
    b. the labour supply curve for these workers is negatively sloped.
    c. these workers are obeying the law of supply.
    d. the demand for these workers is derived.
    e. the marginal product of these workers is negative.

2. Which one of the following would NOT be considered a possible response to a higher wage rate for computer technicians in Vancouver?

    a. A decrease in the amount of hours worked.
    b. An increase in the amount of hours worked.
    c. An increase in the number of individuals who pick computer technician over other occupations.
    d. Migration to Vancouver.
    e. All of the above.

3. Which one of the following is an explanation for why the long-run demand curve for labour is negatively sloped?

    a. An increase in the wage rate raises the price at which output is sold and, thus, increases the profits of firms.
    b. A decrease in the wage rate causes fewer people to be willing to work.
    c. A decrease in the wage rate lowers the cost of labour and causes firms to use more labour instead of other more expensive inputs.
    d. An increase in the wage rate reduces the productivity of workers.
    e. All of the above.

4. In which country would labour be likely to be most expensive?

    a. India.
    b. Haiti.
    c. Mexico.
    d. Italy.
    e. The Philippines.

5. Consider the market for lawyers. Suppose the number of lawyers passing the Bar exam in 2001 is larger than it has ever been in the past. What effect would this have on the market for lawyers?

    a. A decrease in the wage rate (salary) paid to lawyers and an increase in the demand for lawyers.
    b. A decrease in the wage rate (salary) paid to lawyers and an increase in the supply of lawyers.
    c. An increase in the wage rate (salary) paid to lawyers and a decrease in the demand for lawyers.
    d. An increase in the wage rate (salary) paid to lawyers and an increase in the supply of lawyers.
    e. (a) and (b).

6. Which one of the following would increase the demand for labour?

    a. An increase in the price of output that labour produces.
    b. An increase in the productivity of labour.
    c. An increase in the price of capital.
    d. A minimum wage law.
    e. (a), (b), and (c).

7. Which one of the following is a reason for why the relative wage of certain occupations is high?

    a. Few people who have the skills necessary to perform the job.
    b. High education and training costs.
    c. Undesirable job features.
    d. Licensing restrictions.
    e. All of the above.

8. Which one of the following has NOT been suggested as an explanation for the gender and race gap in earnings?

    a. Women and minorities have, on average, less education than white males.
    b. Women and minorities have, on average, less work experience than white males.
    c. Gender/race discrimination.
    d. Women and minorities are only a small percentage of the total work force.
    e. All of the above.

9. Which one of the following statements is true?

   a. In 1995, a typical university graduate earned 54% more than the typical high-school graduate in Canada.
   b. A university education provides a signal to a potential employer that the job candidate has desirable skills.
   c. The "learning effect" of a university education is that students learn new skills that enable them to work in higher-skill jobs.
   d. Over the last twenty years, technological change has created a big increase in the demand for high-skilled, workers.
   e. All of the above.

10. Suppose the current wage rate in the service industry is $5.00/hour. A minimum wage policy for the service industry that sets the minimum wage at $5.25 will create a _____ of jobs and a minimum wage policy for the service industry that sets the minimum wage at $4.50 will create a _____ of jobs.

    a. loss; gain
    b. gain; loss
    c. loss; no effect
    d. no effect; gain
    e. loss; loss

11. Which one of the following statements is true?

    a. A minimum wage policy may lead to a decrease in the price of output that minimum wage workers produce.
    b. A pay equity policy is designed to reduce the wage rate that men earn.
    c. An example of occupational licensing is a requirement that a worker complete a certain number of hours of education and retraining every three years in order to remain licensed.
    d. A labour union has monopsony power.
    e. None of the above is true.

12. Occupational licensing schemes:

    a. restrict entry into the profession.
    b. increase wages.
    c. increase production costs.
    d. are designed to protect consumers.
    e. all of the above.

13. Unions attempt to increase the wages of their members by:

    a. negotiating with the firm.
    b. advertisements that encourage people to buy products with the union label.
    c. featherbedding.
    d. striking.
    e. all of the above.

14. Which one of the following statements is true?

    a. A firm that pays efficiency wages may see an increased work effort by its employees as well as a reduction in absenteeism and turnover.
    b. Featherbedding may lead to lower costs of production.
    c. A firm knows more about the productivity and skill level of a potential employee than the potential employee knows about his or her own productivity and skill level.
    d. The labour market is a fixed market.
    e. A monopsonist in the labour market uses its power to increase the wage rate.

VI.   PRACTICE EXAM: ESSAY QUESTIONS

15. Consider the market for graphic designers in Toronto. Let the current equilibrium wage be $20/hour. Suppose that the demand for graphic designers in Toronto increases by 10%. Discuss what will happen to the equilibrium wage in the short and long run. Be sure to explain why the results are different. Assume the elasticity of labour supply in the short run is 0.5 and in the long run is 2.

16. Discuss the purpose of unions and their intended impact on wages and employment. What are some ways in which union membership leads to more productive workers?

VII. ANSWER KEY: MULTIPLE CHOICE QUESTIONS

1.   Correct answer: b.

Discussion: The labour supply curve is a graph of the wage rate against the amount of labour (or labour time) supplied. An increase in the wage rate that reduces the amount of labour supplied reflects a negative or inverse relationship between the wage rate and the amount of labour supplied.

Statement a is not correct based on the above reasoning. Statement c is not correct because, if the workers were obeying the law of supply, then the labour supply curve would be positively sloped. Statement d is not correct because the relationship between the wage rate and labour supplied tells us nothing about the demand for labour. Statement e is not correct because the marginal product of labour is a component of the demand for labour, not the supply. Furthermore, if the marginal product of workers were negative, no firm would hire them.

2.   Correct answer: e.

Discussion: A higher wage rate may induce some workers to work fewer hours (because they can maintain the same income at a higher wage but working fewer hours) and, thus, take more leisure time. Some workers may do the opposite – they may choose to work more hours and thereby increase their earnings substantially. The choice depends on the workers' preferences for leisure time over income (and increased consumption and saving). A higher wage rate also has the effect of attracting workers to the profession. Many students choose university majors based on what they expect the wage (salary) to be for that particular job when they graduate. Higher expected wages tend to attract students into those majors. A higher wage rate also causes people to move to those places where they can earn a higher wage.

3. Correct answer: c.

Discussion: A decrease in the wage rate creates a substitution effect – the firm finds it less costly to use labour to help produce output than to use other relatively more expensive inputs. Thus, the firm will decide to use more labour and fewer of the other inputs (e.g., conveyor belt) as a less costly alternative way to produce output.

Statement a is not correct because it is not an explanation for why the demand curve is negatively sloped. It is also not a correct statement because a higher wage (unless it is an efficiency wage that creates offsetting productivity gains) typically reduces a firm's profits. Statement b is not correct because it is a reference to labour supply not labour demand. Statement d is not correct because it is not an explanation for why the demand curve is negatively sloped. Since statements a, b, and d are not correct, statement e cannot be correct.

4. Correct answer: d.

Discussion: Labour is likely to be most expensive in countries where the population is relatively small and/or where the skill level of workers is high. Conversely, labour is likely to be less expensive in countries where labour is abundant (big population) and/or the skill level of workers is low. India, Haiti, Mexico, and the Philippines are all countries with big populations and low skilled-workers. Italy, a western European country, has relatively more skilled workers and a relatively smaller population.

5. Correct answer: b.

Discussion: The big increase in the number of lawyers passing the Bar exam would be represented by a rightward shift in the supply of lawyers. The shift would have the effect of lowering the equilibrium wage (salary) paid to lawyers. As the wage decreased, the quantity of lawyers demanded (movement along the labour demand curve) would increase.

Statement a is not correct because the demand for lawyers does not increase (i.e., labour demand does not shift to the right); the quantity of lawyers demanded increases (movement along the labour demand curve). Statements c and d are not correct because the wage rate decreases, not increases, Statement e is not correct because statement a is not correct.

6. Correct answer: e.

Discussion: Statement a will cause an increase in the demand for labour. When the price of output that labour produces increases, the marginal revenue each worker generates for the firm increases and, thus, workers become more valuable to the firm. This would lead to an increase in the demand for labour. Statement b will also cause an increase in the demand for labour. More productive (higher marginal product) workers are more beneficial to a firm (generate more output and, thus, more revenue). Thus, firms will demand more labour when workers' productivity increases. Statement c will also cause an increase in the demand for labour. When capital becomes more expensive, firms will decide to substitute labour in production for capital (since labour would be relatively less costly). Statement d will cause a decrease in the quantity of labour demanded. That is, a minimum wage policy causes a movement along the demand curve, but not a shift in the demand for labour (decrease in demand).

7. Correct answer: e.

Discussion: Higher wages are paid to workers who have skills that few people have. This is why chemical engineers are paid more than a clerk at a shoe store. Doctors, professors, lawyers, veterinarians, etc., are all professions that entail more than a university education and, thus, are more costly professions to enter. Jobs with undesirable features (perhaps risky jobs like oil rig drillers) tend to be paid more because there are fewer people willing to work in dangerous situations. Thus, the supply of labour in these professions is typically not as large as in, say, retail sales, and the wages are

Chapter 17

correspondingly higher. Licensing restrictions limit the supply of workers in the licensed professions. This, too, leads to correspondingly higher wages.

8. Correct answer: d.

    Discussion: Statement d has not been used as an explanation for the gender and race gap. The gender and race gap in earnings is that women and minorities typically earn less than a white male counterpart who is doing the same job. The difference in earnings has been explained in several ways (that are not necessarily mutually exclusive). The gender gap may be due to the fact that women and minorities typically have less education and less work experience than white males. That is, these groups of workers, on average, are less valuable to a firm than a worker with more education and work experience. Gender and race discrimination have also been suggested as explanations for the earnings gaps between men and women and white males and minorities.

9. Correct answer: e.

    Discussion: All of the above are true. Statement a provides evidence that workers that have more education are better paid. Statement b is an example of the "screening" or "signalling" effect that graduation from university provides to potential employers. Statement c suggests that a university education produces workers with higher skills and thereby, admission into better paid professions. Statement d suggests that workers in fields like engineering and computer technology have seen (and may continue to see) increases in wages bigger than those in other professions.

10. Correct answer: c.

    Discussion: A minimum wage is a floor below which the wage may not drop. A minimum wage law set at $5.25/hour is a policy that will not permit the wage to drop below that rate. Since the current wage is $5.00/hour, the minimum wage policy raises the wage to $5.25/hour. The increase in the wage rate reduces the quantity of labour demanded (movement along the demand curve) and, thus, causes a loss of jobs. An increase in the wage rate also raises the quantity of labour supplied (movement along the supply curve). A minimum wage of $4.50/hour is not effective because the equilibrium wage is $5.00/hour. Since $5.00/hour is an equilibrium wage, there is no tendency for it to drop below $5.00/hour. Thus, a restriction that the wage not be permitted to fall below $4.50 is meaningless. This means that the policy will not have an effect on the quantity of labour demanded or supplied or on the equilibrium wage of $5.00/hour. Therefore, statement c is the only correct answer.

11. Correct answer: c.

    Discussion: Occupational licensing requirements typically place restrictions on workers in the profession. Workers typically must fulfill a certain set of conditions in order to become licensed or remain licensed. The conditions may be that the workers meet certain educational requirements or a specified number of hours spent on the job per year.

    Statement a is not correct because a minimum wage typically raises the price of output that minimum wage workers produce. This is because a minimum wage typically raises a firm's cost of production (without leading to increased worker productivity), which is passed on to consumers in the form of higher prices. Statement b is not correct because a pay equity policy is designed to raise the level of wages of women to that of men (not to bring the wages of men down). Statement d is not correct because a labour union is a seller of labour in the labour market. A monopsonist in the labour market is defined as a single buyer of labour (not seller). Since statement c is true, statement e cannot be correct.

12. Correct answer: e.

    Discussion: All of the above are true. However, while occupational licensing schemes are designed to protect consumers from incompetent workers, such schemes may not always be effective. To wit, there are surgeons who are licensed to practice who have amputated the wrong leg or removed the wrong kidney from a patient.

13. Correct answer: e.

    Labour unions attempt to increase the wages of their members as well as to improve working conditions and enhance fringe benefits. Unions do this, (1) by negotiating with the firm (which may lead to a strike as part of the negotiation tactic), (2) by creating a demand for the product they produce (remember that the demand for labour is a derived demand: the stronger the demand for output, the higher the wage paid to employees that produce the output), and/or (3) by featherbedding (dictating that a firm must hire so many workers for a particular task'). That is, featherbedding is designed to increase the demand for labour and, thus, the wage. Featherbedding, however, can backfire and actually reduce the wage paid to workers. This can happen if featherbedding leads to higher production costs and, thus, a higher price for the output the workers produce. If the price of the output rises, the amount sold will decline and this will have a tendency to reduce the demand for labour and reduce the wage.

14. Correct answer: a.

Discussion: Efficiency wages may lead workers to work harder (and not shirk), and also to reduce the frequency with which they call in sick and their desire to quit the job. When Henry Ford raised the wage he paid his workers from $3/day to $5/day, he effectively paid them an efficiency wage since the going market rate was $3/day.

Statement b is not true because featherbedding raises costs of production. Statement c is not correct because employees know more about their own productivity and skill level than does a potential employer. Statement d is not correct; a labour market is a mixed market, meaning that both high and low-skill workers exist in the market, and it can be difficult for a firm to know which type of worker it is hiring. Statement e is not correct because a monopsonist uses its power in the market to reduce the wage rate.

VIII. ANSWER KEY: ESSAY QUESTIONS

15. An increase in the demand for graphic designers would be represented by a rightward shift in the demand for graphic designers. The increased demand for graphic designers would raise the wage above $20/hour. The degree to which the wage rises depends on how elastic the labour supply curve is. In the short run, the supply of labour is less elastic than in the long run. This means that the short-run supply of graphic designers will be steeper than the long-run supply of graphic designers. In the short run, the influence of migration and choice of graphic designer as an occupation cannot be felt on the labour market. That is, the short run is a time period that is not long enough to allow for individuals to migrate to Toronto to fill the increased demand for graphic designers or for university students and others to alter their career decisions so that they can be hired as a graphic designer. Thus, the increased demand puts a lot more pressure on the wage to rise (because of the limited response on the supply side). If the short-run elasticity of supply were 0.5 and the demand for graphic designers increased by 10%, then the increase in the wage rate would be 20%. The formula to be used is analogous to the elasticity of demand formula that was covered in Chapter 5 of your textbook and is reviewed in Chapter 5 of the Study Guide.

The formula is:

Elasticity (E) = %ΔQ/%ΔP

Where in this case, you know that the elasticity of supply is 0.5 and that the %ΔQ is 10% since that is how many more graphic designers are demanded. Since we are analyzing the labour market, the %ΔP is the %Δwage. (The wage rate is the price of labour). Thus, plugging in the numbers and solving for %ΔP yields:

%ΔP (i.e., wage) = %ΔQ/E = 10%/0.5 = 20%.

Thus, in the short run, the wage rises by 20% which, in dollar terms, is equal to (0.20 * $20/hour) = $4.00. The new wage, in the short run, is $24.00/hour.

In the long run, the higher wage and demand for graphic designers causes people to migrate to Toronto and enter the profession of graphic design. This takes some pressure off of the wage. With a long-run elasticity of supply of 2, the equilibrium wage in the long run will change by:

$\%\Delta P = 10\%/2 = 5\%$

Thus, in the long run, the wage rises by 5% which in dollar terms is equal to $(0.05 * \$20/\text{hour}) = \$1.00$. The new wage, in the long run, is $21.00/hour.

In the long: run, the wage rises by less than in the short run because the increased demand for graphic designers is matched by a bigger pool of available graphic designers. Existing firms do not have to compete as strongly with each other (by offering better wage rates) in order to attract graphic designers to work for them as they do in the short run when the pool of available graphic designers is limited.

16. Unions (which came into being in the late 1800s) are organized groups of employees that attempt to negotiate with the firm for higher wages, better working conditions, and better benefits. Unions also attempt to maintain employment for the union members. Since a union is an organization within a firm, the union has more power than an individual in negotiating with the management of the firm.

While unions attempt to increase the wages of the union members, they confront a problem. A negotiation for higher wages may raise production costs and, thus, the price of the output the firm sells. If the higher price reduces the amount of output the firm is able to sell, the firm has an incentive to lay-off workers. (Remember that the demand for labour is derived from how much output and at what price the output can be sold.) Naturally, unions want to avoid any loss of employment for their union members. This is why some unions try to hold membership down. A smaller membership means that a firm would have to think twice about laying off some of its workers because these employees are vital to the firm's operation. Without them, the firm may not be able to operate at all.

Unions also recognize that there are other ways to increase wages without directly asking for higher wages. Unions may promote products produced under the union label. That is, unions attempt (through advertising) to increase the demand for the product(s) that they produce. Unions may also advocate work rules that establish how many workers must be used to fulfill certain tasks. This is called "featherbedding." For example, unions may dictate that a roadside construction crew consist of 4 workers when perhaps 3 could do the job just as well. Featherbedding thus leads to an artificially increased demand for labour and supposedly would lead to a higher wage – just what the union is after in the first place. However, featherbedding can backfire. If featherbedding leads to higher production costs and thereby a higher price for the output the workers are producing, the demand for labour could actually decline. This is because a higher price of output will reduce the amount of output sold so that fewer workers are needed.

In terms of our demand and supply model, featherbedding is designed to shift out (to the right) the demand for labour. Thus, the wage will rise and employment will increase. However, as the price of output rises, the demand for labour shifts back in (to the left). If the price increase in the output market is big enough, the demand for labour could shift back to left by enough that the new wage and employment level are below what the initial wage and employment level were.

This point is illustrated in Figure 17-1.

The curves labelled S and D are the initial supply and demand curves prior to featherbedding. The desired impact of featherbedding is to increase the demand for labour to D(a). However, as the price of output rises (because of production cost increases associated with the featherbedding), the demand curve may shift back to D or even worse D(b). At D(b), the new equilibrium wage and employment level is below what the starting wage and employment level were.

Figure 17-1

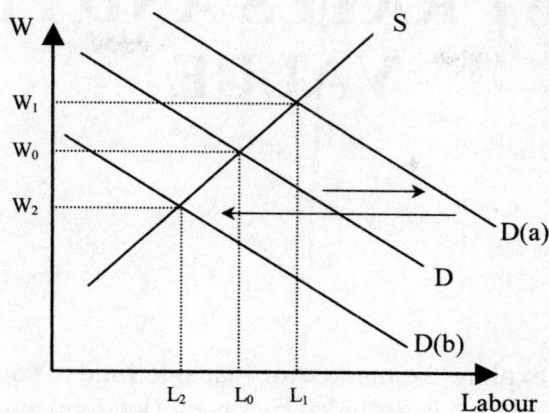

One of the assumptions so far has been that the higher wage that union members are paid is not offset by an increase in union member productivity. That is, the higher wage (without any corresponding rise in worker productivity) is what leads to higher production costs and a higher price for the output, which, unfortunately for the union, reduces the demand for labour. However, this turn of events can be avoided if the higher wage leads to more productive workers. That is, if the higher wage is offset by employees becoming more productive, the firm's production costs may not increase and, thus, the price at which output is sold need not necessarily increase with the higher wage rate. There are two ways in which union members may have an incentive to be more productive. First, since the union promotes communication between the management of the firm and the workers, workers may be more satisfied on the job because management may deal with any problems they have more swiftly. Furthermore, the more satisfied workers are, the less likely they are to quit. Thus, turnover rates of union members may be lower. This translates to more experienced workers (the longer one stays on the job the more experienced one becomes). More experienced workers are assumed to be more productive. Second, the higher wage may be viewed as an "efficiency" wage in the sense that the higher wage motivates workers to work hard (so as to keep their well-paying jobs).

CHAPTER 18
INTEREST RATES AND PRESENT VALUE

I. OVERVIEW

In this chapter, you will explore the market for loanable funds. You will explore the supply of loanable funds, which is provided by savers (lenders) and the demand for loanable funds, which is used by borrowers. You will learn why households and businesses save and how the interest rate influences total saving each year. You will learn why households, businesses, and the government borrow and how the interest rate influences how much, in total, is borrowed each year. You will use supply and demand analysis to examine the effects of changes in the supply and demand of loanable funds on the price of loanable funds, which is the interest rate. You will learn that more risky financial assets typically pay a higher interest rate to the lender. You will learn about stocks and how the effective interest that they pay is determined differently from savings accounts and bonds. You will revisit the problems associated with asymmetric information in a market and apply them to the market for loanable funds. You will learn about how to make wise investment decisions (financial or otherwise). This requires that you compare the present value of different options under different interest rates. You will learn how to calculate the present value of a future payment if you receive the future payment, say, at the end of ten years, versus receiving a payment once each year for ten years.

II. CHECKLIST

By the end of this chapter, you should be able to:
- ❑ Explain the slope of the supply curve for loanable funds.
- ❑ Explain the slope of the demand curve for loanable funds.
- ❑ Explain what would cause the supply and demand curves of loanable funds to shift.
- ❑ Explain what would cause the interest rate to change.
- ❑ Explain the effect of taxes on the payments a saver actually receives.
- ❑ Discuss the problems of asymmetric information in the loanable funds market and why lenders (e.g. banks) may credit ration.
- ❑ Explain the importance of making present value calculations in deciding on different investment options.

- ❑ Calculate the present value of $X paid in Y years to the present value of $X paid each year for Y years.
- ❑ Use present value calculations to make a decision about whether or not to undertake a particular investment that carries a future payment.

III. KEY TERMS

Market for loanable funds: a market in which savers (the suppliers of funds) and borrowers (the demanders of funds) interact to determine the equilibrium interest rate (the price of loanable funds).

Interest rate: the amount of money paid for the use of a dollar for a year.

Supply curve for loanable funds: a curve that shows the relationship between the interest rate and the quantity of loanable funds supplied by savers.

Demand curve for loanable funds: a curve that shows the relationship between the interest rate and the quantity of loanable funds demanded by borrowers.

Personal savings rate: the fraction of personal disposable income (income after taxes) that is saved rather than used for consumption; sometimes called the household savings ratio.

Capital gains: the monetary gain from the sale of a capital asset (stock, bond, real estate, antique, or art) that is bought and resold.

Corporate or government bond: a promissory note issued by a corporation or a government when it borrows money.

Corporation: a legal entity that is owned by people who purchase stock in the corporation.

Corporate stock: a certificate that reflects ownership in a corporation and gives the holder the right to receive a fraction of the corporation's profit.

Dividends: the part of a corporation's profit paid to stockholders.

Credit rationing: the practice of limiting the amount of credit available to individual borrowers.

Present value: the maximum amount a person is willing to pay today for a payment to be received in the future.

IV. PERFORMANCE ENHANCING TIPS

PET # 1

Factors other than a change in the interest rate, which are relevant to the market for loanable funds, may cause the demand and supply curves for loanable funds to shift. Changes in the interest rate cause a movement along the demand and supply curves.

For review of this concept, see PET #1 of Chapter 1 of the Study Guide as well as PET's #1-5 of Chapter 4 of the Study Guide.

PET #2

The suppliers of loanable funds are "savers" who can also be referred to as "lenders." The demanders of loanable funds are "borrowers."

PET #3

Present value calculations can be used to determine how much money you would have to save or put away today in order to accumulate a certain sum of money in the future.

Suppose that you would like to have $500 in one year in order to purchase a new kitchen table and chairs set. Further, suppose that the rate of interest that you could earn if you put your money into a money market account is 6% per year. How much would you have to put away today in order to have $500 in the future? That is, what is the present value of a future payment of $500 in one year?

The formula that you would use (from the book) is:

$$\text{Present Value} = \frac{\text{Future Value}}{(1 + \text{interest rate})^t}$$

Here, the future value is $500, the interest rate is 6% and t = 1 year. Thus, the present value is:

$$\text{Present Value} = \frac{\$500}{(1 + 0.06)^1} = \$471.70$$

This means that you would have to put $471.70 in the bank today in order to amass $500 one year from today.

Suppose you were going to save for three years instead of one year. How much would you have to put away today in order to amass $500 in three years? Assume the interest rate you can earn is fixed at 6% per year.

Obviously, you will have to put away less than $471.70 since you will be accumulating interest for two additional years. Let's see how much you would have to put away:

$$\text{Present Value} = \frac{\$500}{(1 + 0.06)^3} = \$419.81$$

Thus, you would have to put $419.81 in a bank today in order to have $500 three years from today given that the current interest rate is 6%.

<u>PET #4</u>

The present value of an investment decision which yields $X dollars in Y periods is calculated differently from an investment decision that yields $X/Y dollars each period for Y periods.

There is a subtle but significant difference between the two investment plans stated above. A failure to understand or be aware of the difference could lead to poor financial decisions or, worse, incorrect answers on an exam! Let's explore the difference by using a concrete example.

Suppose you are told that you will receive a future payment of $10,000 in 5 years. This is different from receiving a payment of $2,000 each year for 5 years for a total of $10,000. To see this, calculate the present value of each payment, being sure to use the correct formula. Assume the current interest rate is 8%.

The present value of a $10,000 payment 5 years from today is:

$$\text{Present Value} = \frac{\$10,000}{(1+0.08)^5} = \$6,805.83$$

In other words, if you were given $6,805.83 today and put it in the bank for 5 years at 8% interest per year, you would have $10,000 at the end of 5 years. In effect, you may be indifferent between receiving $6,805.83 today or $10,000 in the future.

In contrast, the present value of a $2,000 payment starting today (t = 0) for 5 years (until t = 4) is:

$$\text{Present Value} = \frac{\$2,000}{(1+0.08)^0} + \frac{\$2,000}{(1+0.08)^1} + \frac{\$2,000}{(1+0.08)^2} + \frac{\$2,000}{(1+0.08)^3} + \frac{\$2,000}{(1+0.08)^4} = \$8,624.25$$

Note: $(1.08)^0$ is equal to 1.0 which means that the present value of $2,000 (i.e. $2,000/(1.08)^0$) paid to you today is $2,000. (As an algebra point, any number raised to the zero power is equal to 1.0).

Notice that the present value of receiving payments of $2,000 every year for 5 years starting today for a total of $10,000 is greater than the present value of a $10,000 payment 5 years from today. The reason is that, when you are paid a stream of money each year, you can invest it at the current interest rate and make money on it. If you are paid $2,000 once each year for 5 years starting today, you could put the $2.000 into the bank and earn an 8% interest rate on the first $2,000 for 5 years; the next year when you receive another $2,000, you will earn an 8% interest rate on that $2,000 for the remaining 4 years and so on for the remaining payments of $2,000. In effect, you accumulate more interest earnings by getting $2,000 every year for 5 years compared to receiving $10,000 at the end of 5 years. That is why the present value of a stream of $2,000 payments received every year for 5 years is greater than the present value of receiving $10,000 in 5 years.

<u>PET #5</u>

You should compare the present value of future payment(s) to the current (today) cost of a project or investment in order to decide whether it is worthwhile to undertake a project. Do NOT compare the anticipated value of the future payment(s) to the current (today) cost.

For example, suppose your firm is considering opening a new factory. The cost is $1,000,000. However, the factory will be in operation one year from now at which time you anticipate earning profits of $200,000 every year for 10 years. Should your firm undertake the project of opening a new factory?

It is NOT correct to compute the benefits by simply multiplying the $200,000 in profits earned every year by 10 years. That is, it would not be correct to say that the benefit of opening the factory is $2,000,000. Nor is it correct to then compare this figure to the $1,000,000 start-up cost and conclude that the factory should be opened because the benefit exceeds the cost.

The correct way to decide whether it is worthwhile to pay $1,000,000 to open up a factory that will produce a stream of "future payments" (benefits) of $200,000 each year starting one year from now is to compare the start-up cost to the *present value* of the payments of $200,000. In order to make a present value calculation, you must know what the current interest rate is. Suppose the interest rate is 10%. What is the present value of receiving future payments of $200,000 for 10 years starting one year from today (t = 1).

$$\text{Present Value} = \frac{\$200,000}{(1+0.10)^1} + \frac{\$200,000}{(1+0.10)^2} + \ldots + \frac{\$200,000}{(1+0.10)^9} + \frac{\$200,000}{(1+0.10)^{10}} = \$1,228,913.42$$

Since the present value of the future benefits is greater than the start-up cost, the project is worthwhile to undertake. If the present value had been less than the start-up cost of $1,000,000 it would not be wise for your firm to open the new factory. It would be wiser for your firm to put the $1,000,000 into a financial asset that will earn 10% interest each year for 10 years.

<u>PET #6</u>

Taxes reduce the effective interest rate that a saver earns on invested funds.

Suppose that you invest $1,000 in a GIC (guaranteed investment certificate) that has a 7% annual interest rate. At the end of one year, you will have $1,000 * (1.07) = $1,070. You earned $70 in interest on your $1,000 investment. However, suppose that your income is taxed at a rate of 25%. You will have to pay the government 25% of your interest earnings. What are your effective (or after-tax) interest earnings and the effective (or after-tax) interest rate?

Since you earned $70 in interest, you must pay 25% to the government. 25% of $70 = 0.25 * $70 = $17.50. Thus, you are left with $70 - $17.50 = $52.50. These are your effective interest earnings. Your effective interest rate is the percent of $1,000 that you earned. Taking $52.50 and dividing it by $1,000 and then multiplying that number by 100 would calculate this. Thus, the effective interest rate would be [$52.50/$1,000] * 100 = 5.25%.

Another formula that you can use to calculate the effective interest rate (or after-tax interest rate) is:

$$\text{Before tax interest rate} * \left(1 - \frac{\text{tax rate}}{100}\right) = \text{Effective Interest Rate}$$

Thus, you would have 7% * [1 - 25%/100] = 7% * [1-0.25] = 7% * [0.75] = 5.25%

V.   PRACTICE EXAM: MULTIPLE CHOICE QUESTIONS

1.   The supply curve for loanable funds:

   a.   shows how much borrowers, in total, would be willing to borrow at various interest rates.
   b.   shows how much savers, in total, would be willing to save at various interest rates.
   c.   is negatively sloped.
   d.   does not depend on the interest rate.
   e.   (b) and (c).

2.   The demand curve for loanable funds:

   a.   is negatively sloped.
   b.   shows that, at higher interest rates, total saving rises.
   c.   shows that, at higher interest rates, total borrowing decreases.
   d.   (a) and (b).
   e.   (a) and (c).

3.   Which one of the following statements is true?

   a.   Governments may cover the difference between their tax revenues and their expenditures by borrowing (issuing government bonds).
   b.   Taxes increase the net benefit from saving.
   c.   An increase in the interest rate will cause firms to borrow more money.
   d.   Savers provide the demand for loanable funds.
   e.   None of the above statements are true.

4. If firms decide to expand their production facilities because the economy is booming:

    a. the supply of loanable funds will decrease.
    b. the demand for loanable funds will decrease.
    c. the interest rate will rise.
    d. borrowing will decline.
    e. (a) and (c).

5. Suppose that the government increases it's spending to fund health care. At the same time, the government cuts taxes on households. What will be the combined effect of these two policies?

    a. The interest rate will rise and the equilibrium quantity of loanable funds will rise.
    b. The interest rate will fall and the equilibrium quantity of loanable funds will rise.
    c. The interest rate will rise and the equilibrium quantity of loanable funds will decline.
    d. The effect on the interest rate is ambiguous but the equilibrium quantity of loanable funds will rise.
    e. The interest rate will rise but the effect on the equilibrium quantity of loanable funds is ambiguous.

Use Figure 18-1 to answer the following question.

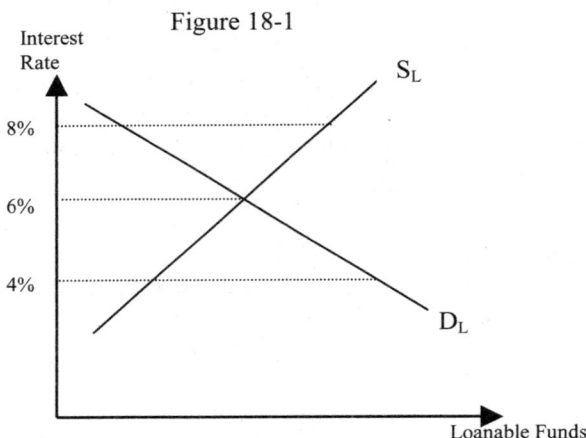

Figure 18-1

6. Which one of the following statements is true?

    a. If households decide to consume less today, the interest rate will rise.
    b. If the government fixes the interest rate at 4%, there will be a shortage of loanable funds.
    c. If the government fixes the interest rate at 8%, there will be a shortage of loanable funds.
    d. A decline in the equilibrium interest rate will reduce the amount of borrowing.
    e. An increase in the supply of loanable funds and a decrease in the demand for loanable funds will have an ambiguous effect on the interest rate.

7. Which one of the following statements is true?

a. The federal government insures savings accounts for $1 million dollars.
b. Government bonds are more risky than corporate bonds.
c. Different financial assets pay different interest rates because of differences in their riskiness.
d. A purchase of stock in a corporation entitles you to receive a fixed dividend payment every quarter.
e. A capital gain is an increase in the profits of a firm.

8. Which one of the following statements is NOT true?

a. At higher interest rates, a lender faces a higher risk (probability) of lending to individuals who will default on their loans.
b. The adverse-selection problem faced by lenders arises because the pool of borrowers at higher interest rates is composed of a greater percentage of borrowers that will default than at lower interest rates.
c. Credit rationing is the practice of limiting the amount of credit (loan) available to individual borrowers.
d. The market for loanable funds is a mixed market because there are high-quality borrowers (those not likely to default on their loans) and low-quality borrowers (those likely to default on their loans) and lenders do not know with perfect certainty which borrower type they are lending to.
e. The market for loanable funds is characterized by adverse information.

9. Suppose you are working for a non-profit organization and one of your donors has bequeathed $25,000 to your organization. However, the $25,000 will not be paid to your organization until 3 years from today. What is the present value of the future payment of $25,000? Assume the current interest rate is 7.5%.

a. $25,000.00
b. $20,124.01
c. $4,664.72
d. $31,057.42
e. $5,925.93

10. Which one of the following statements is correct?

   a. Produce a new line of fad products that will cost $10,000 to produce but will generate a 3-year stream of profits of $4,000 starting one year from today. The current interest rate is 10%.
   b. The present value of $5,000 to be paid 5 years from today is $4,796.37 assuming the interest rate is 3%.
   c. The present value of $25,000 paid every year for 4 years starting today is greater than the present value of $100,000 paid in 4 years, assuming the current interest rate is 8%.
   d. The present value of $10,000 paid in 1 year assuming an interest rate of 10% is less than the present value of $10,000 paid in 2 years assuming an interest rate of 6%.
   e. None of the above.

VI. PRACTICE EXAM: ESSAY QUESTIONS

11. Explain the effects of an increase in government borrowing on the loanable funds market. What will happen to total saving? Will every saver choose to save more?

12. Suppose you work as a financial advisor for a corporation. The corporation is considering two options. The first option is to open up a glass factory in Calgary. The cost of start up is $100,000 and it is expected that, one year after the factory is opened, $40,000 a year in profits will be made for 5 years. The interest rate is 10% per year. The second option is invest the $100,000 in a government bond that pays 10% per year for 5 years. What would you advise your company to do?

VII. ANSWER KEY: MULTIPLE CHOICE QUESTIONS

1. Correct answer: b.

   Discussion: The supply of loanable funds comes from savers – that is, savers lend funds to borrowers. The price of loanable funds is the interest rate. You know from Chapter 4 that, as the price of a good rises, the quantity supplied increases, i.e. the supply curve is positively sloped. The same is true for the supply curve for loanable funds. It, too, is positively sloped. Thus, statement c is not correct, nor is statement e. Statement a is not correct; borrowers are demanders of loanable funds. Statement d is not correct because the supply of loanable funds does depend on the interest rate.

2. Correct answer: e.

   Discussion: The demand curve for loanable funds represents, at various interest rates, how much borrowers would be willing to borrow. At higher interest rates, it becomes more costly to borrow (i.e. the price of borrowing increases), so total borrowing declines. This means that there is a negative relationship between the interest rate and borrowing. Thus, statements a and c are correct. The demand curve for loanable funds does not tell us anything about the behaviour of savers, so statement b is not correct.

3. Correct answer: a.

Discussion: The government can be a borrower, just like an individual, household, or firm can be. The government borrows when its tax revenues are not enough to cover its expenditures. (The government is said to run a budget deficit). In order to cover its expenditures, the government borrows funds from the private sector by issuing bonds (promissory notes).

Statement b is not true because taxes decrease the net benefit from saving. Statement c is not true because an increase in the interest rate will cause firms to borrow less money. Statement d is not correct because the demand for loanable funds comes from borrowers, not savers.

4. Correct answer: c.

Discussion: When firms decide to expand their production facilities (build new factories, enlarge and renovate existing ones), they typically must borrow the funds necessary for the expansion. Thus, the demand for loanable funds will increase. As the demand for loanable funds increases, the price of loanable funds, the interest rate, rises. For this reason, statement c is correct and statement b and d are incorrect. Statement a is not correct because the supply of loanable funds does not decrease, nor does it increase (i.e., there is no shift in the supply curve).

5. Correct answer: d.

Discussion: The government increase in spending on health care is financed through government borrowing. This raises the demand for loanable funds (demand for loanable funds shifts right) and by itself increases the equilibrium interest rate and the equilibrium quantity of loanable funds. The tax cut raises the benefit to savers of saving and, thus, increases the supply of loanable funds. This increases the supply of loanable funds (supply of loanable funds shifts right) and by itself, lowers the equilibrium interest rate and increases the equilibrium quantity of loanable funds. Since the two shifts have opposite effects on the interest rate, the change in the interest rate is ambiguous. However, both shifts raise the equilibrium quantity of loanable funds. Thus, statement d is the only correct option.

6. Correct answer: b.

Discussion: Statement b is an example of a "maximum price" that you learned about in Chapter 6. If the government fixes the interest rate at 4% and the current equilibrium interest rate is 6%, then the government is not permitting the interest rate to rise to what would be its equilibrium value. At an interest rate of 4%, the quantity of loanable funds demanded exceeds the quantity of loanable funds supplied and so there will be a shortage of loanable funds.

Statement a is not correct because a decrease in consumption today is the flip side of increased saving today which would be represented by an increase in the supply of loanable funds (supply shifts right). Statement c is not correct; if the government fixed the interest rate at 8%, there would be a surplus of loanable funds. Statement d is not correct because a decline in the equilibrium interest rate will increase the amount of borrowing (movement along the demand curve). Statement e is not correct. An increase in the supply of loanable funds (supply shifts right) reduces the interest rate. A decrease in the demand for loanable funds (demand shifts left) reduces the interest rate. Both actions reduce the interest rate so that there is no ambiguity about what will happen to it.

7. Correct answer: c.

Discussion: There are many different interest rates in the financial market. Higher interest rates are typically paid on financial assets that are more risky in order to entice lenders (savers) into lending their funds to the borrowers. If two bonds were both paying an 8% interest rate but one was riskier than another, which bond would you invest in? Naturally, you would want the lower-risk bond. However, if the riskier bond was paying 15% interest, you may be willing to invest in it despite the fact that it is riskier.

Statement a is not correct; savings accounts are insured by the federal government for up to $100,000. Statement b is not correct because government bonds are less risky than corporate bonds. The view is that the government is less likely to default on its bonds than is a corporation. Statement d is not correct because a dividend payment is not fixed. It may vary from quarter to quarter depending on the financial health (profitability) of the firm. For example, one quarter, a corporation may pay $0.25 in dividends on each stock and another quarter pay only $0.10 in dividends. Statement e is not correct because a capital gain is defined as an increase in the price of a stock. (The price of the stock may rise because the firm's profits increase but there are numerous other reasons why a firm's stock price may increase.)

8. Correct answer: e.

    Discussion: The market for loanable funds is characterized by asymmetric information, not adverse information. All of the other statements are true.

9. Correct answer: b.

    Discussion: The present value of a $25,000 payment 3 years from today is calculated by dividing $25,000 by $(1.075)^3$. That is, $25,000/1.2423 = $20,124.01$.

    Statement a cannot be correct. The present value of a future sum of money is always less than the future sum (unless the interest rate is zero). For the same reason, statement d cannot be correct (unless the interest rate was negative). Based on the calculations above, statements c and e are also not correct.

10. Correct answer: c.

    Discussion: The present value of $25,000 paid every year for 4 years starting today at an interest rate of 8% is $25,000 + $25,000/1.08 + $25,000/(1.08)^2 + $25,000/(1.08)^3 = $89,427.43$. The present value of $100,000 paid in 4 years is $100,000/(1.08)^4 = $73,502.99$.

    Statement a is not correct. The cost is $10,000 and the present value of the future payments (benefits) is $4,000/(1.10)^1 + $4,000/(1.10)^2 + $4,000/(1.10)^3 = $9,947.41$. Since the cost exceeds the present value of the benefits, the project should not be undertaken. Statement b is not correct because the present value of $5,000 paid in 5 years assuming the interest rate is 3% is $= $5,000/(1.03)^5 = $4,313.04$. Statement d is not correct because the present value of $10,000 paid in one year at an interest rate of 10% is $10.000/1.10 = $9,090.91$ and is greater than the present value of $10,000 paid in 2 years at an interest rate of 6% is $10,000/(1.06)^2 = $8,899.96$.

VIII. ANSWER KEY: ESSAY QUESTIONS

11. An increase in government borrowing, which the government undertakes by issuing government bonds that savers purchase (thereby lending their funds to the government), represents an increase in the demand for loanable funds. An increase in the demand for loanable funds raises the price of loanable funds like an increase in the demand for a good raises the price of the good. The price of loanable funds is the interest rate, so the interest rate rises. As the interest rate rises, the quantity of loanable funds supplied by savers rises. This is represented as a movement along the supply of loanable funds curve. Thus, the equilibrium quantity of total saving rises to meet the increased demand for loanable funds. However, even though the interest rate is higher and the quantity of total saving is higher, not every saver may have decided to save more in response to the higher interest rate. Some may have chosen to save less since the higher interest rate means that their savings are earning more interest. (These savers are the "party hearty" crowd your book refers to). Some savers may not change the amount they save; they're just happy that they are making more money each year in interest than before the interest rate had gone up. Since total saving rises, however, the people who do decide to save more as the interest rate goes up collectively bring enough saving into the market for loanable funds to more than offset the reduction in saving coming from the "party hearty" crowd. Thus, on net, the total level of saving rises as the interest rate rises.

12. I would start by computing the present value of the project and compare it to the cost. The present value is calculated as:

$40,000/(1.10) + \$40,000/(1.10)^1 + \$40,000/(1.10)^2 + \$40,000/(1.10)^3 + \$40,000/(1.10)^4 + \$40,000/(1.10)^5 = \$151,631.50$

Since the cost of the project is less than the present value, it appears that the project would be worthwhile. The company comes out ahead by $51,631.50 since it spends (costs) $100,000 today and gets back (in present value terms) $151,631.50. That is, the benefit in today's term is $51,631.50. However, the company could just hold onto the $100,000 today. The benefit of $100,000 in today's terms is $100,000, which exceeds the benefit from the project. Thus, it would make more sense for the company to hold on to the $100,000. In fact, if the company invests the $100,000 into an account earning 10% for five years, the $100,000 will be worth $161,051 in 5 years [= $100,000 * (1.10)^5]. Therefore, while the firm makes $61,051 in interest, it also keeps the $100,000 investment. Thus, it would be even better for the company to simply invest the money into an account earning 10% per year for the next five years since it will have $161,051 in five years.

CHAPTER 19
INTERNATIONAL TRADE AND PUBLIC POLICY

I.   OVERVIEW

In this chapter, you will learn why trade can be mutually beneficial to countries. You will re-encounter the principle of opportunity cost and use it to determine comparative advantage. You will learn that free trade can lower the price that consumers would pay for goods compared to the prices they would pay if they did not trade (autarky). You will also learn that there are resource movements from one industry to another associated with moving from a position of no trade (autarky) to a position of free trade. These resource movements mean that free trade will, in the short run, create employment losses and factory closings in some industries but expansion in others. You will learn about policies that restrict trade – tariffs, bans on imports, quotas, and voluntary export restraints. You will learn that protectionist trade policies are typically designed to protect job losses in specific industries. However, protectionist trade policies impose costs on consumers. Thus, you will see that protectionism creates some winners and losers within a country. You will learn that protectionist trade policies initiated by one country may invite retaliation by a trading partner. You will learn about the rationale for protectionist trade policies and criticisms of these arguments. You will learn about some recent trade policy debates over foreign producers "dumping" their products in a foreign country, over the impact of trade agreements on the environment, and about whether freer trade causes income inequality. You will also learn about some recent trade agreements.

II.   CHECKLIST

By the end of this chapter, you should be able to:
- Explain the benefits from specialization and trade as compared to autarky.
- Use an output table to calculate the opportunity costs of production in two countries for two different types of goods and determine in which good a country has a comparative advantage.
- Draw a production possibilities curve using information from an output table.
- Explain what the different points on the production possibilities curve represent.
- Explain what determines the range of terms of trade that would be mutually beneficial to two countries.
- Draw a consumption possibilities curve using information about the terms of trade.

- Explain what the, different points on the consumption possibilities curve represent.
- Describe the employment effects of free trade.
- Explain whom the winners and losers are from free trade.
- List the different types of protectionist trade policies.
- Explain how the different protectionist trade policies work and their effects on import prices.
- Compare and contrast the effects of an import ban to an import quota on equilibrium price and quantity using demand and supply curves.
- Explain how the threat of retaliation by one country can persuade another country to loosen its protectionist policies.
- Explain why import restrictions might lead to smuggling.
- Discuss some arguments (or rationales) for protectionist trade policies.
- Describe the practice of dumping and predatory dumping (pricing).
- Explain why some firms might dump their products in other countries.
- Discuss why trade policy and environmental issues have become linked.
- Explain how trade might cause income inequality to widen.
- Discuss some recent trade agreements.

III. KEY TERMS

Production possibilities curve: a curve showing the combinations of two goods that can be produced by an economy, assuming that all resources are fully employed.

Autarky: a situation in which each country is self-sufficient, so there is no trade.

Absolute advantage: the ability of one person or nation to produce a particular good at a lower absolute cost than that of another person or nation.

Comparative advantage: the ability of one nation to produce a particular good at an opportunity cost lower than the opportunity cost of another nation.

Terms of trade: the rate at which two goods will be exchanged.

Consumption possibilities curve: a curve showing the combinations of two goods that can be consumed when a nation specializes in a particular good and trades with another nation.

Import quota: a limit on the amount of a good that can be imported.

Voluntary export restraint (VER): a scheme under which an exporting country "voluntarily" decreases its exports.

Tariff: a tax on an imported good.

Learning by doing: the knowledge gained during production that increases productivity.

Infant industry: a new industry that is protected from foreign competitors.

Dumping: a situation in which the price a firm charges in a foreign market is lower than either the price it charges in its home market or the production cost.

IV. PERFORMANCE ENHANCING TIPS (PETS)

PET # 1

In autarky, a country is constrained to consume what it produces. With trade, a country is able to consume a bundle of goods different from what it produces. Trade permits consumption beyond the production possibilities frontier and thus makes a country potentially better off.

PET #2

Opportunity cost calculations used to determine comparative advantage should be based on a per unit comparison.

Suppose you are given the following information:

Table 19-1

	Country A	Country B
Wood Products	10 units/hour	8 units/hour
High-tech products	15 units/hour	4 units/hour

The information in the Table 19-1 tells you that Country A can produce 10 units of wood products in one hour (with its resources) and 15 units of high-tech products in one hour. Country B can produce 8 units of wood products in one hour (with its resources) and 4 units of high-tech products in one hour. How can this information be used to determine which country has a comparative advantage in wood production and which country has a comparative advantage in high-tech production?

As a side point, you may wish to note that Country A has an absolute advantage in the production of both wood and high-tech products since it can produce more per hour of either good than can Country B. But, absolute advantage does NOT determine the basis for trade.

The easiest way to compute comparative advantage is to determine what the opportunity cost of production is for each good for each country, on a per unit basis. To do this, you must first answer how much Country A must give up if it were to specialize in the production of wood. For every additional hour of effort devoted to producing wood products, Country A would give up the production of 15 units of high-tech products. (Of course, it is then able to produce 10 more units of wood products.) On a per unit basis, Country A must give up 1.5 units of high-tech products for each 1 unit of wood products (15 high-tech products/hour)/(10 wood products/hour). You would read this as follows: "for Country A, the opportunity cost of 1 wood product is 1.5 high-tech products." For Country B, for every additional hour of effort devoted to producing wood products, it must give up 4 units of high-tech products. (Of course, it is then able to produce 8 more units of wood products.) On a per unit basis, Country B must give up 0.5 units of high-tech products for each 1 unit of wood products (4 high-tech products/hour)/(8 wood products/hour). You would read this as follows: "for Country B, the opportunity cost of 1 wood product is 0.5 high-tech products." Thus, Country B has the lower opportunity cost of producing wood products since it has to give up fewer high-tech products.

Since Country B has the lower opportunity cost of wood production, it should specialize in wood production. (Wood production is "less costly" in Country B than in Country A). If this is true, then it must also be true that Country A has the lower opportunity cost of high-tech production and thus should specialize in producing high-tech goods.
Let's see if this is true using the numbers from the Table 19-1. For Country A, the opportunity cost of producing more high-tech products is that for every additional hour of producing high-tech products, it must give up producing 10 units of wood products. (Of course, it is then able to produce 15 more units of high-tech products.) On a per unit basis, Country A must give up 0.67 wood products for every 1 high-tech product (10 wood products/hour)/(15 high-tech products per hour). You would read this as follows: "for Country A, the opportunity cost of 1 high-tech product is 0.67 wood products." For Country B, the opportunity cost of producing more high-tech products is that for every additional hour of producing high-tech products, it must give up producing 8 units of wood products. (Of course, it is then able to produce 4 more units of high-tech products.) On a per unit basis, Country B must give up 2 wood products for every one unit of high-tech products (8 wood products/hour)/(4 high-tech products/hour). Thus, Country A has the lower opportunity cost of producing high-tech products since it has to give up fewer wood products. (High-tech production is "less costly" in Country A than in Country B.)

PET #3

Opportunity cost calculations used to determine comparative advantage are also used to determine a range for the terms of trade that would create mutually beneficial exchanges between two countries.

In PET #2 above, the opportunity cost in Country A of producing wood products is 1.5 high-tech products (i.e., 1.5 high-tech products/1 wood product). In Country B, the opportunity cost of producing wood products is 0.5 high-tech products (i.e., 0.5 high-tech products/1 wood product). Thus, the terms of trade range that would be beneficial to both countries must be between 0.5 high tech/1 wood product and 1.5 high-tech products/1 wood product.

For example, mutually beneficial terms of trade might be 1 high-tech product/1 wood product. Country A would only have to give up (trade) 1 high-tech product in return for 1 wood product if it trades. If Country A produces for itself, it will have to cut production by 1.5 high-tech products to get back 1 wood product.

The extra 0.5 high-tech products the country "saves" can then be used to buy more from the foreign county. Thus, Country A gains from trade. On the other hand, Country B would give up (trade) 1 wood product to Country A and get in return 1 high-tech product. If Country B produces for itself, it will only get back 0.5 high-tech products by reducing wood production by 1 unit. Thus, Country B gains, as well.

PET #4

Trade protection reduces the total supply of a good in a country. The reduced supply will increase the price a country pays for the protected good.

Your textbook mentions different types of trade protection – import bans, import quotas, voluntary export restraints, and tariffs – all of which act to raise the price of the goods and services that a country imports from other countries. Protectionist trade policies effectively reduce the total supply of a good (where the total supply comes from domestic production plus foreign imports) by restricting the amount of foreign imports. Thus, in terms of supply and demand analysis, protectionist trade policies shift the supply curve to the left. A leftward shift in the supply curve raises the price of a good. (See Table 4-2 in PET #7 of Chapter 4 for review.)

V.   PRACTICE EXAM: MULTIPLE CHOICE QUESTIONS

Use the table 19-2 to answer the following question. Assume that each country can use its resources to produce either stuffed animals or pineapples.

Table 19-2

	Country A	Country B
Stuffed Toys (per day)	200	300
Pineapples (per day)	400	900

1. Which one of the following statements is true?

   a. Country B has a comparative advantage in the production of both goods.
   b. Country A has a comparative advantage in the production of stuffed toys and Country B has a comparative advantage in the production of pineapples.
   c. Country B has a comparative advantage in the production of stuffed toys and Country A has a comparative advantage in the production of pineapples.
   d. Country A has a comparative advantage in the production of both goods.
   e. Neither country has a comparative advantage in the production of stuffed toys.

2. Suppose the opportunity cost of producing one unit of lumber in Canada is 3 units of auto parts and that the opportunity cost of producing one unit of lumber in Japan is 6 units of auto pans. If the terms of trade are one unit of lumber for 8 auto parts, then:

   a. Canada and Japan will be able to engage in mutually beneficial trade.
   b. Japan will benefit from trade but Canada will not.
   c. Canada will benefit from trade but Japan will not.
   d. Canada will specialize in the production of auto parts.
   e. (a) and (d).

3. Which one of the following is NOT an example of a protectionist trade policy?

    a. Ban on imports.
    b. Voluntary export restraint.
    c. Tariff.
    d. Import quota.
    e. All of the above are protectionist trade policies.

Use Figures 19-1 and 19-2 to answer the following question.

Figure 19-1

Indonesia

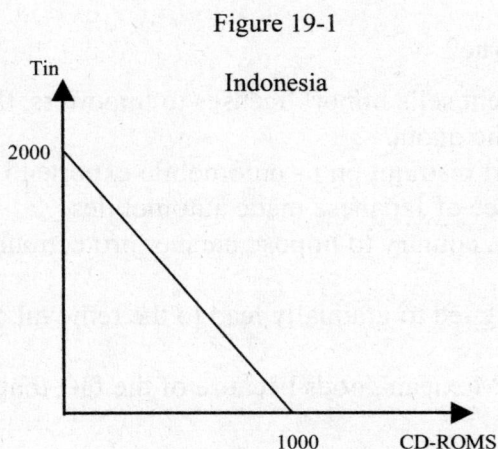

Figure 19-2

South Korea

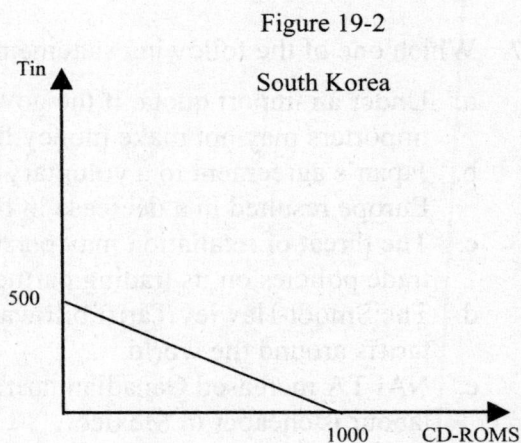

4. Which one of the following statements is true?

    a. Indonesia will specialize in tin production.
    b. Terms of trade of 250 units of tin for 100 CD ROMs will lead to greater consumption possibilities for Indonesia than its consumption possibilities in autarky.
    c. Mutually beneficial terms of trade would be 1.5 units of tin for 1.0 unit of CD ROMs.
    d. If trade occurs, workers in the CD ROM industry in South Korea will become unemployed.
    e. (a) and (c).

5. Which one of the following trade policies would create the biggest increase in the price of the protected good?

    a. An import ban.
    b. A voluntary export restraint.
    c. An import quota.
    d. A tariff.
    e. A WTO license.

Chapter 19

6. Which one of the following would NOT be a result of a tariff imposed by Canada on footwear imported from Brazil?

    a. Canadian footwear firms will be winners.
    b. Employment in the Canadian footwear industry will be higher than compared to a situation of free trade.
    c. The price that Canadian consumers pay for footwear produced in the Canada will be lower than compared to a situation of free trade.
    d. Canadian citizens should prefer a tariff on footwear to an import quota.
    e. All of the above would result from the tariff on Brazilian footwear.

7. Which one of the following statements is true?

    a. Under an import quota, if the government sells import licenses to importers, then importers may not make money from the quota.
    b. Japan's agreement to a voluntary export restraint on its automobile exports to Europe resulted in a decrease in the price of Japanese made automobiles.
    c. The threat of retaliation may persuade a country to impose harsher protectionist trade policies on its trading partners.
    d. The Smoot-Hawley Tariff bill was designed to gradually lead to the removal of tariffs around the world.
    e. NAFTA increased Canadian tariffs on Mexican goods because of the fact that labour is cheaper in Mexico.

8. Which one of the following would NOT be a likely result of protectionist trade policies?

    a. Retaliation.
    b. Smuggling.
    c. Consumers paying a higher price for the protected good.
    d. Unemployment in the protected industry.
    e. Inefficient production.

9. Which one of the following statements is true?

    a. Protectionist trade policies often obtain government approval because of the lobbying efforts of individuals who otherwise would become unemployed under free trade.
    b. The infant industry argument for trade protection is that it promotes learning by doing and thus can enable a new industry to be able to compete with other producers from around the world.
    c. A problem with granting trade protection to an infant industry is that the protection is not likely to be removed as the industry matures.
    d. By protecting infant industries from foreign competition, trade protection may lead to inefficient production by the protected industries.
    e. All of the above are true.

International Trade and Public Policy

10. Which one of the following is a problem with a government subsidizing an industry in the hope of establishing a worldwide monopoly?

    a. The taxpayers ultimately pay for the government subsidy.
    b. There is no guarantee that country will be able to profit from securing the monopoly.
    c. Another country may also grant a subsidy to the same industry.
    d. The government may end up subsidizing an industry in which there are not economies of scale.
    e. All of the above are problems.

11. Which one of the following statements is NOT true?

    a. Dumping occurs when firms charge a price in a foreign market that is below its cost of production.
    b. Dumping is illegal under international trade agreements.
    c. Predatory dumping is an attempt to drive competitors out of the industry so that the dumping firm can gain monopoly status.
    d. Countries are permitted to restrict imports from other countries if the production methods used by other countries cause harm to the environment.
    e. The wages of skilled labour in Canada have risen relative to the wages of unskilled labour as world trade has increased.

VI. PRACTICE EXAM: ESSAY QUESTIONS

12. Suppose Canada initially has no trade restrictions on imports of copper. Explain how a tariff on copper creates winners and losers within Canada. Where might resources (labour and capital) move after the tariff is imposed? Be sure to address the government's use of the tax revenues earned by the tariff. Use demand and supply analysis to show the effects of the tariff.

13. Discuss some of the arguments made in favour of trade protection.

VII. ANSWER KEY: MULTIPLE CHOICE QUESTIONS

1.   Correct answer: b.

    Discussion: Country A's opportunity cost of producing 1 stuffed toy is 2 pineapples (i.e., 400 pineapples per day/200 stuffed toys per day = 2 pineapples/1 stuffed toy). That is, in order to produce 1 more stuffed toy, Country A would have to take resources out of pineapple production and put them into stuffed toy production. Thus, pineapple production would decrease by 2 units. Country B's opportunity cost of producing 1 stuffed toy is 3 pineapples (i.e., 900 pineapples per day/300 stuffed toys per day = 3 pineapples/1 stuffed toy). That is, in order to produce 1 more stuffed toy, Country, B would have to take resources out of pineapple production and put them into stuffed toy production. Thus, pineapple production would decrease by 3 units in Country B. Thus, it "costs" less to produce stuffed toys in Country A (in terms of what must be given up) than it does in Country B. Since Country A has the comparative advantage in stuffed toy production, Country B must have a comparative advantage in pineapple production. To assure yourself that this is true, you can invert the ratios above so that Country A must give up producing 1/2 stuffed toy in order to produce 1 more pineapple whereas Country B must give up producing 1/3 stuffed toy in order to produce 1 more pineapple. Thus, pineapple production is less "costly" (in terms of what must be given up) in Country B than in Country A.

Based on the above discussion, none of the other statements are correct.

2. Correct answer: c.

Discussion: Mutually beneficial terms of trade must be between 3 auto parts/1 unit of lumber and 6 auto parts/1 unit of lumber. Since Canada's opportunity cost of producing lumber is less than Japan's opportunity cost of producing lumber, Canada has a comparative advantage in lumber production and thus should trade lumber for auto parts. Japan should do the reverse. At a terms of trade of 8 auto parts/1 unit of lumber, Canada will benefit since in autarky, she could only exchange one unit of lumber for 3 auto parts: with trade she would get 5 more auto parts per unit of lumber. However, at a terms of trade of 8 auto parts/1 unit of lumber, Japan will not benefit since in autarky, she would have to give up 6 auto parts in order to produce one unit of lumber whereas with trade, she would have to give up 2 more auto parts in order to purchase lumber from Canada. Thus, Japan would be worse off with trade than producing lumber for herself. (See PET #3 above for review.)

Statement a is not correct. For trade to benefit both countries, the terms of trade must range between 3 auto parts/1 unit of lumber and 6 auto parts/1 unit of lumber. Otherwise, one country will gain and the other country will lose. Statement b is not correct based on the discussion above. Statement d is not correct because Canada will specialize in lumber production. Statement e is not correct because neither statement a or d are correct.

3. Correct answer: e.

Discussion: None necessary.

4. Correct answer: e.

Discussion: The slope of the production possibilities curve gives the opportunity cost of producing tin (or CD ROMs). The slope of the production possibilities curve for Indonesia shows that the production of 1 CD ROM "costs" 2 units of tin. For South Korea, the opportunity cost of producing 1 CD ROM is 0.5 units of tin. Since CD ROMs incur a lower opportunity cost in South Korea than Indonesia, South Korea will specialize in and export CD ROMs while Indonesia will specialize in and export tin. Thus, statement a is correct. Since the terms of trade are between 0.5 units of tin/1 CD ROM and 2 units of tin/1 CD ROM, trade can be mutually beneficial. Thus, statement c is correct.

Statement b is not correct. Statement b implies a terms of trade of 2.5 units of tin/1 CD ROM. While these terms of trade would be beneficial to South Korea, it would not be beneficial to Indonesia. (See PET #3 above for review.) Statement d is not correct. Since South Korea will specialize in CD ROM production, labour and capital will have to move to the CD ROM industry. Thus, workers will become, at least temporarily, unemployed in the tin industry, not in the CD ROM industry.

5. Correct answer: a.

Discussion: An import ban completely eliminates any imports of the good. For example, an import ban on cigarettes imposed by the Canada would mean that no cigarettes produced in foreign countries would be permitted into Canada. Thus, the total supply of cigarettes available to the Canadian market would be reduced. In this case, the total supply of cigarettes available to the Canadian market would have to come solely from Canadian production of cigarettes. The import ban would thus be represented by a leftward shift in the supply curve where the new supply curve would now be that attributed to domestic production only. Since this policy is the most restrictive on imports, the increase in the price of cigarettes will be the biggest of any of the policies.

Statement b, c, and d are not correct. An import quota and a voluntary export restraint do not drive imports to zero but instead simply restrict the amount of imports to some number (greater than zero). A tariff is a tax on the price of the imported good and also act to reduce the supply of the imported good, but not to zero. Statement e is not correct. There is no such thing as a WTO license.

6. Correct answer: c.

Discussion: Statement c is not correct. A tariff on footwear from Brazil will raise the price to Canadian consumers of footwear, regardless of whether the footwear is produced in Brazil or Canada

Statement a is correct. Canadian footwear firms will be winners in the sense that they will be able to get a higher price for the footwear that they sell to Canadian consumers. Statement b is correct. In free trade, there would be less production of footwear by Canadian producers and more by foreign producers. Thus, under free trade employment in the Canadian footwear industry would be lower than when footwear is subject to a tariff. Alternatively, employment in the Canadian footwear industry would be higher with the tariff than in free trade. Statement d is correct. A tariff raises the price of the protected good (footwear in this case) less than does an import quota. Moreover, the government collects tariff revenue that the government could then use to fund government programs that benefit consumers (or to even give them tax refunds!).

7. Correct answer: a.

Discussion: When the government establishes an import quota, it gives licenses to importers. The size of the quota determines how much of a good they are permitted to import. Naturally, importers are aware that they can profit by having an import license because they can buy the good from the foreign Country at the unrestricted price and sell in the home Country at the quota-induced price that is higher. However, if importers have to pay for the import licenses, then some of the profit that they expect to make from the import quota will be "eaten up" by the cost of the import license. That is, paying for the import license is a cost that an importer would have to consider in determining how profitable it would be to have the license.

Statement b is not true. Japan's agreement to a voluntary export restraint (VER) on its automobile exports to Europe resulted in a higher, not lower price of Japanese made automobiles. European consumers paid anywhere from 1% to 55% more for Japanese made automobiles after the VER. Statement c is not true. The threat of retaliation may persuade a country to impose less harsh (i.e., less restrictive) protectionist trade policies on its trading partners, not harsher policies. Statement d is not correct. The Smoot-Hawley Tariff bill raised U.S. tariffs by an average of 60% and is pointed to as a policy that may have worsened the global depression of the 1930s. Statement e is not correct. NAFTA is to be implemented over a period of 15 years and is to eventually lead to the elimination of all tariffs and other trade barriers between Canada, Mexico and the United States.

8. Correct answer: d.

Discussion: Protectionist trade policies are "protectionist" because they protect workers in the domestic industry from job losses that might occur were the industry left open to foreign competition. Thus, protectionist trade policies typically (at least in the short run) enhance employment in the protected industry.

All of the others may be a result of protectionist trade policies.

9. Correct answer: e.

Discussion: None necessary.

10. Correct answer: e.

Discussion: When a government subsidizes an industry, it gives money to the industry. Taxpayers ultimately provide the money the government has to give to the industry. There is no guarantee that a country will be able to profit from securing a monopoly in a particular industry since other governments may have, at the same time, chosen to subsidize the same industry. In this case, one or both countries may end up suffering losses. The government may also choose to subsidize an industry thinking that the industry has large economies of scale (low average cost of production at very high levels of output) and is much more likely to exist as a monopoly (single producer). However, if it turns out that the industry is actually able to exist with more than one producer, the government subsidized industry may find itself having to compete with producers from other firms around the world. In this case, monopoly profits anticipated by the government may not materialize.

Chapter 19

11. Correct answer: d.

Discussion: Statement d is not true. Countries are NOT permitted to restrict imports from other countries if the production methods used by other countries cause harm to the environment. For example, suppose that Chile produces aluminium using a method that creates a lot of air pollution (more than what would be permitted under Canadian standards). Under World Trade Organization (WTO) laws, Canada would not be permitted to restrict the importation of Chilean aluminium into the Canada even though the production methods used by Chilean producers would be outlawed in Canada.

VIII. ANSWER KEY: ESSAY QUESTIONS

12. First of all one might wonder why Canada decided to institute a tariff on a previously freely traded good. There are a few explanations. One explanation might be that Canada imposed the tariff as a retaliatory action to its trading partner's decision to impose a tariff on a Canadian good(s). The retaliation may be used as a device to prompt the trading partner to remove their tariff on a Canadian good(s). An alternative explanation might be that workers in the Canadian copper industry felt threatened by the competition from copper producers in foreign countries. Fearing that the competition might mean that Canadian copper producers would lose their market to foreign producers (and thus jobs and profits), workers/management in the Canadian copper industry may have lobbied Parliament for trade protection.

When a tariff is introduced on foreign imports of copper, there will be winners and losers in Canada. The winners will be the copper producers and workers in the copper industry. The price at which producers can sell copper will increase (as Figure 19-3 shows) and thus their profits may increase as well.

Figure 19-3

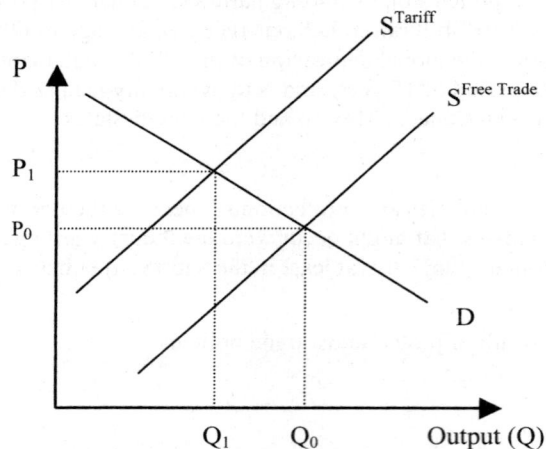

More workers and capital may now be needed in the copper industry, so resources may be taken out of other industries and moved into copper production. Thus, workers with skills in the copper industry will benefit. However, since the tariff raises the price of copper, users (buyers) of copper will lose.

Since the tariff generates tariff revenue for the government, the government may be able to use the revenue to offset some of the higher costs to copper users (i.e., subsidize copper users). Alternatively, the government may be able to use the tariff revenue to reduce income taxes on all workers, i.e., all workers might be given a tax refund. Or, the government could use the tariff revenue to help pay for other government programs that the citizens of the country feel are worth supporting.

International Trade and Public Policy

13. There are several arguments made in favour of trade protection. One argument is that trade protection should be granted to industries that are just starting out – so-called "infant industries." The argument is that the infant industries need protection from international competition in the early stages of development so that they become competitive themselves. Without the protection, the industry may not be successful, so the country loses out on establishing an industry that it may want.

Another argument made in favour of trade protection is that trade protection "keeps jobs at home." Here, the argument is that without trade protection, the industry will be unable to compete against foreign competitors and so the domestic industry will go out of business. Thus, by granting protection to a domestic industry, a government can prevent the industry from going out of business and thereby prevent any attendant job losses that would result.

Another argument made in favour of protection is that monopoly profits may be obtained. In this case, protection would be granted to industries which are likely to survive as monopolies. By granting protection to a monopoly industry, the Country becomes the sole producer of the industry output and may thus be able to extract monopoly profits from sales around the world. The government may encourage this if it is able to share in the profits with the producer.

Another argument that can be made in favour of protection is that it can be used to get trading partners to loosen their trade restrictions. For example, a country may threaten to or actually impose stiff tariffs against a good or set of goods imported from another country to prompt the country to reduce its tariffs. The U.S. used this type of threat against Japan and was successful in getting Japan to loosen some of its trade restrictions against the U.S.

One final argument made in favour of protection is that it will "level the playing field." This is a tit-for-tat application of protectionism. For example, if one country's government subsidizes a particular industry, then its production costs are unfairly low relative to the production costs of the same industry in other country that is not subsidizing the industry. Thus, to compete on a level ground, trade protection is considered to be a fair response.

This discussion provides arguments made in favour of trade protection. To be sure, there are many arguments that can be made against trade protection.

CHAPTER 20
MICROECONOMICS IN THE TWENTY-FIRST CENTURY

I.   OVERVIEW

As the title to this chapter suggests, you will learn about some of the major microeconomic challenges confronting Canada in the twenty-first century. You will learn about poverty, how it is measured, how it has changed, what may cause it, and some public policies aimed at reducing poverty. You will learn about the distribution of income and how it is measured, how it has changed, and what may cause it to have changed. You will also learn about some public policies that may be viewed as worthwhile if a more even distribution of income is desired. You will also learn about government-funded health care programs and the costs and benefits associated with them. You will learn about the challenges of reforming the health care system. You will learn about the Kyoto Protocol. You will also learn about some of the costs associated with complying with the Protocol.

II.   CHECKLIST

By the end of this chapter, you should be able to:
- Explain what the three major microeconomic challenges facing Canada are as outlined in your textbook.
- Describe how the government defines who is considered to be "poor" or living in poverty.
- Offer some explanations for what causes poverty.
- Define and discuss what a progressive tax system is.
- Define and discuss what a regressive tax system is.
- Define and discuss what a proportional tax system is.
- Discuss some public policies that might lead to a more equal distribution of income.
- Discuss how the Canadian health-care system has recently fallen into disrepair.
- Discuss the reform proposals that have been advanced for improving the health care system.
- Define and discuss the Kyoto Protocol.
- Outline some of the costs associated with complying with the Protocol and some of the costs of not complying.

III. KEY TERMS

Efficient market: a market in which there exists *no* additional trades that would mutually benefit a buyer and a seller.

Equitable distribution: a fair distribution of the goods and services produced in an economy.

Low-income cut-off: the level of income at which a household devotes more than 55% of its income to food, shelter, and clothing.

Progressive tax: a tax that takes away a greater percentage of a person's income as his income level rises; average tax rate increases with income.

Proportional tax: a tax that takes away a constant percentage of a person's income at all income levels; average tax rate is constant.

Regressive tax: a tax that takes away a lower percentage of a person's income as his income level rises; average tax rate decreases with income.

Average tax rate: total taxes paid divided by income.

Tax brackets: income ranges over which the average tax rate is constant.

Taxable income: the income upon which a person pays tax; may be less than a person's earned income if there are deductions.

Marginal tax rate: the percentage tax paid on the last dollar of taxable income.

Welfare trap: a situation in which it is better to remain on welfare rather than taking a low-income job because the combination of welfare income and benefits is higher than the income from the job.

Capital gains: the monetary gain from the sale of a capital asset (stock, bond, real estate, antique, or art) that is bought and resold.

Consumption taxes: taxes based on the amount an individual consumes.

Negative income tax: an income tax with a constant marginal tax rate and a guaranteed level of income.

Service sector inflation: in sectors where a large fraction of the work is done by people, wages must rise by the inflation rate or greater, because labour-saving technology cannot replace workers.

Health maintenance organization (HMO): a business that receives an annual fee for each person it provides medical coverage to, and makes a profit by limiting the cost of providing health care services to its members.

Two-tiered system: a system that offers both publicly-funded and privately paid health care.

International emissions trading system: a provision under the Kyoto Protocol to allow for internationally marketable pollution permits between industrialized nations.

Clean development mechanism: a provision in the Kyoto Protocol which allows an industrialized country to meet part of its GHG emission reduction goal by paying for GHG emission reduction in a lesser developed country.

Joint implementation: a provision in the Kyoto Protocol, which allows nations to share credit for emission reduction.

IV. PERFORMANCE ENHANCING TIPS (PETS)

PET #1

Debate over an economic problem may have three sources: (1) how the problem is defined; (2) how the problem is interpreted; and (3) solutions presented for dealing with the problem.

It is particularly important for you to consider the first two potential sources of debate before you argue for or against a solution to a problem. For example, you have learned that poverty is based on what a family's total income is relative to its expenditures on food, shelter and clothing. If you disagree with the government's figure (perhaps because of how it was calculated), you may end up concluding that poverty isn't as big a problem as that reported by the government. Secondly, even if you agree with the government's definition of who is classified as living in poverty, you may not agree with the interpretation of the problem. For example, suppose the government reports that 12.2% of the population lives below the poverty line. The government may deem this to be a major problem. You may disagree. You may think that 12.2% is a fairly small proportion of the overall population and, thus, may feel that there are other more pressing problems that the government should focus on. Thirdly, even if you agree with the government's method for measuring a problem and their interpretation of it, you may disagree with the current public policy for dealing with the problem or over the reforms that have been suggested.

As you can see, there are several points at which you and your classmates may debate. An understanding of where your points of views differ from those of your classmates will help clarify your discussion.

PET #2

Interpret statistics with care.

Statistics are often used to add legitimacy to a person's argument. You should always remember that, to use statistics correctly, you should know how they are calculated. For example, suppose that for the entire Canadian population, 3.6 million people live below the poverty line in 2000. That is, 12.0% of the total Canadian population live below the poverty line.

Suppose further that the number of people living in poverty rose to 3.8 million in 2001. You may want to conclude that poverty is now a much larger problem because of the increase in the number of people in poverty. You should, however, check to see what has happened to the population over this same period of time. Suppose the population increased by 6% from 2000 to 2001 (we realize that this is an unrealistic population growth rate for Canada, but is used for illustration purposes only). What has happened to the poverty rate for the entire population?

We initially assumed that there were 30 million people living in Canada in 2000 (i.e. $(3.6/30) * 100 = 12.2\%$ poverty rate). With a 6% growth rate, the population is now 31.8

million people in 2001. Therefore, the poverty rate is now 11.94%. Although the change is not large, we do see that the poverty has fallen. Therefore, the news is not all that bad (although, some may argue that it could be better).

PET #3

The median and the average are not necessarily the same number.

Consider the following five observations on income:

Obs. #1	Obs. #2	Obs; #3	Obs; #4	Obs. #5
$20,000	$30,000	$10,000	$100,000	$40,000.

The average is computed as the sum of the numbers divided by the sample size. In this case, the sum is $200,000 and the sample size is 5. Thus, the average is $200,000/5 = $40,000. In this example, there is one observation with an income above the average; the remaining four observations are for incomes below the average.

The median is the number corresponding to the midpoint observation number in the sample (when the sample is ranked from lowest to highest or vice-versa).

First, the sample above must be ranked from lowest to highest income. Thus, we would have:

Obs. #1	Obs. #2	Obs. #3	Obs. #4	Obs. #5
$10,000	$20,000	$30,000	$40,000	$100,000.

In this case, the midpoint observation number is 3 (2 observations below it, 2 observations above it). The number corresponding to the midpoint observation number is $30,000. Thus, the median income is $30,000. In this sample, there are an equal number of incomes below $30,000 as there are above $30,000.

The example shows that an average is influenced by extreme high (or low) numbers whereas a median is not.

V.   PRACTICE EXAM: MULTIPLE CHOICE QUESTIONS

1. According to the Canadian government, a poor family is one:
    a. whose total income plus wealth is less than the amount required to satisfy the family's "minimum needs."
    b. whose debts exceed the value of their assets.
    c. who has four or more dependents and only one working family member.
    d. whose total income is less than the amount required to satisfy the family's "minimum needs."
    e. who has no shelter, food, or clothing.

2. Which one of the following is NOT true based on the numbers given:

Persons in poverty	4.0 million
Total population	24.0 million
Persons under age 18 living in poverty	1.6 million
Persons with no high school diploma living in poverty	0.8 million
Total population under age 18	8.0 million
Total population (persons with no high school diploma)	3.2 million

   a. 16.7% of the population lives in poverty.
   b. 40% of those living in poverty are under age 18.
   c. 13.3% of the population does not have a high school diploma.
   d. 33.3% of those under age 18 live in poverty.
   e. 25% of those without a high school degree live in poverty.

3. Which of the following does NOT cause a regressive tax system?

   a. The goods and services tax (GST).
   b. Taxes on tobacco and alcohol.
   c. RRSP contributions.
   d. Capital gains taxes.
   e. All of the above will tend to create a regressive tax system.

4. Which one of the following does the Canadian government NOT use to equalize the income distribution?

   a. Old age security.
   b. Tax credits and tax incentive schemes.
   c. Canada pension plan.
   d. Universal medical care.
   e. All of the above are currently in used.

5. Which one of the following statements is true?

   a. If Bob earns $30,000 a year and pays $3,000 in taxes whereas Sally earns $40,000 a year and pays $4,000 in taxes, then the income tax system is progressive.
   b. If Bob earns $30,000 a year and pays $3,000 in taxes whereas Sally earns $40,000 a year and pays $3,000 in taxes, then the income tax system is progressive.
   c. If Bob earns $30,000 a year and pays $3,000 in taxes whereas Sally earns $40,000 a year and pays $5,000 in taxes, then the income tax system is progressive.
   d. If Bob earns $30,000 a year and pays $1,500 in taxes whereas Sally earns $40,000 a year and pays $1,600 in taxes, then the income tax system is progressive.
   e. All of the above are true.

6. Because health care is funded largely through transfer payments from governments:

    a. people tend to over consume health services because the marginal cost to an individual of any additional service is less than the marginal benefit of that service.

    b. doctor's tend to perform too many tests because the marginal cost to the doctor of any additional test less than the marginal benefit of that service.

    c. it creates a negative spillover.

    d. there is a shortage of doctors and nurses.

    e. all of the above are a consequence of the way health care is funded.

7. According to the World Health Organization's year 2000 health report, which of the following statements is true?

    a. Canada has the best health care system in the world.

    b. The United States has the worst health care system in the world.

    c. Canada is ranked 30th in the world.

    d. The United Kingdom's health care system is worse than Canada's.

    e. None of the above.

8. Which of the following is NOT a potential solution to Canada's current health care problems?

    a. Regionalize health care and reorganize how medical labour is allocated within regions.

    b. Ration services to those most deserving – (i.e. smokers do not qualify for lung cancer treatments, drinkers cannot have liver transplants, etc.)

    c. Create a two-tiered system.

    d. Institute a user fee system with rebates for low-income individuals.

    e. Increase government funding.

9. Which of the following is an instrument that can be used in the reduction of greenhouse gas emissions as outlined in the Kyoto Protocol?

    a. Command and control policies managed by the World Bank.

    b. Global pollution taxes.

    c. Non-marketable permits issued by the World Bank.

    d. International marketable pollution permits.

    e. None of the above.

Chapter 20

10. Under the Kyoto Protocol, cooperation between countries has been hard to organize because:

   a. Countries that reduce their emissions receive 100% of the benefits but only have to incur a fraction of the cost.
   b. We must produce the current level of greenhouse gases in order to maintain our standard of living.
   c. Countries that reduce their emissions receive only a fraction of the benefits but have to incur 100% of the cost.
   d. There does not exist a world body to enforce emission reduction and to penalize cheaters
   e. Both (c) and (d) are correct.

11. Which one of the following is NOT true of global warming?

   a. It is due to an accumulation of carbon dioxide in the atmosphere.
   b. There is uncertainty about how much the earth's temperature will actually rise.
   c. Total rainfall is expected to decrease.
   d. A carbon tax (a tax on the burning of fossil fuels like oil, coal, and gasoline) is one solution aimed at reducing the pace of global warming.
   e. Sea levels are expected to increase.

VI.   PRACTICE EXAM: ESSAY QUESTIONS

12. Define poverty. Explain some causes of poverty. Discuss some of the Canadian programs that help reduce poverty.

13. Discuss the problems with the Canadian system of health care and policy reform proposals that have been suggested.

VII.   ANSWER KEY: MULTIPLE CHOICE QUESTIONS

1. Correct answer: d.

   Discussion: The Canadian government defines a family to be poor based on their income earnings (from working and from interest earned on financial investments) relative to an income level that is deemed necessary to must meet a family's "minimum needs." These minimum needs include, but are not limited to, food, shelter, and clothing.

   Statement a is not correct because the wealth of a family is not (at least directly) considered. It is indirectly considered in that income earned from financial investment would obviously be larger for wealthier families. Statement b is not correct because income, not assets minus debts (or net worth), is considered. Statement c is not correct because the poor are not defined by how many dependents relative to working members there are in a family (although the low income cut-off line does increase as the number of persons in a households increases). Statement e is not correct although it may describe whom we consider to be poor.

2. Correct answer: d.

    Discussion: Statement d is not correct. There are 8.0 million people under the age of 18. Of that 8.0 million, 1.6 million of those live in poverty. The calculation is (1.6/8.0) * 100 = 20%. Thus, the correct answer is 20%.

    Statement a is correct. The total population is 24.0 million, and 4.0 million of those live in poverty. The calculation is (4.0/24.0) * 100 = 16.7%. Statement b is correct. The number of people living in poverty is 4.0 million. Of those 4.0 million, 1.6 million are under the age of 18. The calculation is (16/40) * 100 = 40%. Statement c is correct. The total population is 24.0 million, and 3.2 million of this population do not have a high school diploma. The calculation is (3.2/24.0) * 100 = 13.3%. Statement e is correct. There are 3.2 million people without a high school degree. Of that 3.2 million, 0.8 million live in poverty. The calculation is (0.8/3.2) * 100 = 25%,

3. Correct answer: e.

    Discussion: Recall that a regressive tax is one where the government takes away a lower percentage of a person's income as his income level rises (or a higher percentage of a person's income as his income falls). Consumption taxes like the GST and 'sin taxes' such as those on alcohol and cigarettes are regressive because, independent of the persons income level, they must pay the same dollar amount for the purchase of the good. Therefore, individuals who earn less income must pay a higher percentage of that income in consumption taxes. RRSP deductions are regressive tax break, because as people earn more income they can put a larger dollar amount into their RRSP thereby reducing their taxable income. It is possible that someone who earns more income and invests in an RRSP will pay fewer taxes than someone else that is currently earning less and not investing in an RRSP. Capital gains taxes are regressive because only two-thirds of the capital gains are taxable.

4. Correct answer: e.

    Discussion: Statements a, b, c and d all refer to specific or general mechanisms used by provincial and federal governments to reduce poverty, stabilize people's income when they are out of work, assist people during their old age.

5. Correct answer: c.

    Discussion: Recall that the definition of a progressive tax system is a tax that takes away a greater percentage of a person's income as his income level rises. Alternatively, we could say that the average tax rate increases with income. If Bob makes $30,000 per year and pays $3,000 in taxes, then he pays 10% ($3,000/$30,000*100) of his income in taxes. If Sally makes $40,000 per year and pays $5,000 in taxes, then she pays 12.5% ($5,000/$40,000*100) of her income in taxes. Since the percentage of the person's income paid in taxes rose with the tax rate, the tax system is progressive.

    Statement a is not correct because both Bob and Sally pay 10% of their income in taxes. This is an example of a proportional tax. Statement b is not correct because Bob pays 10% of his income in taxes whereas Sally only pays 7.5% of her income in taxes. This is an example of a regressive tax. Statement d is not correct because Bob pays 5% of his income in taxes whereas Sally only pays 4% of her income in taxes. This is an example of a regressive tax.

6. Correct answer: e

    Discussion: Statements a – d are all examples of what happens when the marginal principle is violated. People tend to consume too many services and doctors tend to ask for too many tests because the cost to the individual is so low (it is generally always less than the expected benefit). Furthermore, when the government funds healthcare through a tax and transfer system, some people incur the cost (pay taxes) while other receive the benefit. This is an example of a negative spillover.

7. Correct answer: c.

    Discussion: According to Table 20-2 in your text, Canada is ranked 30th overall. We can also see that the U.S. health care system is close to Canada in 37th place – this is far from the bottom of the list. The United Kingdom is ranked 18th which is better than Canada.

8. Correct answer: b.

   Discussion: Although this is one possible solution, it is currently not being considered as a solution to the current crisis. The universality of Canada's health care system would make it difficult to institute such reforms (let alone the moral and ethical questions that would need to be answered prior to instituting such reforms). All of the other statements have been proposed as solutions to the crisis.

9. Correct answer: d.

   Discussion: The protocol outlines three economic instruments that can be used: international emissions trading system (marketable pollution permits), the clean development mechanism and joint implementation to share credit for emission reduction between countries.

   Although the Kyoto Protocol set specific targets for greenhouse gas reductions, it does not use a command and control approach to pollution abatement. Thus, statement a and b are incorrect. Statement c is incorrect because the protocol sets up a marketable system, not a non-marketable system.

10. Correct answer: e.

    Discussion: Statement c is just an example of the spillover principle where some of the benefits associated with emission reduction are not confined to the country that decides to reduce its production of greenhouse gases. Statement d is correct because each nation has its own sets of laws and institutions and cannot be forced to comply with a voluntary protocol like the Kyoto protocol. Until nations develop a mechanism to force compliance, the free rider problem will exist.

    Statement a is incorrect because countries incur 100% of the costs yet receive only some of the benefits because of the nature of the good – global pollution falls, not just pollution over a specific country who happens to reduce emissions. Statement b is incorrect because it ignores the possibility of technological change. It is possible to maintain our standard of living while at the same time reducing harmful emissions. Discovering alternative energy sources, or developing new technologies for cleaning smokestacks are a couple of examples where we can continue to maintain our current level of production and reduce emissions.

11. Correct answer: c.

    Discussion: Global warming is expected to increase, not decrease, the amount of rainfall. All of the other statements are true.

VIII. ANSWER KEY: ESSAY QUESTIONS

12. Poverty is defined with respect to family size and income earnings relative to a minimum income level established by the government. The minimum income level is based on an income that would satisfy a family's "minimum needs." For example, for a four-person family living in a large (population greater than 500,000 people) urban area, the low-income cut-off is $33,063. Four-person families with an income above $33,063 are not considered to be poor while those four-person families with income at or below $33,063 are defined as "poor."

    Poverty has many causes. An obvious answer to what causes poverty would simply be to say that it is caused by not working (or not working enough). Without a job, and therefore, without an income, an individual cannot provide for him- or herself (or their family) which is what leads to poverty. However, a deeper answer needs to examine what causes individuals to be out of work or to lack the earning power necessary to keep them out of poverty. Thus, some explain poverty as a result of a lack of education (and, therefore, skills). A minimum wage earner, who typically has little education and low skills, that is providing for a family of four, may not be able to produce an income above the poverty line. Some explain poverty based on poor health (physical or mental) or disabilities. These workers have difficulty finding or maintaining employment and consequently end up without a reasonable and stable source of income.

Another explanation for poverty is that some people are limited in their ability, to work because of family commitments – raising children or caring for a sick or disabled family member.

There are numerous government programs that help to reduce poverty, either explicitly through cash or non-cash assistance, or through education and training. The welfare system is a cash-assistance programs that is explicitly aimed at the poor. The earned-income-tax-credit is a redistributive arm of the Canadian tax system aimed at giving tax refunds to the working poor. In addition to these programs that are explicitly aimed at the poor, there are worker retraining programs, unemployment compensation plans, financial assistance for education (student loans), etc., which may indirectly help to alleviate the sources of poverty.

13. The Canadian system of health care is considered to be problematic largely because of the rising costs of health care; – increases in the price of health care outpace price increases in just about every other industrial sector. And, there seems to be no slowing down. Furthermore, governments have failed to increase funding (and in some cases cut funding). A consequence of this funding crunch is that there are insufficient resources to meet the current demand. The aging of the Canadian society also elevates the potential cost of funding government health care. As more and more citizens reach the age of 65, they require more medical care than is currently being provided. Finally, because of the way health care is financed, each person consumes health care services at a relatively low marginal cost. As we have seen throughout this book, as the marginal costs of any activity fall, people tend to consume more of the activity than what is optimal.

There is an opportunity cost to the rising level of government spending on health care. For a given source of tax revenue, the government will be forced to cut other government programs in order to fund health care. Alternatively, and still an opportunity cost to consider, the government might increase taxes so that it has more revenue to spend on health care and yet be able to maintain the current level of funding of other programs.

There are several reform measures that have been suggested. Some of the reform measures are aimed at controlling the costs of health care (which, will in turn, help reduce the government funding needs of it in the furore). The emergence of health maintenance organizations is one possible reform. HMOs are set up with an objective of providing quality care while at the same time containing health care costs. Another reform proposal is to establish a medical service fee that must be paid by the patient whenever they visit the doctor or go to the emergency room. If people were forced to directly incur some of the health care costs, then they would consume less medical services (think of this as an increase in the marginal cost of visiting the doctor).

Chapter 20

APPENDIX
BASIC ALGEBRAIC RULES

1. The negative of a negative value is positive.

    Example: -(-b) = b

    (You can put in a number, say 3, for "b," if you prefer to use numbers rather than variables.)

    What is really going on is that the negative sign in front of (-b) is really -1. So another way to think of the rule is:

2. Multiplication of a negative value by a negative value returns a positive value.

    Example: (-a)∗(-b) = a∗b.

    (Here again, if you prefer, you can put in numbers for a and b. If a = 1 and b = 3, then (-1) ∗ -3 = 3.)

3. Multiplication of a negative value by a positive value returns a negative value.

    Example: (-a)∗(b)=-a∗b.

    (Here again, if you prefer, you can put in numbers for a and b. If a = 4 and b = 3, then (-4)∗3 = -12.)

4. When moving variables in an equation from one side of the "=" sign to the other, the sign of the variable will change. If the variable was positive, it will now have a negative sign in front of it. If the variable was negative, it will now have a positive sign in front of it.

    Example: Y = a - b∗X

    This can also be written as:

    Y - a = b∗X

    In the example above, "a" was eliminated from the right-hand side of the equation by effectively subtracting it from each side of the equation (as long as you do the same thing to both sides of the equation, its meaning is not altered). That is:

    Y - a = a + b - X - a.

Basic Algebraic Rules

Since a - a = 0, the "a" on the right hand side of the equation is eliminated.

Other ways in which the equation Y = a - b*X can be written are:

Y + b*X = a

Y - a + b*X = 0.

5. A variable multiplied by its reciprocal equals 1.

Example: J*(1/J) = 1.

6. If two variables are multiplied by each other, separation of them requires division.

Example: Y*Z = H

This can also be written as:

Y = H/Z.

In the example above, Z is effectively eliminated from the left hand side of the equation by dividing the left and right-hand side of the equation through by Z. (As long as you do the same thing to both sides of the equation, its meaning is not altered.) Since Z/Z = 1, Z is eliminated from the left-hand side of the equation.

7. Division by a variable is equivalent to multiplying by the reciprocal of the variable.

In the example to rule 4 above, Z was eliminated on the left-hand side of the equation by dividing through each side of the equation by Z. You can also think of this as multiplying each side of the equation by 1/Z. (As long as you do the same thing to both sides of the equation, its meaning is not altered.) That is:

1/Z*Y*Z = H*(1/Z)

Since 1/Z*Z = 1, the equation becomes Y = H/Z.

8. When a set of variables is multiplied (or divided) by a common variable, the common variable can be factored out.

Example: Z - d*Z + h*Z

This can also be written as: Z* (1 - d + h)

Where Z is the common variable.

Example: k/q - d/q + h/q

This can also be written as: (1/q)*(k - d + h)

Where 1/q is the common variable.

9. When given two equations with a common variable, substitutions can be made.

Example: $Y = a + b*X$ and $X = z - v*U$

You may substitute for X from the second equation into the first equation to get:

$Y = a + b*(z - v*U)$

$Y = a + b*z - b*v*U$

Factoring the "b" out of the two last terms on the right-hand side of the equation yields:

$Y = a + b* (z - v*U)$

10. Variables that appear on both sides an equation should be moved to the same side where factoring can be done.

Example: $Y = a + b*z - b*v*Y$

The common variable is Y. By moving the Y term on the right-hand side (along with any variables that it is multiplied or divided by) to the left-hand side (see rule #2 above), the equation becomes:

$Y + b*v*Y = a + b*z$

Factoring out the "Y" on the left-hand side (see rule #8 above) gives:

$Y*(1 + b*v) = a + b*z.$

The term $(1 +b*v)$ can be eliminated from the left-hand side of the equation by dividing through both sides by $(1 +b*v)$. (See rule #6 above). This yields a "solution" for Y as:

$Y = [a + b*z]/[1 + b*v]$